Praise for *Getting to Green*

"This country is ripe for a new era of pragmatic problem-solving. Rich's prescription for ending partisan gridlock on the environment is sensible, based on our shared values as Americans. Tightly argued and persuasive, *Getting to Green* is mandatory reading for anyone who cares about climate change, or about fixing the dysfunction in government."

—U.S. SENATOR EVAN BAYH

"My fellow environmental leaders may not agree with every word, but we ignore this book at our peril. It never occurred to Teddy Roosevelt that Republicans should oppose conservation, and *Getting to Green* persuasively argues that conservatives still should support the responsible stewardship of nature. With a career at the highest levels of global capitalism and as a greatly respected environmental leader, Fred Rich is in a unique position to bring the right and left together to find practical solutions to our environmental challenges."

—RAND WENTWORTH, PRESIDENT, LAND TRUST ALLIANCE

"Rich rethinks the foundations and rewrites the playbook of the American Green movement. In an exploration that is by turns history lesson, political commentary, philosophical analysis, and campaign strategy session, he succeeds in showing that one of the most angrily contested topics in contemporary politics could be, if we can reset some of the basic rules of communication, a place of deep and meaningful consensus. Rich's stimulating book is both a challenging and a well-informed examination of a very important contemporary issue and an insightful starting point, one might hope, for a broad reconsideration of many other issues that now divide us."

—GREGORY E. KAEBNICK, THE HASTINGS CENTER, AUTHOR OF *HUMANS IN NATURE*

"As someone who believes in putting governance ahead of politics, I welcome this call to transcend the partisanship that has stood in the way of urgently needed action on climate change and the environment. Regardless of your place on the political spectrum, there is much to admire in this book, which reminds us that the stewardship of nature is an obligation shared by all Americans."

—U.S. SENATOR ANGUS S. KING JR.

"Dare conservatives ask, 'Can free enterprise solve climate change?' and dare progressives imagine something more efficient than a regulatory solution? If, as Fred Rich suggests, we come together around shared values like love, wisdom, and compassion, then taking action on climate change, now seemingly impossible, will become inevitable without ever passing through the probable. *Getting to Green* shows the way: Conservatives need to be welcomed as the indispensable partners for action on climate and other environmental issues."

—BOB INGLIS, SIX-TERM GOP CONGRESSMAN FROM SOUTH CAROLINA, DEFEATED FOR CHANGING HIS VIEW ON CLIMATE CHANGE; WINNER OF THE 2015 JOHN F. KENNEDY PROFILE IN COURAGE AWARD

"The environmental and conservation communities must learn to work together, as they once did, if we are to successfully safeguard our natural resources for the future. *Getting to Green* presents a thoughtful analysis of where the Green movement is today, and a compelling case for what Greens must do to regain broad public support. Whether you are an environmentalist or a conservationist, liberal or conservative, you must read this book."

—SIMON ROOSEVELT, FOUNDER, CONSERVATION ROUNDTABLE, AND AUTHOR OF *AMERICAN HUNTING AND CONSERVATION* (FORTHCOMING)

GETTING TO GREEN

GETTING TO GREEN

SAVING NATURE:
A BIPARTISAN SOLUTION

Frederic C. Rich

W. W. NORTON & COMPANY
Independent Publishers Since 1923
New York | London

For information about permission to reproduce selections from this book,
write to Permissions, W. W. Norton & Company, Inc.,
500 Fifth Avenue, New York, NY 10110

For information about special discounts for bulk purchases, please contact
W. W. Norton Special Sales at specialsales@wwnorton.com or 800-233-4830

Manufacturing by Berryville Graphics
Book design by Chris Welch Design
Production manager: Julia Druskin

ISBN 978-0-393-29247-3

W. W. Norton & Company, Inc.
500 Fifth Avenue, New York, N.Y. 10110
www.wwnorton.com

W. W. Norton & Company Ltd.
Castle House, 75/76 Wells Street, London W1T 3QT

1 2 3 4 5 6 7 8 9 0

This book is dedicated to the late Frances Stevens Reese.

Contents

GETTING TO GREEN

Prologue

On November 15, 1990, Republican president George H. W. Bush, with Environmental Protection Agency administrator William K. Reilly (who had been president of the World Wildlife Fund before taking the job) at his side, signed the Clean Air Act of 1990, which required that acid rain causing sulfur and nitrogen dioxide emissions be reduced by about 50 percent. The final bill was passed with 89 senators voting yes, and a vote in the House of 401 to 21. Senator Mitch McConnell of Kentucky, today's Republican majority leader in the Senate, voted in favor. Despite the final vote tallies, the path to success had not been smooth. Oil and chemical companies were strongly opposed, and the regional calculus was complicated, causing, for example, coal state West Virginia's two Democratic senators to vote no. But compromise prevailed. The targeted emissions reductions were reduced from the full amount demanded by environmentalists. And to obtain the support of some Republicans, the initial bill was recrafted to take the form of a "cap-and-trade" system, ensuring that the overall reductions could be achieved at the lowest possible cost. It was a landmark in American environmental history and a triumphant success for the Green movement. And now, with the benefit of a quarter century of perspective, we know that the law worked better than its proponents could have hoped, drastically reducing the deposition of atmospheric acids in our forests and waterways at a cost to industry that was far less than originally estimated, and producing benefits (in terms of resource recovery, lower health care costs, etc.) conservatively estimated at 800 percent of those costs.[1]

This was a piece of legislation that actually achieved the reversal of large-scale environmental damage, used a market mechanism dear to conservatives, and avoided the economic sacrifices feared by business while providing net economic benefits to the nation. In a statement following the signing ceremony, Bill Reilly said the legislation would "undoubtedly serve as a model . . . leading to the widespread use of market approaches here and abroad." It seemed that Washington had found a way to satisfy both environmentalists and conservatives, and the Green movement could deploy this template to address a range of other pressing issues. The future looked bright.

Instead, November 15, 1990, marks the day that the Green movement hit a legislative dead end. No president in the quarter century since then has signed a major environmental bill. Every subsequent attempt by the Green movement to forge a national legislative solution to national environmental problems, including global warming, ended in failure.

And what Green issue has Washington, D.C., in its grip today? Climate change and sea level rise? Ocean acidification, perhaps? Water supply and water quality? Species extinction and biodiversity? No. The environmental cause célèbre in America in the early twenty-first century was Keystone XL, the proposal by a Canadian pipeline company to add 875 miles of additional pipeline to the country's existing network of over 190,000 miles of crude and liquid petroleum product pipes and 305,000 miles of inter- and intra-state natural gas transmission pipe. The environmental movement enthroned opposition to Keystone as a litmus test of Green ortho-doxy, despite the fact that the pipeline itself does not present any unusual environmental risks, its approval or nonapproval would not affect the development by our Canadian neighbors of their dirty tar sands (which is a fait accompli), and the impact on carbon emissions would be, according to the *New York Times*, "infinitesimal."

In 1990 the Green movement fought a battle where the prize was a 50 percent reduction in damaging acid rain; in 2015, the Green movement's prize, President Obama's denial of the Keystone permit, was almost wholly symbolic, a tactical "victory" without any meaningful impact on the natural world. And the costs of this six-year campaign by Greens? We created a potent issue that energized the anti-Green right, caused significant political complications for a friendly president, and, most importantly, distracted the public and committed Greens from making real progress on far more pressing environmental issues.

How did this happen?

Environmentalism, one of the most successful mass movements of the modern era, has transformed America. In only five decades it has reversed polluting practices that prevailed since the dawn of the Industrial Revolution, improved air quality, restored many water-ways to a cleanliness not seen since the early nineteenth century, protected vast tracts of wilderness, and attracted millions of adher-ents. It is a breathtaking record of achievement.

Seventy to eighty percent of American adults typically tell poll-sters they consider themselves to be "environmentalists" or are concerned about the environment. The Green movement should be riding high. The tidal wave of Green sensibility and political con-sensus that brought us cleaner air and water in the late twentieth century should now be chalking up victories on the most pressing issues of the twenty-first century.

Instead, the Green movement in America has lost its way. Environmentalists declared climate change to be the first truly global environmental emergency and reoriented the movement toward its prevention. Despite euphoria over the Paris climate agreement in late 2015, virtually nothing real has been achieved. Atmospheric CO_2 continues its relentless climb. After eight years of inaction under a conservative Republican administration, a progressive Democrat took office, but the Green agenda remained largely stalled. Even committed environmental insiders have pronounced "the death of environmentalism," provoking a decade-long bout of angst and self-doubt in the environmental community. What's going on and what can be done about it?

I've always admired John McPhee's 1965 book about Bill Bradley, *A Sense of Where You Are*. New York Knicks star and later U.S. Senator Bradley explains to McPhee that one of his principal basketball strategies was not to focus on where the basket was, but on his position on the court. Know exactly where you are in the field of play, Bradley suggested, and scoring will follow. Focus only on the goal, and you will miss the challenges and opportunities all around you. The Green movement has focused way too much on its goals, such as dramatic reduction of greenhouse gas pollution, and not nearly enough on the question of where the movement itself stands in its field of play: the court of politics and public sentiment in which the game will be won or lost. Bradley played to improve his field position. Once he achieved that objective, scoring followed. Greens should do the same.

So where are we? The bipartisan political consensus that had Republican congressmen voting for, and Richard Nixon signing, the most important environmental legislation of the 1970s has been lost and replaced with what I call the "Great Estrangement": a conservative movement dominated by those deeply suspicious of Green goals and hostile to virtually all policies advocated by environmentalists; and a Green movement that all too often appears hostile to business and economic growth.

A market research firm asks Americans each year if they agree with the statement, "Most of the people actively involved in environmental groups are extremists, not reasonable people." In 1996, 32 percent agreed. By 2004, that number had leapt to an incredible 43 percent.[2] Nine years after the "conservative revolution" of 1995, the newly vigorous right, with aid from missteps by the Green movement itself, had deeply damaged the standing of environmentalism in America. Since then, the partisan gap in attitudes over the environment has grown more than in any other area, and now—according to Pew polling—is one of two topics on which Republicans and Democrats disagree the most.[3]

Most Greens are aware of this sorry state of affairs and uncomfortable with the hyperpartisanship in which the Green agenda is now mired. Gus Speth, formerly dean of the Yale School of Forestry and Environmental Studies and a major figure in modern environmentalism, was typical of movement leaders in 2008 when he argued that getting the environmental movement back on track requires "a new politics," but nowhere does his vision of a new politics acknowledge, address, or involve the nearly sixty million Americans who were then about to vote for John McCain. Speth, like so many in the movement, had simply written off the Republican Party.[4] For too many Greens, it is as if American conservatives do not exist. Presumably they believe that the Green movement's goals can be achieved without the GOP, and also perhaps that it is just not possible to persuade American conservatives to care about the environment. Both of these beliefs are wrongheaded and highly irresponsible.

As early as 2004, before the second Bush term, some Greens started to urge the movement to "rethink everything." Two environmental insiders, Michael Shellenberger and Ted Nordhaus, caused a firestorm of controversy with their essay, *The Death of Environmentalism,* which was followed two months later by a speech by Adam Werbach, former head of the Sierra Club, titled *The Death of Environmentalism and the Birth of the Commons Movement.*[5] Werbach, a wunderkind who became president of the Sierra Club at age twenty-three, declared to his audience at the Commonwealth Club of California, "I am here to perform an autopsy. . . . I am done calling myself an environmentalist." These disenchanted environmentalists went on to offer similar solutions, a call for Greens to broaden their scope and merge the environmental movement into an undifferentiated leftist/progressive agenda.

Although in my opinion their prescription for the environmental movement was wrong, they were correct about one thing: simply adjusting course is not sufficient. Shellenberger and Nordhaus argued, "We will never be able to turn things around as long as we understand our failures as essentially tactical, and make proposals that are essentially technical."[6] But, from the perspective of only one decade later, it seems that they too were merely tactical in advocating continuing the "war" to "overcome the alliance of neoconservative ideologues and industry interests in Washington, D.C."[7] It was all too easy to blame the Green movement's failures on business and "neoconservative ideologues." We now know, after seven years of a progressive president and a 2014 midterm election that returned control of both houses of Congress to the right, that those ideological conservatives and "industry interests" are here to stay. Greens have fought the "war" against them to paralysis, and the planet is paying the price. It's time to try something else.

What is that something else? I believe that getting the Green movement back on track requires change in three main areas. First, instead of giving up on conservatives, we must seek to reconnect a critical mass of moderates and conservatives with their long tradition of support for conservation. Second, to succeed in the next fifty years, environmentalism needs a coherent, strong, and sustainable rationale, and one that answers the charge that Greens care more about nature than they do about people. If we cannot articulate an answer to the question "Why save nature?" that is persuasive to ordinary Americans and consistent with their needs and aspirations, then the Green movement is unlikely to flourish. And, finally, the modern Green movement, which is now a half-century old, must look honestly at its own failings and limitations, and get its house in order for the challenges ahead. This includes putting to rest the old Green refrain that economic growth and big corporations are the enemy.

The Great Estrangement will not end with conservative capitulation to the compelling urgency of the Green agenda; instead, the Green movement will need to listen to conservatives, take a few steps in their direction, and focus on that space where the values of right and left overlap, which I call "Center Green." Center Green takes as its model the national land trust movement, a corner of the environmental movement that has succeeded in maintaining vigorous bipartisan support. Center Green is a modest change in approach rooted in the way America is, not a utopian vision of what it could become. It is, above all, pragmatic and nonideological, where policy is measured not by whether it is the optimum solution, but by the two-part test of whether it would make a meaningful contribution to an environmental problem, and whether it is achievable politically.

Most books dealing with environmental politics—especially those aimed at "turning" conservatives to the Green side—start by trying to convince the reader about the urgency of the planet's problems and the necessity of implementing the Green movement's solutions. This book does not. It contains no descriptions of dying coral reefs, disappearing rain forests, floating islands of plastic waste, or predictions of climate apocalypse. I assume that if you are reading this book you are already interested in environmental issues, familiar with the environmental problems we face, and desirous of seeing at least some of the Green agenda implemented. However, I do not assume that you buy in to the entire

Green agenda. You may come to your environmentalism through a particular interest in saving land, birds, or fish; working on ocean acidification; conserving energy; cleaning up a river; promoting recycling; saving a community garden in your urban neighborhood; or any other particular cause. And your Green credentials are welcome here regardless of your views on what we should do about climate change.

The message of this book is aimed at Greens of all political hues: learn how to make major chunks of the Green agenda relevant and acceptable to a sustainable majority of Americans, or fail. This message does not presume that either the right or the left has a monopoly on virtue or the capacity to save the planet. But it does presume that American conservatism has been, and will continue to be, a powerful and occasionally predominant force in American life for the foreseeable future, and thus that American Greens should have no higher priority than escaping from hyperpartisan paralysis and recapturing the bipartisan support that characterized the modern American environmental movement at its inception.

——————

A 1931 song about the struggles of coal-mine workers in Harlan County, Kentucky, asks the question, "Which side are you on, boys?" and resonates deeply with most Americans. You've got to pick a side. And now social psychologists such as Jonathan Haidt tell us this is not just a cultural preference, but also the way our brains are wired.[8] When someone speaks or writes, my brain wants to know whose side is he on—my team, or the other one? If my team, his words will be greeted with a presumption of validity and my brain will work hard to convince me that he's right. If the other team, my brain will be in skeptical mode, working overtime to find flaws in his arguments.

This means that you, the reader, may still be trying to figure out which side your author is on. You probably made an assumption about that question when choosing to read this book, and whether you continue beyond this prologue may well turn on what you decide. Am I a liberal Green making crafty arguments in an attempt to sell the Green agenda to conservatives? Or am I a right-winger, making a pathetic attempt to argue that my ideology won't lead inevitably to the death of the planet? You want to know.

If the social psychologists are right, you won't like my answer, because I do not fit neatly into the boxes with which you are most comfortable. I have a foot in both camps. Yes, I am a "Green." I call myself an environmentalist. I have been deeply involved with land conservation, at the local, regional, and national levels, for a quarter century. I have served on the boards of various local and national environmental, conservation, and parks organizations and have provided support and counsel to many of them. I head an ad hoc group of environmental leaders in New York State. And, as an amateur horticulturalist, I have an emotional attachment to the inanimate side of life on earth, and a gardener's appreciation for the risks (and rewards) to the natural world of human activity. I have experienced the redemptive power of nature.

Although I have devoted a great deal of time and energy to Green causes, my "day job" gives me a perspective on environmental issues that few of my fellow Greens share. For the past three decades I worked as a Wall Street lawyer at the heart of global capitalism. Most of my clients have been large multinational companies, including some of the leading resource and energy companies so often vilified by Greens.[9] As head of my law firm's global project development and finance practice, I have worked on the financing of large mining, oil, gas, pipeline, and other infrastructure projects—exactly the sorts of projects against which Green NGOs so often campaign. My work has given me the chance to see the main actors in these environmental dramas at work.

Friends have long joked that my environmental work must be atonement for my career in financing large resource and energy projects. But I have found that having a foot in each camp makes me both a better environmentalist and a better counselor to business. And it is my decades of straddling the line between the worlds of the multinational corporation and the Green NGO that gave rise to, and make possible, this book.

Okay, you say, but this book is about politics. And here you really need to know, which side am I on? I'm not sure you will like this answer much better. Following the arc (if not exact timing) of the advice that any man under twenty-five who is not a socialist has no heart, and any man over twenty-five who is a socialist has no head, I delivered a rousing nominating speech for George McGovern at my high school's Mock Democratic Convention in 1972, but in my mid-twenties was pulled toward the GOP for two principal reasons. The first was my exposure in the late 1970s to pre-Thatcher Britain, where the corrosive effects of European socialism—on both the economy and culture—were dramatically obvious. Second was the receipt of my first paycheck as a lawyer, where the corrosive effects of federal, state, and New York City income taxes were illustrated with equal vividness. During my thirties and forties, I was viewed as a reasonably firm fiscal and smaller-government conservative, albeit one with no sympathy for the "culture war" agenda of the GOP.

The Bush years were tough ones for New York Republicans like me. We were appalled by the gradual take-over of the national party by movement conservatives and evangelicals, by a cultural agenda that seemed so at odds with the libertarian flavor of American conservatism, and by the overall dumbing down of the GOP (especially in economic and fiscal matters, where the party's rejection of Keynesian stimulus in times of crisis seemed to betray deliberate ignorance of history). I voted for George Bush *père* with some enthusiasm and George Bush *fils* once without enthusiasm. But after Tom DeLay, Gale Norton, the hypocrisy of the Terri Schiavo affair, "faith-based funding," and bans on stem-cell research, I couldn't pull the lever for Bush a second time. When 2011 rolled around, with the Republican Party firmly under the influence of its "Teavangelical" wing and offering the nation candidates such as Michele Bachmann, Mike Huckabee, Rick Perry, and Rick Santorum, I could not in good faith remain enrolled in the GOP. Before the 2012 election, having been a registered Republican since I was first eligible to vote, I reregistered as "unaffiliated" and joined the 42 percent of my compatriots who self-identify as "independent."[10]

So I leave it to you to judge which side I am on. I hope you conclude at least that I am not wholly in the enemy camp, and perhaps that my history of sympathy with your team (whichever one that may be) means that there might be something in this book worth reading.

1

THE GREEN AGENDA IN A HYPERPARTISAN AMERICA

The Green agenda is at a standstill. During the past twenty-five years, not only have we failed to move any piece of landmark federal environmental legislation, but federal spending on environment and conservation shrank from about 4 percent of the nation's budget to less than 1 percent.[1] And what did the Green movement do during this time? It totally realigned itself to address climate change, a problem that should have galvanized the nation into action. Instead, after two decades of effort, Americans remain deeply split over whether climate change is a problem and the American public consistently tells pollsters that the Green movement's issues are not near the top of its list of priorities. Mainstream Greens, even with a friend in the White House, find themselves stuck playing defense as environmental challenges escalate. Despite the conservative origins of American conservation, many conservatives would now agree with the Heritage Foundation, which called the environmental movement "the greatest single threat to the American economy." The Green movement finds itself mired in the vortex of hyperpartisan fury that dominates Washington and from which there appears to be no escape.

Of course I recognize that over the same period the American environmental movement has done much good work and achieved a great deal. Green organizations have litigated and lobbied on every Green issue, and achieved important victories before federal regulators and courts. At the state and local levels Green organizations have decades of legislative accomplishments. The Green movement has increased fuel efficiency and limited vehicle emissions, convinced regulators to reduce allowable emissions of numerous toxic substances, stopped hundreds of environmentally damaging projects, restored fisheries, increased food safety, protected countless wilderness and conservation areas, changed the behavior of dozens of the world's largest corporations, educated millions of children about environmental issues, and profoundly changed the landscape of American opinion and practice in relation to recycling and energy conservation. But this does not change two essential facts: during the 1970s and 1980s the movement measured success largely by its achievements in Washington, D.C., and the most critical problems of the twenty-first century, which cannot be solved in the statehouse or by changing individual behavior, also require political victories at the federal level. When environmentalism is viewed against the critical tests of federal legislation, federal spending, progress on climate, and public opinion, the failure of the environmental movement comes into clear focus.

During the past quarter century, the Green movement's main message has been clear and simple: reduce greenhouse gas emissions by 70 percent (now 80 percent) as soon as possible or else a disaster of epic proportions will befall you and your children. With a vice president and presidential candidate as its main spokesman on the issue, all the tools of modern media and communication at its disposal, hundreds of millions of charitable dollars diverted from other priorities to fund a response to the crisis, *both* presidential candidates in 2008 supporting climate cap-and-trade legislation, and the new president pledged to make it one of his highest priorities, the Green movement has achieved . . . nothing. The culmination of all of that effort, the Waxman-Markey cap-and-trade bill, died in 2010 without even being brought to the Senate floor for a vote.

Even worse, the American public is far from agreeing that climate change is a problem, much less coming to a consensus around a solution. According to recent Pew Research Center polling, only 40–42 percent of Americans believe that global warming is caused by human activity.[2] Twenty-six years after NASA first alerted us to the fact of climate change, the Green movement has managed to convince only four out of ten of us that it is a problem that we caused and can correct. This is an astonishing failure.[3]

It gets worse. Since the failure of Waxman-Markey in 2010 the antienvironmental right has seized the initiative and the paralysis has deepened. The subject of climate change was not raised by any reporter, or either candidate, in any of the 2012 presidential debates. There is, by universal consensus, no prospect of federal legislation of any sort dealing with climate change. Instead, in 2011 and 2012 Republicans rallied around legislation called the Energy Tax Prevention Act, designed to reverse the Supreme Court's decision allowing the EPA to regulate emissions of greenhouse gases, and also sought to slash the budget of that agency to prevent it from acting on climate even were it to retain the authority. After the 2010 elections, seventy-six of the eighty-five GOP congressional freshmen signed the "no climate tax pledge" (to oppose "any legislation relating to climate change that includes a net increase in government revenue"). "Americans for Prosperity," a Koch-funded group, announced that the entire GOP House leadership had signed the pledge, and in 2013 the group cited a report estimating that a quarter of the Senate and a third of the House had signed. The antienvironmental legislative activism is not limited to climate. A study commissioned by congressmen Waxman and Markey reports that the House voted 247 times on proposals to undermine the framework of federal environmental law that has existed for decades.[4]

Signaling the hopelessness of any sort of legislative action, the president decided to act unilaterally. Waiting three years after the demise of Waxman-Markey, President Obama in 2013 gave a speech at Georgetown University in which he unveiled "The President's Climate Action Plan," a collection of measures that the executive branch of the U.S. government would take to combat climate change, none of which require legislative sanction. The centerpiece was a proposed regulatory limit on greenhouse gas emissions from newly built electric power plants, known as the Clean Power Plan, which was finally adopted by the EPA in August 2015. Although the status of greenhouse gasses as "pollutants" for purposes of the Clean Air Act was confirmed by the U.S. Supreme Court in 2007 (in the context of motor vehicle emissions) and 2014 (with respect to already-regulated "stationary sources," like power plants), within 12 hours of its publication in the Federal Register, it became the most heavily contested environmental regulation ever. Twenty-five states and numerous industry groups commenced litigation, and many of the plaintiffs asked that the regulation be stayed, or prevented from taking effect, until the litigation was resolved. Most commentators believe that this litigation will be finally decided only by the Supreme Court, and perhaps as late as 2018.[5] Even if the new EPA rules survive legal challenge, Congress has voted once to overturn them (blocked by a presidential veto) and could do so again. In the long run, it is highly doubtful that regulation and executive action alone will be sufficient to comply with the commitments made by the United States at the Paris conference and to effect the necessary shift in America's energy policy. In addition, as a regulation and not a law, the Clean Power Plan simply could be rescinded by a subsequent administration. Although the president has taken an important step to seize the initiative from the opponents of climate action, every sign indicates that hyperpartisanship will continue to paralyze the federal government, preventing it from acting in any meaningful and permanent way in relation to the Green movement's number one priority.

The quarter-century drought in federal environmental legislation not only resulted in our inability to deal with newly presented challenges such as climate change, but also resulted in the erosion of the federal government's effectiveness in dealing with air and water quality, toxics, and other threats. The basic legislative framework that gives the federal government its environmental protection powers was enacted during the 1970s and was designed to evolve in response to experience and technological developments. These laws were periodically reauthorized and amended during the period up to 1990, but have been largely unchanged since then. This is a problem. Environmental technologies and economics have evolved significantly, and our experience under these statutes has resulted in both left and right concluding that changes are necessary to make them more effective, efficient, and fair. But frozen by toxic politics, Congress has failed to act, and now our country's core environmental laws are a quarter-century stale.

Federal spending on the environment is another measure of the Green movement's moxie in federal politics. Each year, Congress must appropriate billions of dollars to allow federal regulators to do their work and federal investment in the environment to continue. An analysis of the nation's Green spending produces an equally disturbing metric. The federal budget is divided into approximately twenty categories that group spending by function (or subject matter). It provides a convenient way to measure long-term trends in budget priorities. According to the House Committee on the Budget, "Function 300" spending includes "programs concerned with environmental protection and enhancement; recreation and wildlife areas; and the development and management of the nation's land, water, and mineral resources." A review of Function 300 over the past few decades tells a distressing story. Prior to 1984, spending in this function category accounted for about 4 percent of the nation's budget. Recently, it has fallen to less than 1 percent.[6] This means that environmental spending as a percentage of the total budget is now less than one-quarter of what it used to be. As the federal budget approximately doubled between 1980 and 2010, items grouped in Function 300 increased by only 2 percent.[7]

Part of this is due to the uncontrolled growth in "entitlement" spending and corresponding decrease in all discretionary spending as part of the total federal budget (per the Congressional Budget Office, only 40 percent of the total federal outlays in 2011 were "discretionary," with half of that devoted to defense).[8] But even if analyzed solely in the context of nondefense discretionary funding, the picture is still grim. An analysis by the Boone and Crockett Club shows that in 1975 Function 300 accounted for 11.5 percent of nondefense discretionary spending; by 2010 it had fallen to only 6.5 percent.[9] By any measure, we cannot say that the environmental movement has succeeded in convincing Congress to prioritize environmental needs.

The state of the environmental movement itself, four decades after approximately twenty million Americans took to the streets on the first Earth Day, is not much better. It is true that 70–80 percent of Americans typically tell pollsters that they are "environmentalists" or support strong standards for clean air and water.[10] But those numbers tell us nothing about how much voters *care* about those issues, or how they *prioritize* environmental issues when casting their votes. Looked at from that perspective, the results are alarming. Over and over, when asked to compare various issues in terms of importance, either generally or to the respondent's community, environment fares badly, typically ranking far below concerns such as the economy, jobs, health care, social security, education, terrorism, moral values, taxes, and other things.[11] A Gallup poll in March 2012 found that Americans' concerns about air and drinking water pollution had fallen to all-time lows, with all environmental issues included in the poll showing sharp drops in concern since 2000.[12] This growing indifference to the environmental cause cannot be blamed simply on the financial crisis of 2008 and the resulting reluctance of legislators and citizens alike to take actions that could harm the recovery. The boom periods prior to 2008, when marginal declines in the rate of economic growth could have been more easily tolerated, were times of even greater hostility toward the climate-change agenda.

So what is the explanation? How is it possible that, at the same time when the need for environmental action has never been more compelling, the Green agenda has been stalled, with half the country actively hostile, and the other half not caring very much? The answer is clear: politics.

There are several reasons to believe that the hyperpartisanship that has prevailed in Washington during the past two decades is the major factor contributing to the impasse. First is that, as chronicled in the next chapter, virtually every major advance of the environmental agenda in America for the past century has been the result of *bipartisan* action.[13] There is simply no historical precedent for any major Green bill progressing into law unless at least some segment of each party has been willing to work with the other. Also, while the United States has suffered partisan paralysis, other countries not similarly afflicted have made substantial progress on environmental issues, including greenhouse gas emissions. South Korea set up an emissions trading scheme that commenced in 2015, and both Japan and Australia introduced carbon taxes.[14] A study by a group of legislators from around the world indicated that of sixty-six countries studied (accounting for 88 percent of human greenhouse gas emissions), sixty-one now have some sort of basic domestic legislation designed to address the climate crisis.[15] During 2012 alone, when the United States could not even pass a budget, this group of countries passed twenty new environmental laws.[16]

What was the difference? Pew polling has confirmed what most of us already knew: the value gap between Republicans and Democrats has grown to a chasm, and each side is waging the partisan battle with unprecedented vigor. Measured across forty-eight different values, the policy gap between the two sides nearly *doubled* between 1987 and 2012.[17] Other metrics of partisanship, "party unity" (the number of times that representatives vote together with the majority of their own party), tracked by *Congressional Quarterly* since the 1950s, together with partisan animosity, as measured by Pew, also have risen to all-time highs. And in even broader historical perspective, a recent study has demonstrated that partisanship has risen steadily since the late 1970s, reaching levels not seen in this country since the time of Reconstruction following the Civil War.[18]

This same steep curve of rising partisan rancor plots the corresponding loss of environmental bipartisanship that was the foundation for the Green movement in the decade following the first Earth Day. Pew polling shows that between 1987 and 2012, the partisan divide in the area of the environment grew from a gap of only 5 percentage points to a gap of 39 percentage points, the greatest change in any of the fifteen subject-matter values studied by Pew. The falloff in support from Republicans was astonishing: in 1992 86 percent of GOP members agreed that "there needs to be stricter laws and regulations to protect the environment"; by 2012 that number had plummeted to 47 percent. This contrasts with 93 percent of 2012 Democrats who recognize the need for better environmental regulation.

In absolute terms, the partisan difference regarding environment is now the second largest of any of the partisan gaps examined by Pew, only slightly behind the issues of whether the social safety net should be expanded. This bears repeating: as of 2012, the environment was one of two things about which Republicans and Democrats disagreed most, more than they disagree about labor unions, the scope of government, immigration, business, or religiosity.[19]

As a result, the national Green movement is now tightly allied with the Democratic Party, and the GOP hardly bothers to contest the environmental vote. The League of Conservation Voters' annual scorecard demonstrates virtually no engagement between the parties on the federal legislation scored by that organization. In the League scorecards from 2009 to 2012, the average scores for the Democratic House leadership are 93, 100, 94, and 86. For the Republican leadership in the House in the same years: 0, 0, 9, and 6. Tea Party activists and GOP primary voters vigilantly discipline any Republican congressman who strays from the antienvironmental line, and the occupancy of approximately two hundred House seats is effectively determined in the Republican primary, as the result of gerrymandering that makes it virtually impossible for the other party to successfully contest the general election.[20] So even as the power of the Tea Party and "establishment" factions of the GOP waxes and wanes, most political analysts cannot yet see any path to a politics where the GOP is released from the grip of the anti-Green force.

Finding a path out of the hyperpartisan vortex requires three things: an understanding that a century of conservative leadership of the conservation movement set the stage for the bipartisan consensus of the 1970s; an analysis of the causes of the great environmental estrangement between right and left that began in the mid-1990s; and a frank analysis of the strengths and weakness of the half-century-old Green movement.

2

IT WASN'T ALWAYS THIS WAY

A Brief History of Conservation and the Right

> The nation behaves well if it treats the natural
> resources as assets which it must turn over to the next
> generation increased, and not impaired, in value.
>
> —THEODORE ROOSEVELT

Political battles are fought on many fronts, and one of them is the struggle to take control of history. Given the extreme politicization of environmental issues, it should be no surprise that we also find dueling narratives of the history of the Green movement itself. According to one, the Green movement is a progressive social movement with its roots in the counterculture of the 1960s, kin to the civil rights and antiwar movements of that era. According to the other, the movement has its roots deep in the transcendentalist thinking of the nineteenth century, and stands on the shoulders of Emerson, Thoreau, and Burroughs, with Muir, Pinchot, and Teddy Roosevelt then translating this sensibility into a call to conservation action. Of course neither narrative is entirely accurate. The truth is more complex: the Green movement is woven from many different strands of philosophy, ideology, interests, values, and politics, and the complexity and diversity of its ideological and political origins is—or at least can be—one of its great strengths.

Allocating "credit" for the origins of the American Green movement is a tricky business, and I am not making any historical or phil-osophical claim that environmentalism "belongs" to either party or ideology. But we now suffer from a sort of historical blind spot that does need to be addressed in order for the environmental agenda to advance. Many of the contemporary conservatives who are now so hostile to the Green movement have no idea of the role that con-servatives played in advancing and shaping that movement over the course of the twentieth century.

American conservation is a plant with deep and vigorous roots, some extending back to the mother country where the so-called cult of nature flourished in conservative circles, and Tories joined with radicals in recoiling against the industrial revolution and industrial farming.[1] In the New World, Whigs and conservatives played a simi-lar role after the Civil War in setting the foundation for conservation as a political movement. Sometimes called the country's first "con-servationist," George Perkins Marsh was a Whig politician who in 1864 articulated the case for ecological conservation in its modern form, observing that the steady transformation by Americans of the landscape of the New World was a "great revolution . . . vast in its magnitude," presenting American civilization with "contingent and unsought results" that could then only dimly be perceived.[2] As an instinctive conservative, he warned that this power to overturn the natural order implied a weighty responsibility to use that power for the public good and with an eye to preserving the long continuity of civilization.

At the same time that Marsh wrote these words, the American people—only recently exposed to the unique beauty of the Ameri-can West—were shocked by the obvious dwindling of the wilderness they had once perceived as limitless. At the same time, the transcen-dentalist belief in the transformative power of nature, together with the romantic and nationalist tendencies of the age, caused people to perceive meaning and value in the American wilderness in a way that few did in the antebellum culture. This sensibility lead to the creation of Yellowstone National Park in 1872 and Yosemite National Park in 1890 and, in 1892, the moment that probably marks the beginning of conservation as a movement with political aspirations, the formation of the Sierra Club.

The first great flourishing of the conservation movement in America occurred in the twenty years following the turn of the century, and its leader, exemplar, and philosopher was the great Republican president, Theodore Roosevelt. Roosevelt, although "progressive" in his fight against corruption, rejection of monopoly, and embrace of scientific management principles, was a conservative in his nationalist love of country and commitment to capitalism.[3] Like English Tories of a generation before, he was convinced that the materialism of the industrial age threatened the corruption of traditional American values. Only in nature could Americans connect with the honesty, strength, and simple virtue that he believed defined the American character. Because TR came to his love of the land through the camping, fishing, and hunting that were the chief recreations of his class, the conservation imperative for him was deeply personal.

But at the same time, conservation TR-style was largely utilitarian: the goal was the practical and economical use of resources, informed by science and professional expertise. No one could accuse TR of putting the interests of nature above those of man, and his understanding of the relationship between nature and human health has a distinctly twenty-first-century resonance. The nation's first Conservation Conference, organized by Roosevelt at the White House in May 1908, produced a report stating: "The spirit and vigor of our people are the chief glory of the republic. Yet even as we have neglected our natural resources, so have we been thoughtless of life and health."[4] As much as his conservation was animated by his genuine love for the great outdoors, his policies were justified primarily by what nature could do for people and to sustain America's prosperity. The conservation movement that enjoyed such popular support and political success during the first two decades of the century was, in today's jargon, anthropocentric, and comfortable with—indeed convinced of the necessity of—balancing the protection of nature with the economic needs and aspirations of people.

By 1920, Roosevelt's pragmatic flavor of conservation was the prevailing model, and was distinguishable from the approach being taken by the Sierra Club and those who preferred to describe themselves as "preservationists"—those dedicated to the protection of nature for its own sake. This dichotomy played out in the first great environmental battle of the century, the fight over whether to flood the spectacular Hetch Hetchy Valley in Yosemite National Park to create a reliable water supply for the burgeoning city of San Francisco. In defense of the Tuolumne River and the inviolability of the National Park: the Sierra Club and John Muir. On the other side: the utilitarian calculus of Theodore Roosevelt and Gifford Pinchot. The needs of the people of San Francisco won out.

Although with the benefit of hindsight TR was probably wrong about Hetch Hetchy (the inviolability of national parks being a fundamental principle), TR's conservation record is unmatched by that of any other president of either party. Thirteen national parks were created by 1916, when the National Park Service was created, and Roosevelt added 130 million acres to our national forest lands, fifty-one new national wildlife refuges, and eighteen new national monuments. It is a stunning achievement that changed the face of the country.

TR believed that conservation was mandated by the values and principles that he understood to be fundamentally conservative, including a moral duty of responsible stewardship for future generations. Republican leadership of the conservation movement was also, as several historians have pointed out, unsurprising, because both the conservation movement and political conservatism were then dominated by (in the language of the academy) "people of privilege."[5]

Many but by no means all leaders of this first wave of conservation activism shared TR's social standing, influence, wealth, and class values—together with a salutary hankering for public service.[6] TR's friend Gifford Pinchot, perhaps (with the benefit of hindsight) even more influential than TR himself, came from a wealthy family and attended Yale. But to call the early-twentieth-century conservation movement "elitist" is misleading. John Muir was largely self-taught and often impoverished during his early life. And most importantly, conservation was genuinely popular. Only 69,000 people visited the national parks in 1908; by 1915 that number had risen to 335,000.

Following this energetic burst during the first two decades of the century, neither party had much use for conservation during the heady days of the 1920s, during which Republican Warren Harding foreshadowed some of the active antipathy to conservation that would arise again in the 1980s. He appointed a secretary of the interior dedicated to the unmanaged exploitation of resources, an enthusiasm that led him to issue leases over federal oil reserves in return for bribes, leading to the infamous "Teapot Dome" scandal. Interestingly, although history paints him as obsessively laissez-faire, the next Republican president, Calvin Coolidge, has been called by some historians "the first conservationist President since Theodore Roosevelt"; he supported legislation to regulate the Alaska salmon fisheries, limit water pollution, and conserve mineral resources.[7]

With a few notable exceptions, conservation did not return to the first rank of political discourse during the years of the Depression, the Second World War, and the 1950s.[8] But heading into the latter decades of the twentieth century, a few things were incontestable: conservation had deep roots in conservative thinking and shared several important core constituencies with the GOP; the golden age of conservation activism had occurred under a Republican president; and the issue did not belong to either of the political parties.

On January 22, 1970, three months before the first Earth Day, President Richard Nixon delivered his first State of the Union Address. The domestic-policy part of the speech reflected a conservative agenda: reinvigorated states' rights, balanced budgets, and increased law enforcement. But the longest part of the speech, greeted with vigorous applause from both sides of the aisle, was dedicated to the environment, and included the following:

> [I]n the year 1980 will the President standing in this place . . . look back on a decade in which 70 percent of our people lived in metropolitan areas choked by traffic, suffocated by smog, poisoned by water, deafened by noise? . . . The great question of the seventies is, shall we surrender to our surroundings, or shall we make peace with nature and begin to make reparations for the damage we have done to our air, to our land, and to our water? . . . It has become a common cause of all the people of this country. . . . Clean air, clean water, open spaces—these should once again be the birthright of every American.[9]

It is difficult to imagine anyone in the Republican leadership today giving such a speech. But the 1970s was a decade when partisanship was eclipsed by what William F. Buckley referred to as our "common revulsion" at environmental damage.[10] There was no reason to think that Republicans or conservatives would be less concerned than anyone else about being sickened by the air they breathed or the water they drank, and indeed they were not. American hero and archconservative Charles Lindbergh had emerged from his cocoon of privacy to campaign for conservation.[11] As late as 1990, polling indicated that among respondents calling themselves "active environmentalists," an equal portion self-described as "liberal" and "conservative."[12] Richard Nixon called environmentalism "a cause beyond party and beyond factions." Barry Goldwater was a member of both the Sierra Club and Republicans for Environmental Protection.[13]

The rise of the environmental movement during the 1960s has been well chronicled. The customary narrative focuses on specific incidents like the burning of the Cuyahoga River, the Santa Barbara oil spill, and the coining of the word "smog" for the new plague that afflicted Los Angeles.[14] But the key point is that the consequences of underregulated economic growth were ubiquitous, and experienced personally by a plurality of American citizens, both rural and urban. They gazed on rivers and lakes that seemed irredeemably fouled, the air was visibly dirty and hard to breathe, and litter covered the streets of cities where buildings were black with soot. The farms, forests, and open spaces that before the war had surrounded those cities now were gone, and suburbs gobbled up open lands at an alarming rate. Their government had allowed thalidomide to be sold as part of a "clinical trial" and their neighbors' children suffered hideous birth defects, and now Rachel Carson warned them that DDT and the hundreds of other chemicals that before had seemed to define modernity could actually be damaging their family's health. And all this at the exact time postwar America had created a broad middle class that expected a country in which it could enjoy its newfound affluence. The new environmental agenda was not about far-off wilderness, but about the pollution and ugliness that plagued their lives every day. Americans optimistically believed that these problems, like disease and poverty, could be solved by a country that seemed as powerful and prosperous as any in history.

Americans wanted pollution to be addressed by their national government and so the issue now known as "the environment" catapulted to the front lines of national politics.[15] The number of Americans telling pollsters that "reducing pollution of air and water" should be one of the top three priorities of government had climbed from 17 percent in 1965 to 53 percent on the eve of Nixon's inauguration.[16] As Nixon's cabinet secretary wrote in an article many years later, "When President Nixon and his staff walked into the White House on January 20, 1969, we were totally unprepared for the tidal wave of public opinion in favor of cleaning the nation's environment that was about to engulf us."[17]

The near universality of these concerns allowed the environment, unlike the rest of the social agenda of the 1960s, to avoid the deeply partisan reaction that greeted the movements for civil rights, social justice, and peace in Vietnam. As one historian explains, "Of all the suggestions and protests of the 1960s, environmentalism was the one that most easily found a place in the mainstream. . . . Instead of becoming oppositional in the manner of the leftist politics of the decade, environmentalism became a point of healing in the culture wars that racked the United States. . . . Unlike radical politics, which withered as American involvement in Vietnam slowed . . . environmentalism gained and retained a political and cultural resonance. As the 1970s began, environmentalists and their supporters had many reasons for optimism."[18]

That optimism proved to be well founded. The first Earth Day, on April 22, 1970, launched a decade of extraordinary legislative achievement, when the modern framework for American environmental policy, law, and regulation was created. In a sign of the bipartisan tone that would prevail for much of the next ten years, Earth Day itself had bipartisan sponsorship. The idea was that of Democratic senator Gaylord Nelson, who reportedly aimed not only to galvanize the nascent environmental movement, but also "to limit its links with the New Left that was so prominent on American college campuses at the time."[19] Early in the process, he recruited California Republican Paul (Pete) McCloskey to co-chair the Earth Day Steering Committee. Congress adjourned that April 22 to permit its members to speak at Earth Day events, and two-thirds of its members did. The head of the national coordinating group was explicit about his goal to create a centrist event: "We didn't want to lose the 'Silent Majority' just because of style issues."[20] By all reports, they succeeded. Many sources repeat the anecdote, which may nonetheless be apocryphal, of Richard Nixon looking out the window of the White House at the Earth Day rally on Pennsylvania Avenue and, seeing the well-dressed crowd, commenting, "Those are Republicans."[21] But even if that particular comment is apocryphal, there is other evidence of Nixon's evolving view of environmentalism. In his privately published memoir, Russell Train remembers sitting next to the president at a dinner for the transition task forces shortly before the inauguration. He reports that the president was keenly aware of and interested in the political calculus of the environment, expressing his conviction that the environmental agenda could serve as a unifying political force.[22]

The single event that best illustrates the bipartisan consensus that prevailed at the dawn of modern environmentalism is the passage of the statute that provides the key architecture for our federal environmental law and regulations, the National Environmental Policy Act of 1969 (NEPA). NEPA passed the U.S. Senate unanimously, with all forty-three GOP senators voting in favor. In the House, 192 Republican congressmen voted yes and only 7 Republicans opposed the bill. NEPA, which imposed the requirement for environmental assessments and environmental impact statements on all projects taken or funded by federal agencies, was conceived by Democratic senator "Scoop" Jackson, but quickly endorsed by the politically savvy Nixon. The president wanted to sign the bill at the symbolically powerful midnight turn of the new decade, but was persuaded to wait and sign on the morning of January 1, 1970, when press coverage would be better.[23] In his signing statement, Nixon said, "By my participation in these efforts I have become further convinced that the 1970's absolutely must be the years when America pays its debt to the past by reclaiming the purity of its air, its waters, and our living environment. It is literally now or never."[24] Few people realize that later that year, in December, Nixon on his own motion created the Environmental Protection Agency as part of an executive branch reorganization.

Around the time of the adoption of NEPA by Congress, popular and political sentiment seemed to reach a tipping point, allowing for the first time rejection of potent symbols of modern progress on the basis of their environmental impact. Congress voted to end the U.S. supersonic aircraft project, largely in response to grassroots unhappiness at adding the sonic boom to the other burdens of modern life. President Nixon, acting by executive order, stopped the Army Corps of Engineers from completing the proposed Cross-Florida Barge Canal, which would have destroyed the Everglades. The rejection of projects like these, which once had seemed inevitable and unstoppable, together with the GOP having made the astute political calculation that fixing the environment could not be left to the other party, set the stage for a decade of largely bipartisan action during which the entire architecture of federal environmental regulation and policy—now so reviled by the right—came to life.

The relatively smooth passage of the many pieces of environmental legislation over the course of the decade does not mean that these bills were free from debate. The industrial sectors affected by clean air and water standards lobbied hard, and the debates reveal many differences over how to craft and implement the new requirements.[25] But to a political observer accustomed to the type of partisanship that prevailed during and after the 1990s, the record is startling. The 1970 Clean Air Act, 1972 Clean Water Act, Marine Protection, Research, and Sanctuaries Act of 1972, and even the legislation that within a decade would become the subject of GOP ridicule, the Endangered Species Act of 1973, all were passed by unanimous votes in the Senate (and the remaining legislation attracted overwhelming support from Republican senators, with only a handful in opposition). In the House, strong majorities of the GOP members supported every one of the landmark environmental bills during the decade.

	Number and Percentage of House Republicans Voting in Favor
1970 Clean Air Act [26]	165 (85%)
1972 Clean Water Act	142 (79%)
1972 Marine Protection, Research, and Sanctuaries Act of 1972	126 (70%)
1973 Endangered Species Act	160 (83%)
1974 Safe Drinking Water Act	116 (60%)
1975 Toxic Substances Control Act	95 (66%)
1976 Resource Conservation and Recovery Act	116 (81%)
1977 Water Pollution Control Act Amendments	108 (76%)
1980 Comprehensive Environmental Response, Compensation, and Liability Act (Superfund)	123 (78%)

The final act in this decade-long legislative surge, propelled in part by the Love Canal debacle in 1978–79, was the passage on December 11, 1980, of the Comprehensive Environmental Response, Compensation, and Liability Act (CERCLA), more widely known as "Superfund" for the fund it created for the cleanup of toxic waste sites. President Carter signed the new law with only six weeks left in his term. This historic wave of legislative action that ended with CERCLA in 1980 not only depended on a bipartisan political consensus, but it created a safe place in American politics where the divisive effects of the Vietnam War and the convulsions of the sexual revolution were held at bay. Professor Hal Rothman observed, "For a brief moment, it seemed as if the broad spectrum of support for environmental quality would heal the immense political rift in American society. Here was an issue that a wide range of Americans, from the leaders of industry to the political left, could embrace as a social objective."[27] The idea of the bipartisan consensus is not simply a construct imposed by historians with the benefit of hindsight, but was observed and understood at the time. Russell Kirk, who Ronald Reagan called "the prophet of American conservatism," wrote in 1971, "The issue of environmental quality is one which transcends traditional political boundaries. It is a cause which can attract, and very sincerely, liberals, conservatives, radicals, reactionaries, freaks and middle-class straights."[28]

Even though the bipartisan consensus started to fall apart with the "Reagan Revolution" in 1981, the spirit of bipartisan compromise produced several more important environmental achievements before disappearing completely in the mid-1990s. Before President George H. W. Bush tackled acid rain with the landmark Clean Air Act of 1990, the Reagan administration negotiated a treaty, the Montreal Protocol, to protect the Earth's ozone layer from the depleting effect of a class of industrial chemicals called chlorofluorocarbons (CFCs), then in common use as refrigerants and aerosols. The treaty required the phaseout of around one hundred different CFCs. Dramatic pictures of "holes" in that part of the atmosphere that protects us from harmful ultraviolet radiation helped to mobilize public support. Even though Tom DeLay and other doctrinaire conservatives opposed it, the effort attracted broad bipartisan support and was signed by President Reagan. Unlike similar efforts in relation to carbon dioxide, most countries honored their obligations, and the treaty proved to be a great success. According to one recent scientific study, these same CFCs are also now understood to be powerful greenhouse gases, and the Montreal Protocol has had the unintended effect of achieving a significant slowdown in atmospheric warming.[29] If this is correct, then we can draw the ironic conclusion that it was conservative heroes Ronald Reagan and Margaret Thatcher who championed one of the few initiatives to actually reduce the pace of global warming.

The lessons of this brief survey are clear: America's Green movement has deep roots in conservative thinking, was championed during the first stage of its evolution by Republican leaders, and morphed into modern environmentalism with the participation and support of both right and left. Every significant piece of environmental legislation resulted from bipartisan action.

So what went wrong? What took us from a place where Republicans could take the lead on environmental solutions to a place where Republicans can barely admit that there are such things as environmental problems? What happened is what I refer to as the Great Estrangement, a hard tack to the right by conservatives, a drift to the left by Greens, and the disastrous transformation of the environment from common cause to divisive wedge.

3

WHAT WENT WRONG

The Great Estrangement

Most environmental historians attribute the Great Estrangement, whereby the bipartisan environmental consensus of the 1960s and 1970s was lost, to the end of America's postwar economic expansion, specifically the decline in real wages starting in the mid-1970s and the oil shocks of 1973 and 1979. By 1976, 70 percent of Americans named "the economy" as their primary concern, and so it would continue, with only a few brief interruptions, for the next three decades.[1] This had profound implications for the young Green movement. Environmental historian Hal Rothman sees it as a relatively straightforward case of cause and effect: "In an era of prosperity it was easy to place the goals of environmentalism beside an expanding economy. As the economy slowed, these values overlapped. The result was first a fracturing of the bipartisan consensus and later the polarization of the dialogue about environmental issues."[2]

While it is true that over time support for the Green agenda somewhat correlates with the state of the economy, it also is clear that the end of the bipartisan consensus was as much a function of politics

as of economics. When Theda Skocpol of Harvard compared the gap
on Green issues between Republican and Democratic *voters* shown by
Gallup polling over the past forty years with the gap on environment
between Republican and Democratic *lawmakers* as revealed by the
League of Conservation Voters (LCV) National Environmental Scorecard, she found that public opinion did not polarize anywhere near
as much as congressional voting did.[3] This suggests to me that voters
and their increased concern with economic issues may not have been
the primary driver of the Great Estrangement. A 2014 study by three
social scientists supports the same conclusion, demonstrating that
antipathy toward environmental spending by the government originated with political elites, with public opinion only slowly changing
as individuals adjusted their opinions to conform to the new positions of their political parties.[4]

Whatever the cause, the result was clear. In Congress the partisan
gap on environment was modest and relatively stable between 1970
and 1990, but doubled between 1990 and 2000 and widened further
by 2010.[5] These metrics show that during the 1980s the bipartisan
consensus came under attack, during the 1990s it started to fall
apart, and by 2000 it was lost completely. Figuring out what happened is the first step in analyzing how to reclaim bipartisan support and move the Green agenda forward.

––––––––––––––

Upon moving into the White House, one of Ronald Reagan's first
acts was to remove the solar panels installed by President Carter, a
highly symbolic act that was quickly followed by a more substantive
anti-Green agenda. Reagan did not bother to nominate a person to
fill the vacant top job at the EPA for over a year, and when he did, the
woman he chose, Anne Gorsuch Burford, neutered the agency by cutting its budget and staff. One scholar observed: "She seemed more
determined to dismantle the EPA than [to] administer it."[6] Even

more fanatical was Reagan's secretary of the interior, James Watt, who brought evangelical certainty and "impregnable self-righteousness"[7] to the job of dismantling protections for Federal lands and opening natural resources to private sector exploitation.

The beginning of the Reagan administration marked a political shift, largely occurring within the Republican Party, that would come to full fruition fourteen years later with the 104th Congress. The Republican worthies who had been the stewards and proponents of the GOP's long tradition of conservation, men like Russell Train, Nathaniel Reed, William Ruckelshaus, and Nelson Rockefeller—largely establishment figures from the Northeast—were eclipsed by a new wave of western Republicans, resentful at the extent of federal government land ownership in the West, anxious to return control of land use to the states (the cause of the so-called Sagebrush Rebellion), ideologically libertarian, dismissive of environmentalists as a remote elite, and as willing as the left to unleash the dogs of class warfare against their enemies within the party.

The president's infectious optimism also may have encouraged some conservatives to dismiss environmental concerns and instead rely on a cheerful Reaganesque faith that these sorts of problems would simply take care of themselves, or, as one historian put it, should properly be viewed as mere "transitory irritants that would easily be resolved by the marketplace."[8] New conservative ideologues took particular exception to science's evolving understanding of the carcinogenic effects of certain toxins (called by one conservative commentator, the "big lie"),[9] an attitude foreshadowing the willful blindness that came to be embraced by so many conservatives in relation to climate change.

Despite these ominous developments, the country as a whole was not ready to embrace that part of the Reagan revolution that sought to dismantle the Green achievements of the prior decade. Burford was forced to resign as EPA administrator after only two years, and the appointment of GOP establishment figure William D. Ruckelshaus signaled the administration's conclusion that the country was not ready to give up on its adolescent environmental watchdog, and particularly its mission to protect Americans from the scourge of toxic chemicals.

At the same time, the extreme antics of Secretary Watt proved to be a boon to Green groups everywhere. The Sierra Club grew from 181,000 members in 1980 to 346,000 only three years later, and both the Wilderness Society and Audubon achieved similar growth as ordinary citizens looked to environmental NGOs to protect our national parks, national forests, and other public lands from the predations of Jim Watt and his allies.[10] In 1965, the combined annual budgets of the ten largest mainstream Green groups fell short of $10 million; by 1990, they totaled $514 million.[11] The younger activist litigating and lobbying NGOs, such as the Natural Resources Defense Council, also came into their own, effectively leveraging each new outrage from Watt and others in the Reagan administration to more than double their memberships, and attracting significant financial support from foundations, philanthropists, and celebrities. Professor Rothman concludes, "[I]n response to the Reagan revolution, the environmental movement reached a paradoxical maturity."[12] But this maturity brought with it not only the rise of the Green NGOs to their contemporary forms and influence, but also two trends that in the long run cost the movement more than the actions of anti-Green warriors like Burford and Watt: the overall leftward drift of the movement (a natural reaction to the assault from the right), and the radicalization of a part of the Green movement (Greenpeace, Earth First!, Animal Liberation Front, and others) that would thereafter compete with the larger groups for the hearts and souls of Greens, and change the way that ordinary Americans perceived environmentalists.

With millions of signatures on a "Dump Watt" petition drive, GOP reversals in the midterm election in 1982, and anger in Congress, Watt resigned in 1983. Congress managed to renew the Superfund Act in 1986, and the same year reauthorized and expanded the Safe Drinking Water Act, which was signed by President Reagan. The full-on assault on the Green movement had failed. In 1988 a poll of delegates to the Republican National Convention indicated that an overwhelming majority would pay higher taxes for a cleaner environment, and their nominee George H. W. Bush in his 1988 campaign promised to be the "environmental President."[13] He appointed William K. Reilly, then president of the World Wildlife Fund, to be his EPA administrator, and it would have been tempting to think that the early Reagan years had been an anomalous spasm, that the Republican Party was returning to its conservation roots, and that the bipartisan consensus might be restored. Tempting, but wrong.

In January 1993, with Bill Clinton and Al Gore in charge of the executive branch, and Green stalwarts Carol Browner and Bruce Babbitt presiding at the EPA and Department of the Interior, environmentalists were feeling confident. But with the benefit of hindsight, and perhaps informed by our current understanding of the right's superior skill at opposition, we see that President Clinton provided the bogeyman that the anti-Green forces on the right needed to finally and decisively drive an effective wedge between conservatives and the environment. The Sagebrush Rebellion, which burned slowly during the Reagan years, finally caught fire and morphed into the "Wise Use" movement under Clinton. The Wise Users piggybacked the economic aspirations of cattle, timber, and mining interests onto a stew of populist resentments. They promoted a nostalgic vision of land use in the West based on near-absolute private property rights and the return of federal lands to local control. Although burdened by their alleged ties with racist militias and an increasingly active violent fringe, they rose to a position of real influence within the GOP.

Clinton/Gore put environmental issues back on the national

agenda, proposing among other things to elevate the EPA administrator to the cabinet, refresh CERCLA, the Safe Drinking Water
Act, and the Clean Water Act, and reform the laws governing mining on federal lands. But the administration's failed efforts at fiscal
stimulus, health care reform, and dealing with gays in the military,
together with deep popular dissatisfaction with the pace of the
economy, led to historically low approval ratings for the president
and (with the exception of amendments to the Safe Drinking Water
Act passed by Congress and signed by Clinton in 1996) largely stalled
the president's environmental agenda.[14]

Then, in 1994, real disaster struck the Green movement. Republicans won majorities in both houses of Congress for the first time in
forty years, led by Newt Gingrich and dedicated to implementing his
"Contract With America." Speaker Gingrich and his seventy-three
freshmen rebels believed they had a mandate to dismantle the federal environmental regulatory apparatus as it then existed, and allow
industry and landowners to return to the prelapsarian days before
1970. Many of these freshmen found that anti-Green rhetoric was a
big winner in their home districts. For example, one of them, Representative Helen Chenoweth-Hage, a popular Republican from Idaho,
held an "endangered-salmon bake" and declared that "white men
are an endangered species," winning herself a place on the Speaker's
"Endangered Species Task Force."[15]

The phenomenon of the 104th Congress, which introduced the
budget battles, government shutdowns, and hyperpartisan dysfunction that is being replayed in Washington today, has been well
chronicled. The Contract With America was breathtakingly ambitious, and the newly minted GOP warriors in the House were dead
serious about its implementation. The House proceeded to craft and
in many cases pass legislation that attacked the fabric of federal
environmental law from every angle. This was not small-beer politics. The infamous seventeen "riders from hell" were attached to an
EPA appropriations bill and would have crippled that agency. Gin-

grich's warriors also sought to subject every federal environmental rule to a procedure that would have the effect of allowing a regulated industry to block regulation that it opposed, and would have required the federal government to pay regulated businesses for costs they would incur by complying with environmental rules. House Republicans also sought to amend the U.S. Constitution to treat regulation of land use as a "taking" that required government compensation, and then pursued this through ordinary federal legislation when the constitutional amendment failed. A cavalcade of less sweeping initiatives attempted to deaccession or defund national parks, cripple the Endangered Species Act, and implement virtually the entire agenda that had kicked around far-right circles since the early 1980s.

With very few exceptions, they failed, as few of the House bills were able to attract sufficient support in the Senate. But they succeeded in changing the face of American politics.

———

According to Pew polling, in 1987 the gap between Republican and Democratic voters expressing concern about the environment was only five points. By 2012, thanks in large part to the wedge politics that took hold in the mid-1990s, the gap had grown almost *eightfold* to 39 percent.[16] The reasons that the Great Estrangement grew notwithstanding the failure of the 104th Congress to implement its Contract With America, and the explanation for why the Great Estrangement has proven so intractable in the years following, are more complex. The most powerful contributor to the Great Estrangement was the growth of "movement conservatism," sponsored by strategically sophisticated and well-funded interests, and ultimately embraced by an activist plurality of Republicans. But the GOP's tack to the right was not the only factor.

The first generation of Green issues shared a number of characteristics that made them compelling to Americans regardless of

ideology. These problems tended to be obvious and obviously serious: rivers on fire, lakes covered with toxic sludge, malodorous smog
dense enough to block the sun, urban buildings coated in soot, and
beloved natural areas paved over as the suburbs started to spread
from urban centers. The problems were manifest in the mud-brown
skies, the soot on your sheets when hung to dry, and your child's
hacking cough. Scientific explanations were not required to understand that these were problems. And although these problems were
shared by many different parts of the country, individual Americans
experienced them as local. The seeds of the environmental revolution were in everyone's backyard.

By the beginning of the Great Estrangement in the mid-1990s,
the major legislative initiatives of the 1970s were already mitigating
some of the worst problems; water and air were becoming noticeably
cleaner. So the Green movement set its sights on a new, second-order
agenda: biodiversity, persistent toxics, resource scarcity, ozone depletion, acid rain, loss of rain forests and coral reefs in far-off places,
and, eventually, global warming. Some of these new agenda items—
such as protection of rain forests and coral reefs—were tangible,
but of course not local for most Americans. Most of the others were
neither tangible nor intuitively obvious. Fish poisoned with PCBs
look and smell normal. Humans can't tell the difference between 10
and 50 parts per billion of arsenic in their drinking water, and don't
know whether they should care.

The new agenda required the intermediation of science to identify
and explain the problems, and the solutions proposed by the Green
movement were more complex than simply requiring polluters to
clean up their acts. With the corresponding rise of scientific illiter-
acy, millions of Americans neither understood why the things that
upset the Greens were problems, nor trusted that the proffered solutions were appropriate or worthwhile. Even among the scientifically
literate, the more abstract nature of the second wave of Green issues
resulted in personal support that was more rational than emotional,

and less intense than the support that propelled the movement in the 1960s. Because the new Green agenda imposed burdens on individuals as well as corporate polluters, and seemed to call for varying degrees of personal sacrifice, more people were tempted to listen to voices claiming that the problems were not sufficiently serious to warrant incurring any kind of cost or inconvenience.

On the morning of July 26, 2003, I read this sentence in a *Wall Street Journal* editorial: "The grist of modern environmentalism is turning concern for the earth into rage against corporations." Surprised, I tore it from the paper and put it in a file. Later another *Journal* op-ed suggested that environmental groups' "hatred for capitalism seems boundless" and that Green groups were consumed with a "lust for power."[17] At that time (well prior to the "Occupy Wall Street" phenomenon) I was doing lots of environmental work, and didn't know any Greens who raged against corporations, hated capitalism, or lusted for power. Nor did fomenting rage against corporations seem the "grist" for our work. We disapproved, for example, of the way in which General Electric was handling its responsibility to clean up PCBs from the Hudson River, advocated to the EPA that GE should be forced to clean up its mess, and succeeded. But we didn't question GE's legitimacy or otherwise question the role of multinational corporations in the capitalist system. I wondered what the *Journal* was getting at. In many ways, this book had its origins in that moment. Soon, that file was filled with many other examples of hostility directed by right-wing publications and organizations at environmentalists. The Republican chairman of the Senate Environment and Public Works Committee during the Bush administration called the EPA's career staffers "a Gestapo bureaucracy"[18] and others referred to State officials enforcing the protection of endangered salmon as "jack-booted Nazis."[19] Soon, millions of Americans were driving to work listening to Rush Limbaugh mock the "environmentalist wackos," at least on days when he was being polite. The *Wall Street Journal* continued to editorialize against "enviromania" and sowed the seeds of the idea, in full flower today in the garden of right-wing ideology, that environmentalism is a false religion.[20] Obviously, these are not policy arguments but rhetoric whose sole purpose is to arouse emotion—highly personal and deeply felt anger, disdain, and even hatred—directed at environmentalism and the individuals who promote it.

Today, there seems to be no line that the ideologues of movement conservatism will not cross in expressing their hatred for Greens. Spokespersons for the Cornwall Alliance for the Stewardship for Creation, a conservative Christian public policy group that fiercely opposes Green Christianity, have called environmentalism "the greatest threat to Western Civilization" and "the most dangerous agenda on earth." Even as Roman Catholicism under Pope Francis embraces the proposition that environmentalism is a moral imperative, America's fundamentalist evangelicals continue their harsh rhetoric, with some calling belief in climate change "an insult to God" and accusing the Green movement of combining "the utopian vision of Marxism, the scientific fallacy of secular humanism, and the religious fanaticism of jihad."[21]

It is important to put all this in perspective. The simultaneous viciousness and vacuity of political dialogue, and the tendency of politicians to pander to the most extreme parts of their base, are not new phenomena in America, and certainly not confined to political discourse on the environment. In 1937 the lawyer and professor Thurman Arnold suggested we had no reason to expect anything better, arguing that political debate in this country had long been little more than "a series of cheers in which each side strives to build up its own morale."[22] While this may be true of political speech generally, the use of this sort of extreme rhetoric in the environmental policy debate is relatively new, and it cannot be dismissed, as it was, and continues to be, a prime driver of the Great Estrangement. If we are serious about healing the divide, we need to understand better the origins and drivers of this rhetorical campaign against environmentalism.

The campaign to foment right-wing rage against Greens had its origins in the period following the collapse of the Soviet Union in 1991. Without the Soviets to kick around any more, old cold warriors started to redirect their fire from red to Green. For example, conservative columnist George Will wrote in the *Washington Post,* on May 31, 1992, that environmentalism is "a Green tree with red roots . . . a socialist dream . . . dressed up as compassion for the planet." Rush Limbaugh wrote, "With the collapse of Marxism, environmentalism has become the new refuge of socialist thinking."[23] Soon, the Green menace replaced the red menace in the mouths of conservatism's most extreme ideologues.

Although the need for new enemies following the collapse of communism may provide a partial explanation for this rhetorical campaign to cultivate right-wing anger against Greens, the direct cause was a tactical decision by movement conservatism and the institutions that support it. A 2014 study of thirty-nine years of data from the General Social Survey by social scientists from Michigan State, American University, and Oklahoma State identified a process by which "party activists and ideological leaders drive polarization among political elites, and this process sends cues to voters that party positions are changing."[24] This "party sorting theory" holds that when political parties are more polarized, they become better at sorting individuals along ideological lines. During the 1980s and early 1990s, party activists—and not grassroots sentiment, which was still broadly supportive of the environmental agenda—drove the GOP to the right and introduced a fierce antienvironmentalism as a marker of party identity. After what they observe as a pivot point around 1992, the GOP rank and file realigned their opinions to accord with the position of the party.[25]

A slate of hard-right NGOs formed the core of this activist campaign to promote antienvironmentalism. The beer magnate Joseph Coors provided much of the funding for the Mountain States Legal Foundation, which promoted and funded Wise Use groups throughout the West (that clever phrase, which offered the appearance of moderation, wisdom, and balance in questions concerning the use of natural resources, proved instead to be a front for radical resistance to almost any form of public ownership of land or environmental regulation). A group called Defenders of Property Rights was founded in 1991 to promote expanded takings laws and to litigate taking cases. And, in the sort of Orwellian inversion that has been typical of hard-right rhetoric (e.g., Fox News as "fair and balanced"), rabid anti-Greens formed groups purporting to be environmental advocates. One, called the Coalition of Republican Environmental Advocates, a PAC claiming to be a grassroots environmental organization, was called by a real Republican proenvironment group (ConservAmerica, formerly known as Republicans for Environmental Protection) "a transparent attempt to fool voters who care about environmental protection." It was reported that the six members of Congress listed on its honorary board had an average voting score from the League of Conservation Voters of only 5 percent.[26]

It is not entirely clear why these efforts succeeded in arousing in so many conservatives an active antipathy toward Greens. We generally associate the phenomenon of "faith-based knowing" replacing evidence-based reasoning with the later ascendancy of the Christian right and the Tea Party and rise of climate-change denial. But there is evidence that group-think irrationality on Green issues actually had its roots in the preceding decades. In 1995, for example, after a Republican Party official from Indiana had been awakened to the serious dangers of discharging persistent toxins into the Great Lakes, he wrote candidly about the reaction of his fellow Republicans: "My conservative friends still like me, even though I am concerned about the long-term effects of toxic substances. They just think I have been duped somehow, and they continue making sure that they are not exposed to the facts that duped me. Most of my friends are open-minded, inquisitive, seeking new information on almost every issue, except the environment. Why is that? It is a resistant attitude that is seemingly woven into the fabric of our [the conservative movement's] ethos."[27]

This admission is too strange not to be honest, and shines a light on the dynamics still at work within the conservative movement. Although written about toxins in the mid-1990s, you could substitute greenhouse gas emissions and it still has great explanatory power. A conservative who has opened his eyes to the facts must have been "duped," and his fellows huddle up with eyes closed to be sure none of them is "exposed" to the same information. The faith-based influence on policy making is quite clear here and is promoted to this day by politicians such as Sarah Palin, who said, "I never read anything that might conflict with my beliefs."[28]

The rise of antienvironmental rhetoric and the widespread adoption of anti-Green anger as a core marker of conservative orthodoxy made life increasingly difficult for those Republicans and conservatives still faithful to the conservative tradition of support for conservation. The tenure of former Republican New Jersey governor Christine Whitman as George Bush's first EPA administrator provides an instructive example, both of the emerging impossibility to maintain GOP credentials while acting responsibly on the environment, and of the quickness of many Greens to assume that it would be impossible to work productively with a conservative. In a March 4, 2004, speech at Princeton's Woodrow Wilson School of Public and International Affairs, Governor Whitman said: "I came to the job at the EPA with all sorts of good intentions, and got totally whacked. . . . You couldn't have a discussion. . . . You couldn't get a dialogue going in the public arena. Sides were already chosen." Whitman later complained that instead of trying to make regulations better, business executives claimed that virtually any regulation would "drive them out of business," and, she commented, "I sometimes wonder whether those companies spend more money trying to defeat new regulations than they would by simply complying with them."[29] And Green NGOs were often equally guilty of extreme rhetoric, accusing the Bush administration, within only a few months of its taking office, of conducting "war on the environment."[30] When Whitman decided to *toughen* the standard for arsenic in drinking water from that in effect during all eight years of the Clinton administration—but to reduce the amount of permitted arsenic less than the full reduction advocated by Greens—Senator Joseph Lieberman said that her decision "threaten[ed] to roll us right back to the Stone Age."[31] The DNC ran an ad showing a cute little girl holding out a glass of water, saying, "May I please have some more arsenic in my water, Mommy?" The ad was terrifically effective.[32] Whitman resigned in 2003, a prominent victim of the Great Estrangement. She epitomizes the sort of competent, thoughtful, nonideological conservatives who had been pillars of the conservation movement, but who today are dismissed by movement conservatives as RINOs (Republicans in Name Only).

Although the lion's share of the blame for the Great Estrangement sits with the embrace of market fundamentalism by the right and its abandonment of the conservation tradition, there is some merit to the argument that part of the blame lies with the Green movement's concurrent tack to port. The way Newt Gingrich perceived it, "green conservatives didn't leave the environmental movement; the movement left them."[33] The only thing that is clear is that the rise of movement conservatism set off a nasty political feedback loop: as conservatives abandoned the Green movement, it was left free to drift to the left; the more the movement drifted left, the more justified conservatives felt in abandoning environmentalism as just another liberal special interest. From the 1980s on, influential voices on the left sought to define conservation as an essentially liberal cause, insisting that Greens must adopt an integrated progressive worldview across the entire spectrum of issues. The fewer conservative voices in the Green movement, the easier it was for voices from the far left to pull Greens in that direction. In 1986, for example, the idiosyncratic leftist Kirkpatrick Sale claimed in *Mother Jones* that the true Greens (that is, those who were reliably progressive) had already "become disenchanted with the environmental establishment and [had] in recent years mounted a serious and sweeping attack on it—style, substance, systems, sensibilities and all."[34] This critique from the left has been renewed consistently since then, resonating deeply with the established Green NGOs, which are torn between the more centrist "style, substance, systems, and sensibilities" that their professional convictions tell them are most effective, and a secret fear that they have become too corporate, too moderate, and should therefore heed the call to a broad "progressivism."

Today, many Greens simply assume that it is incoherent to call yourself a Green without supporting the rest of the progressive agenda. As one commentator put it in an online discussion, "I think that being a right-wing environmentalist is about as absurd as being a right-wing feminist or a right-wing civil rights activist. If you're progressive on one issue but you don't fit into the larger picture, you're likely to meet with nothing but confusion and failure."[35] Few if any Green leaders would say such a thing out loud, but many of them agree with the argument. This conviction that being a conservative environmentalist is intellectually incoherent sends a powerful signal that right-wing Greens are not welcome in the movement. Given the large numbers of moderates and conservatives who consider themselves environmentalists—Audubon, for example, estimates that about 40 percent of its members self-identify as "moderate to conservative"—this idea that there is an ideological litmus test to qualify as Green is deeply harmful to the movement.[36]

The leftward drift of the Green movement made it harder and harder for some Green conservatives to maintain their ties with Green organizations. The League of Conservation Voters (and its network of state leagues around the country) is the principal political voice of the Green movement, making endorsements of candidates with the best environmental records, publishing lists of "Environmental Champions" and the "Dirty Dozen" environmental enemies, and providing independent and direct financial support through its two political action committees. Founded in 1969, the League aims to be nonpartisan—i.e., to call each race solely based on specified environmental criteria, without any ideological or partisan preference—and long hosted both Republicans and Democrats on its board of directors. In 2000, the League's only Republican staffer and three out of four Republican board members resigned, reportedly due to what they perceived as growing partisan bias in endorsements.[37] These types of incidents, sometimes repeated at state organizations and local chapters, underscored the difficulty of accommodating conservatives and maintaining nonpartisan balance in a movement that had indeed drifted steadily to the left.

The perception of many conservatives that environmentalism has become a left-wing movement is reinforced by the people who represent the movement to the public, mainly NGO executives, authors, and activists such as Bill McKibben, politicians such as Al Gore, and celebrities such as Leonardo DiCaprio. And with respect to certain parts of the Green movement, that perception is accurate: many of the prominent national Green NGOs are dominated by people who, in their personal politics and personal political philosophies, are Democrats and liberals, operating in a cocoon of fellow liberal Democrats. A survey in 1995 of a hundred prominent environmental leaders revealed that 93 percent of them had voted for Bill Clinton in the most recent presidential election.[38] Getting to Green requires us to understand and accept that the right-wing narrative of the movement's drift to the left is an important part of the explanation for the Great Estrangement.

Finally, the causes of the Great Estrangement were not limited to the changing nature of the Green agenda or to substantive differences. Pew research in 2014 revealed what it described as "a fragmented landscape of increasingly rigid 'ideological silos' that permeate nearly all facets of life—including where people chose to live and whom they choose for friends." This growing culture gap between right and left played a significant role in the estrangement. The *Wall Street Journal* editorial page has a long record of promoting the notion that environmentalism is an elitist movement at odds with mainstream America. The consistent message from talk radio and the evangelical pulpit was that Greens did not live like you or share your problems, that it was they and not you who were out of touch with the mainstream, and that Greens, despite their claims to scientific support, actually had no special expertise or knowledge, but were simply expressing the preferences of their class. The Great Estrangement became *personal*.

This meant that issues that Greens saw as scientific or policy questions—such as the need for a total ban on snowmobiles in national parks—were seen by many of the citizens affected as primarily *cultural*. As Terry Anderson argued in his 1997 debate with Carl Pope of the Sierra Club, "Some people would rather go and watch a roller derby than hike in a redwood . . . forest. . . ." Increasingly, the motives and morals of Greens themselves began to be impugned, including the odd idea that environmentalists are "interested in power more than anything else."

At the same time that conservatives came to see Greens as more and more estranged from the conservatives' lives and values, Greens saw the GOP moving to territory that was equally foreign to most environmentalists. As has been well chronicled, the GOP base shifted west and south, gradually lost support among college-educated voters, and gained the allegiance of the white working class. These working-class whites were hostile to the eastern country-club elites who had at one time dominated the party and led the conservation movement. The religious right began its gradual hijacking of the GOP agenda and rhetoric, and eventually the Tea Party emerged to enforce the new right orthodoxy, completing what *The Economist* referred to as the GOP's "divorce from the intelligentsia."[39] This cultural transition reached a nearly unimaginable extreme during the 2008 and 2012 election cycles, with what Jonathan Chait called "the humiliating and almost surreal anti-intellectualism of Sarah Palin" and the strange announcement by Rick Santorum that "we will never have the elite smart people on our side."[40] In reaction, Greens—dedicated to science and to technocratic solutions to complicated problems—tended to write off the new right as impossibly alien. In a rare moment of frankness, two Green insiders observed that "most of the intellectuals who staff environmental groups are . . . repelled by the right's values."[41] And the half of the population on the other side of the great divide can tell. When Rush Limbaugh explains to his listeners that environmental leaders are far-left activists who hate them, their values, and the way they live, he is actually not too far off the mark.

4

THE ULTIMATE WEDGE ISSUE

Climate Change

The Great Estrangement would have occurred even if the global warming issue had not arisen. But the global warming thesis emerged from NASA's James Hansen in 1988 and the politics of the environment was changed forever. No matter how bitter the debates around jobs vs. owls and dams vs. the snail darters, it was child's play compared to the vitriol, emotion, and division that would emerge from the question of climate change. Global warming proved to be the ultimate wedge issue. It sent right and left flying in different directions and has powered the Great Estrangement for the last two decades.

The Green movement's main message has been simple: to avoid the risk of apocalyptic disaster we must reduce greenhouse gas emissions by 70 percent (now 80 percent)[1] as soon as possible—which is impossible while maintaining anything remotely like the life you currently enjoy. It is probably perfectly true, but it also was a great gift to the antienvironmental right. The essence of the right's initial response was summed up neatly by the *Wall Street Journal* editorial page: "Scientists aren't sure that global warming is taking place, or that if it is it will be bad for us, or that in any case we can do anything about it."[2]

Twelve years later the *Journal's* essential objections had been refined but not really altered: "[How much the human component may have influenced climate change already is] an insoluble noise-to-signal problem. And forecasts of future warming depend on theoretical models that are highly speculative and necessarily suspect. . . . Nothing America could do by itself would make a significant difference. . . . Indeed, a rational case for action on cost-benefit grounds is challenging to make at all."[3]

From the earliest days of the national dialogue on climate change, virtually everything relevant to the issue has been contested: whether or not the planet is actually warming; whether its causes are primarily anthropomorphic (human-caused) or natural; the operation of offsets and feedbacks; the amount, timing, and probability of future warming; how global warming would manifest itself locally if it occurred; the likely human and economic costs of climate change; and the efficacy and cost of various preventive and mitigating measures. The quarter-century-long argument has been remarkably unsatisfying, even by the low standards of U.S. political debate. With occasional exceptions, one side largely relies on carefully worded studies and reports written by large committees of highly qualified scientists, coupled with apocalyptic rhetoric. The other side speaks with the sarcasm, ridicule, exaggeration, and vitriol of talk radio, where "argument" takes the form of impugning the motives, integrity, and bona fides of one's opponents.

One of the landmark events in the deepening division between right and left in relation to climate change was the publication in English in 2001 of a thick tome titled *The Skeptical Environmentalist* by Danish scientist Bjørn Lomborg. In it, he argued that the Green movement and Green policy prescriptions were based on a "litany" of beliefs that were flawed, among them that natural resources were running out, that population growth was a fundamental problem, that the pace of species loss was increasing, and that the air and water were ever more polluted. He systematically attacked this "litany" of the Green movement, and argued that the cost of the effort needed to mitigate global warming was too high and that resources should be spent on higher priorities likes AIDS, malaria, and sanitation. The book caused a firestorm of protest and consternation. A commentator writing in the (London) *Daily Telegraph* called him the "Anti-Christ of the green religion"[4] and *Scientific American* responded with a series of articles by respected scientists purporting to refute each of Lomborg's fundamental assertions, arguing that the book was filled with error and even suggesting that it was intentionally misleading. American conservatives were delighted and the normally reasonable *Economist* became infatuated with the Danish scientist, opining that

> Dr. Lomborg's critics protest too much. They are rattled not because, as they endlessly insist, Dr. Lomborg lacks credentials as an environmental scientist and is of no account, but because his book is such a powerful and persuasive assault on the central tenets of the modern environmental movement. . . . Dr. Lomborg reminds militant greens, and the media that hang on their every exaggerated word about environmental calamity, that environmental policy should be judged by the same criteria as other kinds of policy. Is there a problem? How bad is it? What will it cost to fix? Is that the best way to spend those resources?"[5]

In January 2003 the Danish Committee on Scientific Dishonesty issued a ruling siding with the *Scientific American* authors: "Objectively speaking, the publication of the work under consideration [Lomborg's book] is deemed to fall within the concept of scientific dishonesty." *The Economist's* verdict: "The panel's ruling—objectively speaking—is incompetent and shameful."[6]

Although the Lomborg fracas has now faded to a mere footnote in environmental history, it brought into public focus some of the

Green movement's greatest vulnerabilities (such as the exceptional-ist claim, or appearance of a claim, that addressing climate change trumps all other policy objectives), introduced the contestation of scientific objectivity that has dominated political discourse around climate change ever since, and foreshadowed the shrillness that would only grow over the next decade. Four years later, when Lom-borg tried to "stake out the sensible middle ground" in his book *Cool It*, the *National Review* said it was a "highly valuable contribution to the climate-policy literature," while the *Washington Post* review called it a "stealth attack on humanity's future."[7]

Bona fide arguments like those advanced by Lomborg were soon eclipsed by the far more cynical and far more effective efforts of ideologically motivated funders, conservative think tanks, and cer-tain carbon-based business interests. These efforts have been stud-ied and analyzed by various scholars and journalists.[8] These studies confirm what was anecdotally obvious: wealthy ideologues poured money into an effort to "manufacture uncertainty" about climate science (as was done so successfully for so many years with tobacco science), and create a climate of "environmental skepticism" targeted at undermining the scientists on whom the Green movement relied to advance its claims. They showered support and media attention on the few bona fide climate dissenters, and as these skeptics became increasingly rare in conventional academia, gave a home to a new "counter-intelligentsia" in right-wing think tanks (including at var-ious times the Competitive Enterprise Institute, George C. Marshall Institute, the Greening Earth Society, the Science and Environmen-tal Policy Project, Committee for a Constructive Tomorrow, and the Weidenbaum Center). Three scholars, Peter Jacques, Riley Dunlap, and Mark Freeman, charted the ramp-up of these efforts and their connection to these think tanks by analyzing the 141 antienviron-mental books published in English between 1972 and 2005. The defining theme of these works was the denial of the authenticity of environmental problems, particularly biodiversity and climate change. The pace of these publications rose steeply in the early 1990s and again after 2000, and of the 141 works, the scholars found that 130 were either directly sponsored by conservative think tanks or had authors with demonstrable ties to one or more of those institutions.[9] In the dry language of the academy, they conclude that "[climate] skepticism is a tactic of an elite-driven counter-movement designed to combat environmentalism. . . ."[10]

The steady stream of denial literature was amplified, both deliberately and unwittingly, by the media. Various scholars have exhaustively reviewed the media coverage of climate change and its impact on public opinion.[11] One, who meticulously analyzed Fox coverage during early 2007, demonstrated that Fox was relentless in ridiculing climate experts, telling stories supporting the climate "hoax" hypothesis, and presenting the proponents of climate legislation as socialists with a "religious" adherence to environmentalism who, if left to their own devices, would destroy the lifestyle of ordinary Americans. The analysis of Fox coverage in response to each critical development during the year leaves little doubt that the messaging was coordinated and deliberate. Moreover, it worked. Between 2006 and 2010, the correlation between the number of Fox stories highlighting climate skepticism and the rise in the percentage of GOP voters telling pollsters there is no solid evidence for global warming is extraordinary: as the number of Fox climate stories sounding the hoax/skepticism message rose from 50 percent in 2006 to nearly 90 percent in 2009, the percentage of GOP voters telling Pew pollsters that there is no solid evidence for global warming doubled from about 30 percent to nearly 60 percent.[12] In covering the resulting "controversy," even the mainstream media, perhaps unavoidably, contributed to sowing the seeds of doubt in a broader audience.

Conservative think tanks and their funders did not limit their campaign to supplying a steady stream of ideological deniers to the conservative press. They also pushed a more moderate version of the anti-climate-change message through a sophisticated lobbying effort. This message, stripped of the nonsense that motivates the base on talk radio, simply emphasized uncertainty and doubt, allowing politicians, even moderate Republicans, to appease the hard right, business supporters, and home-state interests without having to sign on to the stranger and more embarrassing fictions that had persuaded their constituents. All they had to do to justify inaction was to repeat the simple mantra that the science was "unsettled." It was a brilliant and effective strategy.

As climate denial started to take hold in certain parts of the right as a core marker of conservative identity, the Green movement was presented with a difficult challenge. Among conservatives, views on climate change have become deeply entwined with an integrated worldview. For a growing group on the right, "true" conservatives don't just disagree that we should make economic sacrifices to abate carbon emissions to the atmosphere, they simply deny as a matter of core faith that the problem exists and thus reject the possibility of evidence that would change their minds. Climate change is no longer an "issue" in the conventional sense, it is a cultural marker trapped in a political vicious circle.

Advocates of science education are justifiably worried. Josh Rosenau of the National Center for Science Education writes, "Just as the creationist movement's persistence grew out of its success in linking religious identity with creationist belief, there is a danger that climate change denial could establish itself as a permanent feature of American politics if denialist beliefs establish themselves as core parts of the conservative identity."[13] Scholars applying the tools of moral psychology and social movement theory have discovered that when a view becomes a marker of community or identity (the falsehood that President Obama was not born within the United States is another example), it becomes "sticky," not easily dislodged by empirical evidence or logic. When the sticky view evolves into a "shibboleth for [a] political faction," it becomes even harder to dislodge because that faction then has a vested interest in its perpetuation. It hardly should be surprising that in 2012 the Texas Republican party explicitly condemned efforts to teach "critical thinking skills" on the ground that such efforts "have the purpose of challenging the student's fixed beliefs and undermining parental authority."[14]

The wedge effect of the climate-change issue was exacerbated by the global nature of the problem, and the international nature of the solutions proffered by the Green movement. The Green movement outside of the United States has always skewed further to the left, and encompassed a challenge to capitalism and globalization. The rhetoric coming from international environmental forums, influenced by these European and other Greens, did not sit well with American conservatives. The treaty solutions that were for many years the principal policy prescription for global warming conflicted with a strain of isolationist sentiment that sees certain sorts of treaty making as a derogation of national sovereignty. The right's long-standing skepticism regarding climate-change treaties, rekindled by the results of the 2015 Paris climate change conference, has been reinforced by the record: few of the nations most responsible for greenhouse gas emissions have met their carbon emission reduction targets, whether self-imposed or imposed by treaty.

Cracks in the wall separating the two parties on climate matters emerged in 2003, when John McCain joined with his friend Joe Lieberman to cosponsor the Climate Stewardship Act, and again in 2005, when the two teamed up to sponsor the Climate Stewardship and Innovation Act. Al Gore's 2006 documentary *An Inconvenient Truth*, together with his receipt (with the Intergovernmental Panel on Climate Change) of the 2007 Nobel Peace Prize, raised the public profile of the issue. In the two years prior to the 2008 election, at least ten different carbon cap-and-trade bills were introduced in the House and Senate. Sensing that some sort of carbon caps were inevitable, major U.S. corporations teamed up with Green NGOs to form the U.S. Climate Action Partnership in support of cap-and-trade. By 2007, public perceptions of the climate threat peaked.[15]

In 2008, with conditions as favorable as they ever had been, Greens hoped that climate change would finally play a major role in the presidential election. Al Gore launched his "We Campaign" (short for "We Can Solve It"), wisely abandoning the warnings of global warming catastrophe and making a commendable effort to bring right and left together in an upbeat call for a quick transition to a renewable-energy future. It was in this campaign that Newt Gingrich sat on a couch with Nancy Pelosi, and Pat Robertson with Al Sharpton, and asked Americans to insist that their political leaders "repower America," with a switch to 100 percent clean energy in ten years. The 2008 Republican Platform's first item under "Environmental Protection" was captioned "Addressing Climate Change Responsibly," and the Platform document stated that "common sense dictates that the United States should take measured and reasonable steps today to reduce any impact."

When Barack Obama was elected in 2008, Greens were elated that they finally had a president publicly pledged to take action on carbon reduction. The long-sought national carbon cap-and-trade system seemed not only possible but inevitable. Only two years later, despite a liberal democrat in the White House and a Democrat-controlled congress, the Waxman-Markey Act (the American Clean Energy and Security Act, which sought to reduce emissions to 83 percent below 2005 levels using the market-based cap-and-trade scheme that worked so well to reduce acid rain) died an ignominious death when Majority Leader Harry Reid announced that he would not bring the bill to the Senate floor for a vote.

The failure to realize the potential of this moment has spurred a small industry of scholars and journalists offering analyses of what went wrong, and a jarring war of internecine recrimination within the Green movement. The resulting post-traumatic stress punctuated the movement's lingering crisis of confidence, and has left the environmental movement still struggling to find its footing. And the failed effort itself, in the words of one of those scholars, "did much to provoke and mobilize fierce enemies and enhance their populist capacities and political clout for future battles."[16]

So the Great Estrangement continues unabated, with climate change retaining its singular power as a wedge issue. The corporate partnerships, outbreaks of bipartisanship, and hopeful moments between 2006 and 2008 appear to have had no lingering effects. High energy prices and a bad economy swamped Gore's "We Campaign," and the partisans who joined each other on Gore's couch largely pretend it never happened. McCain, facing a Tea Party talk show host in the GOP primary, seemed to reverse course and join the "drill, baby, drill" school. Senator Lindsay Graham was rewarded for his initial support of cap-and-trade with formal "censures" from various South Carolina GOP county organizations, and the handful of GOP representatives who supported the bill, like former Rep. Bob Inglis of South Carolina, were defeated in the June 2010 Republican primary. Nineteen of the twenty serious challengers to incumbent GOP senators in 2010 took the position that the science of climate change is inconclusive or flat-out incorrect.[17] It is a sad commentary on the hardwiring of climate-change denial as a GOP litmus test that even Senator Graham felt forced to say after the collapse of Waxman-Markey, "I think they've been alarmist and the science is in question."[18] Most of the GOP has now fallen in with the party line that cap-and-trade constitutes an unacceptable "tax."

Two years later, in the 2012 campaign, the words "global warming" and "climate change" completely dropped out of the Republican Platform document. In contrast to the 2008 "common sense" approach, the document simply promised to end the "war on coal," oppose "any and all cap and trade legislation" (without, strangely, any reference to what might be capped and traded or why), and support legislation to "prohibit the EPA from moving forward with new greenhouse gas regulations."[19]

Ambitious politicians on the right fall over themselves to demonstrate "zero tolerance" for anything that even remotely legitimizes climate change as a bona fide issue. In 2013, Senator Ted Cruz burnished his credentials by objecting to a previously noncontroversial annual Senate resolution commemorating International Women's Day. The reason? The resolution contained the statement that women in developing countries "are disproportionately affected by changes in climate because of their need to secure water, food and fuel for their livelihood." To the climate denier, any mention of climate, no matter how vague or indirect, is now deeply offensive speech that cannot be tolerated. When the Senate "climate caucus" gathered for an all night "talkathon" in March 2014, not a single Republican was with them, and the four most vulnerable Democratic incumbents facing reelection later that year stayed away.[20] Senator James Inhofe of Oklahoma, now chairman of the Senate Environment and Public Works Committee, who once had a lifetime score of 0 out of 100 from the bipartisan League of Conservation Voters, has resumed his campaign against action to mitigate global warming, which he refers to (in speeches and in a 2012 book) as a "hoax." The legislature of North Carolina carried the crusade one step further when it prohibited by law any consideration of future sea level rise in the development of the state's coastal management policy, effectively enshrining willful ignorance as a requirement of North Carolina law. The hugely popular Glenn Beck doesn't mince words: "Global warming is a pile of crap." The same message in the words of the slightly more refined editorial page of the *Wall Street Journal*: "[The climate issue is going] down the drain. That's how thoroughly defunct, dead, expired is the idea that humanity might take charge of earth's atmosphere through some supreme triumph of the global regulatory state over democracy, sovereignty, nationalism and political self-interest, the very facts of political human nature."[21] And so, in six short years from the time the GOP presidential candidate supported sweeping cap-and-trade legislation, climate change has again resumed its place as the principal wedge issue that defines the Great Estrangement, which more and more Americans are starting to accept as a permanent Green gap between the right and left.

MARKET FUNDAMENTALISM

The Antienvironmental Orthodoxy of the Right

The "Republican Revolution" launched in 1995 drove the party hard to starboard by crystallizing and embedding in American conservative culture a new orthodoxy, much of which was deeply hostile to environmental goals. Most enduringly, it succeeded in adding "the environment" to a political litmus test for Republicans that endures to this day: the true conservative must embrace the conviction that environmentalism is an elitist movement whose goals come at the cost of jobs and economic growth and thus is indifferent to the needs of ordinary people; a conservative must reject "command and control" environmental regulation and even the premise that environmental problems require government solutions; and finally a conservative believes that our constitutional "property rights" require us to dismantle our system of public lands and prohibit most ordinary land use regulations. These three major planks of what many call "market fundamentalism" share the same essential flaw: they take old conservative ideas and dumb them down by stripping them of all subtlety and nuance, in the process perverting their meaning to something completely at odds with the traditions of principled conservatism.

These three ideas have sustained the Great Estrangement for the past two decades, and understanding them is key to finding an end to it.

During the cold war, conservatives defended capitalism against competing economic systems, communism and socialism, which had claimed the mantle of history and swept much of the globe. This struggle was difficult and vital, and it preoccupied conservatives between 1917 and the collapse of the Soviet Union in 1991. During this period the more nuanced debate around the appropriate degree of laissez-faire in our market system was less urgent and less intense. After the end of the cold war, the American right turned its sights inward, rejected European models of capitalism that were more social in their orientation, and gradually emerged as the champion of a type of market fundamentalism that provided the intellectual foundation for the new antienvironmental orthodoxies.

The emerging market fundamentalism owed its quick ascendency within the GOP to the concerted efforts of a newly sophisticated network of well-funded organizations such as the Cato Institute, the Heritage Foundation, and the Mountain States Legal Foundation. The anti-Green ideas that the 104th Congress brought to Washington may have gotten their start in the Sagebrush Rebellion of ranchers in Nevada, Utah, and Wyoming, but they were nurtured and given a veneer of legal and intellectual respectability in the conference rooms of inside-the-beltway think tanks, by people whose salaries were paid by foundations with names like Scaife, Koch, Coors, and Olin.[1]

Calvin Coolidge famously said, "The chief business of the American people is business." Market fundamentalists have now perverted this rhetorical tautology into a harmful falsehood: that whatever imposes costs or limits on business has the effect of "killing jobs" and therefore is a bad thing. The false dichotomy between economy and environment has been one of the most insidious—and politically successful—

features of the new-right orthodoxy. It is a paradigm that has no room for nuance, and can be applied indiscriminately to oppose as a "job killer" anything disliked by a specific business or industry. The argument is that if compliance with an environmental law, regulation, or goal costs a company money—and it almost always does in the short term—then it hurts revenues and profits, and thus jobs and the economy. When the choice is formulated as "X vs. jobs," whatever takes the place of X, whether it is spotted owls or snail darters or global sea level rise, loses.

This idea came into full flower in conservative circles in the 1990s. It became a matter of faith among antienvironmentalists that the Green movement's success in having the northern spotted owl listed as "threatened" under the Endangered Species Act cost at least thirty thousand forest industry jobs in the Pacific Northwest, even though mill modernization, overseas competition, and declining demand all may have been equal or greater contributing factors.[2] A decade later, the economic case against environmental protection became a governing principle during the eight years of the George W. Bush administration. His undersecretary for natural resources and environment in the Department of Agriculture, Mark Rey, an advocate for logging the national forests, put it clearly: "We should start with the premise that a policy cannot be good for the environment if it is bad for people."[3] What people want most, the argument goes, is jobs, wealth, and cheap gas; they want a clean environment too, but not at the expense of the things they want more, and they don't really care at all about wilderness, endangered species, minute amounts of toxins, sprawl, predictions of far-off changes in the climate, and the other things that seem to motivate the wonky elites from the coasts. Painting environmental protection as inconsistent with the things that people want most was an astute and successful political strategy for the foes of the Green movement.

The enduring success of that strategy is harder to explain, though, because in most cases the economic-cost argument is simply not true, nor is it accepted by a majority of Americans. Economy vs. environment—no matter how well it plays with the conservative base—is in fact a false dichotomy. Many environmental initiatives, such as the reduction of acid rain, have resulted in net economic benefits to society. Even during the period between 1974 and 1985, when pollution control regulation was indeed imposing significant costs on utilities and industry, a Harvard study found that the investment capital diverted to pollution control reduced gross national product by an average annual rate of less than .2 percent, and that is without in any way accounting for the offsetting economic benefits achieved by cutting pollution, such as the lower cost of health care resulting from reduction in pollution-related illnesses.[4] There is no empirical evidence that sound environmental policy hurts economic competitiveness, and much empirical evidence that the environmental regulation in the latter part of the twentieth century actually spurred both innovation and competitiveness.[5]

Happily, many Americans seem to understand this. In a 2012 bipartisan poll commissioned by The Nature Conservancy, voters were twice as likely to say that protections for land, air, water, and wildlife have a positive impact on jobs (41 percent), rather than a negative impact (17 percent). More voters viewed conservation as having a positive impact than a negative impact in every region of the country, even in the western United States, where there are significant holdings of public lands.

But neither the evidence over a long period of experience with environmental regulations nor the sensible views of a plurality of American voters matters to "movement" conservatives. From the mid-1990s on, right-wing market fundamentalists did what business itself did not succeed in doing in the 1970s and 1980s. They convinced large numbers of otherwise rational people that virtually any further environmentally motivated limitations on business should be opposed as being bad for the economy. By 2002, the

New Yorker was calling this argument the "unwinnable trench war between conservation and commerce."[6] We will never get to Green so long as it continues.

The second plank of the new antienvironmental orthodoxy was antipathy to regulation, especially federal regulation. The anti-Green right accuses environmentalists of knowing no solution to environmental problems other than "mandate, regulate, and litigate," and to the market fundamentalist, no regulatory agency (putting aside the IRS) is more reviled than the EPA.

How did this happen? Environmental legislation in the 1970s relied heavily and necessarily on prescriptive rules: "polluter pays" or straight-up limits on emissions. The initial debates revolved around how those regulations would be administered. For things like toxics and emissions, the EPA advocated a "risk-management" approach, which focused on threats to human health and the environment, and was not sympathetic to the notion that the costs of compliance should outweigh the imperative of control where the substance posed a substantial risk to human health or the environment. Market conservatives, on the other hand, argued that the costs of regulatory compliance often exceeded the value of the benefits achieved and, in some cases, that regulation of any sort was not the most efficient means of achieving the environmental objective. A corollary to this clash between the risk-management and cost-benefit approaches was a debate between Greens and conservatives over the law of diminishing returns. The earliest regulatory initiatives in the 1970s and 1980s achieved significant improvements in environmental quality at modest cost, but as the 1990s wore on, Greens advocated the further tightening of regulatory standards, which were designed to achieve much smaller incremental improvements in environmental quality at ever-increasing cost. In many cases those incremental improvements were fully justified by our evolving understanding of toxics and their peril to human health, but in other cases the concerns about the cost of these diminishing benefits were valid. In addition, as the lines were drawn in this debate, the ability of the political system to respond to newly understood threats, such as the perils of MTBE (a gasoline additive that seriously threatened drinking-water sources and was banned in numerous states), was badly compromised because regulatory ideology, and not science, had become the focus of the debate. The breakdown of any kind of sensible cost-benefit analysis also was facilitated by the chronic tendency of business to grossly overestimate the costs of compliance with environmental regulations, the difficulty of quantifying the benefits of those regulations, and the corresponding tendency of Green lobbyists to overestimate those benefits when defending a regulatory initiative.

The debate over cost-benefit was not the only driver of growing conservative wariness about the entire edifice of environmental regulation. Conservatives have long feared the growth of the large and costly bureaucracies that are the handmaidens of regulatory complexity, and were understandably alert to the tendency of the federal government to tackle problems through regulation that might have been more appropriately handled at a lower level of government.[7] Foreshadowing today's GOP argument that government bureaucracies pervert the market by "picking winners," some conservatives even argued that straightforward bans on emission of dangerous substances were better than any system involving bureaucracies, permits, exemptions, and regulatory discretion.[8] And the libertarian strain of the American right, always alert to the prospect of regulatory infringements on individual rights and freedoms, became particularly fearful of what they perceived as environmentalists' claims of exceptionalism. The George C. Marshall Institute, a conservative think tank, articulated this fear as follows: "If saving the Earth is the overarching principle dictating what government should and should not do . . . [then environmentalists will argue that] government cannot be limited by anything so narrow as civil and political rights. The safety and security of Spaceship Earth overrides the liberty of its passengers."[9] Paranoid, perhaps, but nonetheless a fair point about the dangers of any movement that sees its issues transcending ordinary politics and having a special claim to priority.

By the end of the 1990s, the right's willingness to discriminate between good and bad environmental regulation had withered, and it settled into a mode where, as one conservative environmentalist put it, "Government regulation is something that most every conservative abhors."[10] The western "Sagebrush" rebels' language foreshadowed today's shrill tone, with one conservative think tank referring to environmental regulation as a "two decade old regulatory *jihad* by the Federal Government."[11] Gingrich and the new right were relentless in characterizing any regulatory initiative as "command and control," to be resisted on principle as an incremental step on the slippery slope toward socialism. Senator James Inhofe (now chair of the Senate Environment and Public Works Committee) compared the EPA to the Gestapo,[12] and by 2012 the entire regulatory apparatus was under attack by House Republicans, determined either to limit existing rules or eliminate the funding required to enforce them. In 2012, *Politico* declared "This election year, the EPA is toxic."[13] Now, the *Wall Street Journal* opinion page, which both reflects and leads conservative sentiment, typically refers to any regulatory initiative in the environmental space in inflammatory terms (a "power grab" by the relevant agency, or "brute regulation").[14]

According to Pew polling, Republicans always have been more skeptical about regulation than Democrats, but after 1987 the gap widened and in 2008 exploded, driven, Pew concluded, by Tea Party Republicans, almost 90 percent of whom say "that government regulation of business does more harm than good," compared to only 65 percent of non–Tea Party Republicans.[15] Following the Tea Party's remarkable success in the 2010 midterm elections, David Koch and the head of Americans for Prosperity visited the Speaker and the newly installed House Energy and Commerce Committee chair to rally them against environmental initiatives and urge them to take swift action to curtail the powers of the EPA.[16] The House responded with a flood of bills designed to hobble the agency and reverse decades of regulatory action.

———————

On April 12, 2014, Nevada rancher and Mormon grandfather of fifty-two Cliven Bundy, riding at the head of an armed posse with a copy of the U.S. Constitution tucked into the pocket of his shirt, instructed Clark County Sheriff Doug Gillespie that it was his duty to disarm the Bureau of Land Management and other federal agents then engaged in a roundup of livestock on federal land. Bundy, who had stopped paying grazing fees to the BLM two decades earlier, had been ordered from the land by a federal court. Declining to recognize federal ownership of the land or federal jurisdiction in the matter, he refused, and instantly became a folk hero to the far right. His views about property rights were broadcast to every corner of the nation by Sean Hannity and Fox News. Despite racist comments by Bundy shortly thereafter, which caused many politicians and right-wing journalists to distance themselves from him, a year later a "Bundy Bill" (limiting federal land rights) was introduced in the Nevada legislature (the Nevada bill ultimately failed), and similar bills were introduced in other states. And if you think that all this agitation is limited to the fringier parts of the right, consider that in the spring of 2015, the U.S. Senate voted 51 to 49 in support of an amendment to a nonbinding budget resolution to sell or otherwise dispose of all federal lands other than the national parks and monuments.

The widespread coverage of the Bundy affair was a reminder to the rest of the nation about the enduring strength of the third and final plank of market fundamentalism, a misguided obsession with property rights that grew out of the Wise Use movement in the 1980s and attracted serious money from business interests threatened by land use regulation. Wise Use promoter Alan Gottlieb's paranoia regarding private property knew virtually no bounds, and he was often quoted by journalists as making statements such as "The National Park Service is an empire designed to eliminate all private property within the United States."[17] But behind the "black helicopter" rhetoric was relentless antipathy to public land ownership, zoning, and environmental regulation that had a broad and deep base of public support in the West and rural communities throughout the country, built on long-simmering resentments regarding the vast amounts of land in public ownership and the regulation of private lands by distant bureaucrats. The response was to fetishize "private property" as an unconditional absolute constitutional right—similar to speech rights under the First Amendment—against which all regulations and limitations were seen as tyrannical impositions.

This absolutist approach to private property not only set it above all communitarian interests (such as the public interests in resource management, wilderness, and endangered species protection), but also above any other individual rights that might conflict with property rights. In the battle between property and freedom, property wins, because in this view private property ownership is the only real freedom. The result is what one scholar called a nearly anarchic property-based libertarianism. The Bill of Rights does afford us nearly unlimited freedom of speech, with consequences that are mainly political. But to construe the Fifth Amendment's protection from expropriation without compensation as similarly unlimited would have profound consequences for the ability of the government to exercise a wide range of its "police powers," that is, the powers necessary to protect the public health, safety, and welfare, including those which support virtually all environmental legislation and regulation.

This particular strain of far-right ideology was hardly new. What was new was the willingness of the mainstream GOP and movement funders to lend it legitimacy, the adoption by its proponents of the organizing techniques perfected by the left in the 1960s, and its success in attracting significant popular support. Mimicking the successful scoring system used by the League of Conservation Voters, property rights advocates formed the League of Private Property Voters (now called the American Land Rights Association) and issued their own scorecard. In small towns around America, developers frustrated by local zoning took up the cry of "property rights," and, in the half-dozen years following the millennium, ballot measures treating ordinary zoning and land use regulation as "regulatory takings" requiring compensation appeared in at least seven states. The movement scored a landmark victory in 2004 with voter approval of Measure 37 in Oregon. Measure 37—totally out of step with regulatory taking jurisprudence, which provides for compensation only if the regulation deprives the landowner of *any* economic use of his or her property—required Oregon state and local governments to compensate landowners for the "reduction in the fair market value" resulting from any new environmental or land use regulation. If the government entity fails to pay the compensation within two years, the landowner is in effect exempted from the regulation. In the years following Measure 37, thousands of landowners (many of them developers) brought claims for hundreds of millions of dollars, which—except in a handful of cases—went unpaid, with the result that critical zoning and other land use laws were waived, with often significant adverse effects on neighbors, communities, and the environment. By 2007, in a major backlash against the so-called property rights movement, Oregonians passed Measure 49 with an even greater majority than had supported Measure 37, and eviscerated most of Measure 37's more troublesome provisions.

Ironically, nothing is more insidiously undermining of private property rights in the long term than efforts like these to paint those rights as absolute. This is because it is the boundaries around private property rights—the limitations necessary to accommodate the rights of other property owners and of society—that secure private property's place in a democratic society. No one would enter into a social contract where ownership of private property provided complete absolution from the property owner's interference with the rights and interests of others, or complete immunity from democratic measures necessary for the public health, safety, and welfare. Private property works in a democracy only because its use *is* fettered both by the property owners' responsibility to avoid harm to their neighbors and by the power of the state, most often devolved to the local level, to regulate land use in a way conducive to public health and safety. Nonetheless, property rights fundamentalism profoundly influenced the new-right orthodoxy, and shifted previously uncontroversial zoning and land use practices from the stuff of sleepy meetings of the local planning board to the center of the ideological battleground.

These three strains of market fundamentalism (the beliefs that environmental protection is inconsistent with economic growth, that virtually all regulation is socialistic, and that property rights are nearly absolute) were powerful levers that pried many conservatives loose from the conservation movement they had been part of for a century. The good news is that each of them bears within itself the seeds of a future reconciliation, because each is at odds with the underlying principles of conservatism, and clashes irreconcilably with the even stronger instinct that tells all true conservatives that nature is about something more than price.

UNEASY ABOUT GROWTH

The Anticapitalist Tendency in Environmentalism

W hile market fundamentalism provided the ideological fuel that powered the conservative abandonment of conservation, its evil twin, anticapitalism, gained a troubling foothold among Greens. Environmentalists must transcend their unease with growth, capitalism, and the corporate world if we are to have any hope of healing the Great Estrangement and restoring the bipartisan consensus.

The Green movement had its roots in ideas about scarcity and the limits to growth. Most Greens of my generation and before were nursed on Malthus, the Club of Rome's 1972 *Limits to Growth*, and Paul Ehrlich's *The Population Bomb*. Although the specific predictions made by these seminal works proved to be embarrassingly wrong, their shared conviction that the planet cannot sustain unlimited growth remains an article of faith among many Greens.

This conviction comes in many flavors. Gus Speth[1] and others endorse the Australian economist and ethicist Clive Hamilton's thesis that a "growth fetish" is the fundamental cause of environmental problems, and join in the call for what Hamilton calls a "post-growth" society."[2] Radicals like Hamilton believe that we have already reached the limits to growth, and would like to see output and consumption stabilized at current levels (with, perhaps, some allowance for the developing world to raise itself to a decent standard of living). Others look beyond scarcity, arguing, in effect, that enough is enough. At some point, we will have enough goods, enough wealth, enough leisure, and enough freedom from care that further growth in productivity and wealth will be unnecessary. This view might be coherent with respect to a country with a static population and a high standard of living. But with a forecast increase in the American population of about 100 million by 2050, we need growth sufficient to create somewhere between 90,000 and 125,000 jobs each month just to keep up with the growing labor force.[3]

The more orthodox Green view is not that we already have reached the limits to growth, but that environmental limits to growth are looming realities. The idea of scarcity has been a key part of the thinking and language of the Green movement from its earliest days, and environmentalists continue to make the case that the earth, as provider of our inputs of resources, nonrenewable energy, and food, and as receptacle for our outputs of carbon dioxide, waste, and toxics, is reaching its limits.[4] In the early 1970s, Paul Ehrlich and John Holdren, with the participation of Barry Commoner, introduced the now well-known IPAT equation: $I = P \times A \times T$, where I is environmental impact, P is population, A is affluence, and T is technology.[5] Even if they don't know the equation, many Greens have internalized its core lesson: growing population and affluence are the engines of environmental degradation.

While these modern environmentalists still indulge in the language of scarcity and fret about "peak oil," they also admit that, with the right amount of correction of market failure and government intervention, growth can be rendered more environmentally friendly and thus sustainable. Other Greens argue that affluence is the engine, not the enemy, of environmental concern, and that

environmental solutions will come mainly from advances in technology. But Green orthodoxy in general remains anxious about all
that affluence brings with it in terms of consumption and pollution, and worries whether technological advance will be sufficient
to offset it. Most Greens continue to speak of "acceptable levels" of
growth, and the undercurrent of meaning, to which conservatives
are hypersensitive, is that growth is on balance a thing that needs to
be constrained.

In contrast, most conservatives embrace orthodox market economics, which focuses on prices as the only reliable measure of
scarcity. The two sides of the scarcity debate are well illustrated
by the infamous 1980 bet between ecologist and scarcity guru Paul
Ehrlich and a little-known economist, Julian Simon, over whether
the real prices of five specified metals would increase over the following decade, a proxy for the question of whether the scarcity of the
resources and pressure of population growth would inevitably raise
their prices, as most environmentalists believed, or whether innovations in technology would allow supply to grow along with demand,
resulting in stable or falling prices.[6] A decade later the global population had grown by eight hundred million people, but the prices of
every one of the five metals had declined by an average of about 50
percent. The economist won, became a conservative folk hero, and
is remembered by the annual awarding of a prize in his name by the
Competitive Enterprise Institute for "debunk[ing] the alarmist predictions of eco-doomsayers like Paul Ehrlich."[7] The bet, of course,
really proved nothing, as price trends within a period as short as
a decade have everything to do with commodity price cycles and
macroeconomic conditions, and are not a fair measure of whether
technology will compensate for scarcity and demand growth over
the long term. What was a meaningful indicator of things to come
was the ugly rhetoric between the two, and the manner in which
market fundamentalists used the meaningless outcome to discredit
environmental concerns generally.

The ambivalence about economic growth that many conservatives see as hardwired into the Green movement has contributed mightily to the movement's political failures. When we are feeling prosperous as a nation, we are both more willing to bear the costs of environmental protection and more reluctant to accept greater risks to our quality of life—a virtuous circle that leads to broad support of environmental causes. Conversely, when Americans are feeling economically insecure, they have proved reluctant to make even the smallest sacrifices in the name of sustainability. As a result, Green hostility to economic growth is doubly disadvantageous to the political prospects of the movement: it embodies a preference for economic conditions where popular support of Green causes is minimized, and creates a perfectly valid reason for voters to distrust politicians who seem to be linked with this strain of Green thinking. Ted Nordhaus and Michael Shellenberger are right when they refer to "the albatross we call the politics of limits."[8]

Most Greens today pay lip service to the notion that environment and growth are not incompatible. But this is too little too late. The important truth is that environment and economy are codependent.[9] Without the healthy and durable ecosystem on which all human activity depends, there can be no sustainable economic growth. And without economic growth, we cannot achieve the global affluence to invest in developing the technologies that we will need to save the Earth. In addition, the poor, especially the urban poor, are not likely to prioritize postmaterialist values like the beauty and fulfillment found in nature until they are relieved from the burdens of poverty.[10] So the marriage between economy and environment is not one of transient infatuation, or a mere marriage of convenience. This is a marriage of necessity, and until a majority of Greens embrace this truth, it will be difficult for many conservatives to return to their place within the environmental movement.

Closely allied with the notion that economic growth is the main enemy of a sustainable environment is the conviction that capitalism, so good at producing growth, is a social and economic framework inconsistent with environmental goals. It is tempting but wrong to think of this as a fringe position. This anticapitalist bias arises from a longstanding Green focus on market failure, and has been promoted by some of the most mainstream figures in environmentalism, such as former Yale School of Forestry and Environmental Studies dean Gus Speth, who—not mincing words or evidencing any concern for conservative sensibilities—asserts, "The planet cannot sustain capitalism as we know it."[11] The rapturous reception accorded by many Greens to Naomi Klein's 2014 anticapitalist polemic, *This Changes Everything: Capitalism vs. The Climate*, demonstrates the continuing strength of this bias within the Green movement.

There are few Green books that do not at some point mention Garrett Hardin's 1968 article in *Science*, "The Tragedy of the Commons."[12] This is because most Green engagement with market capitalism starts with the proposition that people acting only as economic animals in their own rational self-interest will be free riders. Free riders take advantage of any opportunity to use (to and past the point of abuse) public or ecological resources (as in the grazing rights on the commons or fish stocks in the ocean). Free riders also impose costs on others or society at large (e.g., through pollution, where the free rider imposes an "externality," or cost, on society that should properly be priced into its own cost of production). This predisposition and ability to abuse public resources and impose externalities in a laissez-faire market system is at the heart of much Green discomfort with leaving everything to the free-market economy.

A similar market failure arises on the value side of the equation: Greens observe that the market prices resources such as timber and minerals, but fails to value "ecological services" (like the role of forests in protecting aquifers or of wetlands in buffering storm surges). These failures are related to the market's difficulty in valuing things that are as intricate as ecological systems, or in accounting for deferred consequences (such as the flood-buffering effects of wetlands over time in the face of sea level rise). As Speth puts it, "The result is that our market economy is operating on wildly wrong market signals, lacks other correcting mechanisms, and is thus out of control environmentally."[13] This much is true. The solution, of course, is not to throw out the market system but to correct the market failures by, for example, a carbon tax that shifts the costs of the externality to the producer.

Market failures are not, however, the exclusive cause of the anti-capitalist tendency among Greens. Parts of the Green movement are influenced by a broad leftist distrust of markets and capitalism. This distrust was exacerbated after the debacle of 2008 and the rise among progressives generally of severe doubts about the particular risks attached to unfettered financial markets. These doubts can, I think, be excused, given the damage done in the last decade by irrational excess, both on Wall Street and in corporate America. The distinction between rational self-interest (good) and excessive greed (bad) is also a critical one for some on the right, as illustrated by Russell Kirk's worrying in 1953 that the withering of religion, with its prohibition against avarice, and "the decay of the old aristocratic prejudices against greedy speculation," could lead to "a vast and voracious concentration upon profits."[14] This sense that "a vast and voracious concentration upon profits" may not be a good thing is shared both by traditional conservatives and the left.

Nonetheless, when Greens like Gus Speth take aim at capitalism, hostile conservatives shine a spotlight on the antimarket rhetoric and use it to paint the movement as socialistic. These old fault lines between socialism and capitalism have been revived by the virulent debate around capping carbon emissions, where forces on the right argue that confronting climate change threatens the free-market system as we know it, and certain forces on the left agree, admitting that lowering global carbon emissions to the levels required to stabilize the climate will indeed be achieved "only by radically reordering our economic and political systems in ways antithetical to [the] 'free market' belief system." Canadian journalist and author Naomi Klein argues that this is a good thing, and that "the real solutions to the climate crisis are also our best hope of building a much more enlightened economic system—one that closes deep inequalities, strengthens and transforms the public sphere, generates plentiful, dignified work and radically reins in corporate power."[15] Her new book calls frankly for redistribution of wealth, what she calls "managed de-growth." She writes that rightist ideologues who argue that action to limit climate change would spell the doom of capitalism actually have a better understanding of what is really required than mainstream environmentalists.

The anticapitalist flavor of "deep ecology" also provides an easy target for conservative critics such as Dinesh D'Souza, who wrote, "[S]ome environmentalists hold that the whole premise of modern technological capitalism, which is to supply the ever-increasing wants of man, is based on the false premise that the biosphere is ours for the ransacking. In the view of 'deep ecologists,' technological capitalism is a vicious, predatory enterprise because nature does not belong to us, we belong to nature."[16]

Finally, despite the current Green movement's broad embrace of "environmental economics" and market-based solutions, thoughtful Greens understand that there remains an apparent disconnect between the deepest values of the Green movement and the mechanistic determinism of the market. The market deals with things that can be priced, and uses their prices to determine their values. When nature is looked at in terms of its values as a resource, as genetic information, and/or as provider of "ecological services," prices *can* be fixed, and used to set priorities and maximize efficiency. But the idea of a transcendent value to nature is deeply embedded in Green thinking. Simply put, some of environmentalism is about saving things whose value just cannot be priced. Aldo Leopold asked, "Do economists know about lupines?" and the question resonates deeply with many Greens, myself included. This sensibility, even if it highlights the *limits* of the market, does not require that market economics should be *replaced* with socialism or anything else. And, importantly, it provides a vital bridge to conservatives, who also recognize that certain values lie in a realm outside of the reach of the market.

Given the Green ambivalence about growth and capitalism, it should be no surprise that the Green movement remains quite conflicted about its relationship with the corporate world. Corporate actions are the most frequent targets of Green criticism, the subject of most environmental laws and regulations, and the target of most of the litigation commenced by Green NGOs. On the other hand, corporations are our funders and from time to time our partners. Their CEOs sit on the boards of many of our NGOs. The relationship between corporations and the Green movement is complex.

The attitude and behavior of the corporate world in relation to environmental issues is diverse: some corporations oppose any Green initiative that would increase short-term costs, while others are converts to the sustainable-business movement; some corporations are guilty of the most cynical type of "greenwashing," while others are purveyors of authentically "green" products. To generalize as if the corporate world were monolithic in its approach to the environment is absurd.

The attitude of Greens toward the corporate world is similarly diverse. The Environmental Defense Fund's Fred Krupp was an early advocate of moving beyond what he called "reactive opposition" to business to a type of positive engagement with the corporate world—what he somewhat optimistically labeled the "third stage" of the environmental movement.[17] This strategy had its denouement in the U.S. Climate Action Partnership between green NGOs and businesses that pushed hard for carbon cap-and-trade legislation in 2008 and 2009.[18] Even Greenpeace worked with McDonald's on Amazon deforestation and with Coca-Cola on more efficient refrigeration, with the Greenpeace chief scientist explaining, "We don't share all the values of these corporations but are pragmatic enough to realize what working with them could deliver."[19] Greens need to understand that at least some of the corporate world's claims to have been converted to sustainability are honest ones.

While the *Wall Street Journal* was incorrect to suggest that the grist of the entire Green movement was to foment "rage against corporations," there are several segments of the Green movement—that small corner that intersects with the international antiglobalization movement—that believe that the existence of the corporate form is part of the problem. John Cavanagh and his coauthors typify this strain of thought, arguing that "[a]t the dawn of the twenty-first century, the global corporation stands as the dominant institutional force at the center of human activity and the planet itself. . . . We must dramatically change the publicly traded, limited liability global corporation, just as previous generations set out to eliminate or control the monarchy."[20] Thank goodness, this "off-with-their-heads" attitude toward corporate America is a fringe voice, but its very existence has done great damage to the Green movement in general and needs to be loudly repudiated by the rest of us.

A more promising path forward is based on the idea that the market can be part of the solution rather than the heart of the problem. The prophets of the sustainable business movement were Amory Lovins and L. Hunter Lovins, founders of the Rocky Mountain Institute, and entrepreneur Paul Hawken (of Smith & Hawken fame) who in 1999 wrote *Natural Capitalism: Creating the Next Industrial Revolution*. The principal promise of natural capitalism is the "triple bottom line" of profits, people, and the planet: if you do the right thing by people and the planet, then competitive advantage and profits will follow. You would think the Green movement would applaud this sort of thinking. But many Greens remain deeply skeptical that any good can come from a for-profit corporation. One, journalist Heather Rogers, points to the phenomenon economists call the "Jevons Paradox," where greater efficiency (such as a business achieves when reducing energy use) leads to *greater* resource use rather than less: "When the Wal-Marts of the world say that they are going to put in different light bulbs and get their trucks to get by on half the fuel, what are they going to do with that savings? They're going to open up another box store somewhere. It's just nuts."[21] When this way of thinking prevails, then the business community cannot do anything right. Business will stop listening to Greens, and Greens will fade into irrelevance, dreaming the impossible dream of the demise of corporate capitalism.

Collaboration with the corporate sector, although vital, can be risky. When the former head of the Sierra Club declared that "big corporations are not always the enemy" and then formed a corporate-sustainability consulting business and took on Walmart as a client (to create a "Personal Sustainability Project" for its employees), he was widely criticized by fellow Greens, lost clients, and even reported receiving death threats.[22]

Tension between the corporate sector and the Green movement is natural. Many of the policies and regulations advocated by Greens limit opportunities and add costs for corporate actors, and large segments of the business community have been and will continue to be shortsighted in opposing as "bad for business" even the most necessary and reasonable environmental initiatives. This sort of crying wolf at everything that adds costs in the short term is a sign of mismanagement, and in my view investors will increasingly favor those companies managed for sustainability. After all, which company is likely to grow and prosper over the long term: the gas driller that is casual about environmental compliance and does the minimum to protect the communities in which it works, or the one that is diligent about compliance, instills a culture of environmental commitment in its employees, and goes the extra mile to protect the communities in which it operates?

All too often Greens seem to suffer from a Manichaean view of corporate America, seeking to divide industries or corporate players into two clear camps: good guys and bad actors. This is a mistake. I have observed and participated in corporate partnerships with Green groups for decades, and know something about corporate decision making in my role as a counselor to those companies. The truth is simple: corporations will oppose the Green movement when they are threatened, and cooperate and partner when it is in their interest to do so. It is legitimate for Greens to hope that corporations will increasingly embrace the long-term, realize their dependence on ecosystem services, understand the damage to their brands when they act irresponsibly, and generally align their investments and activities with the principles of sustainability. But when some do and some don't, Greens must become much more comfortable than they are now in shining a positive spotlight on corporate farsightedness, while at the same time continuing to criticize bad corporate conduct—even when the praiseworthy and blameworthy conduct comes from the same company.

When Bill Ford served as chairman of Ford Motor Company, he was one of the top handful of Green Fortune 500 CEOs in the world and had been an eloquent spokesman for sustainability. In the face of huge skepticism and pressure from fellow CEOs, stockholders, and equity analysts, Ford was doing his best to make the company's operations more sustainable, including making some dramatic investments in green technologies at the carmaker's factories. The movement should have rewarded Ford by picking one of the other major car companies as the particular target for a campaign in favor of improved fuel efficiency. But, quick to wield the stick and slow to offer a carrot, the Green groups chose to aim their campaign against Ford. A former Greenpeace activist was right when he argued at the time, "Going after Ford will mean fewer, not more, CEOs will turn around and say protecting the environment is the right thing to do."[23] Only a few, more sophisticated Green NGOs were able to wield both carrot and stick, praising Ford's commendable green initiatives while at the same time advocating loudly for mileage requirements that would make its marquee SUVs obsolete. This is a good model for the movement to follow as it moves forward.

———————

The final vein of Green orthodoxy that is damaging to its standing with conservatives is an obsessive hostility to fossil fuels paired with an unrealistic delusion that hydrocarbons can be quickly excised from the economy. The one thing that is clear about American energy policy is that in the near to medium term the major part of the country's energy will come from hydrocarbons. Even if every Green proposal for the encouragement and subsidizing of renewable energy were immediately adopted, we would still need massive investment in petroleum infrastructure and development for decades to come in order for the lights to stay on, for planes to fly, and for cars to be driven. There are few uncontested facts in the messy arena of energy policy, but this one of them.

So why do so many environmentalists oppose virtually every project, investment, or activity that is necessary to keep the needed hydrocarbon fuel sources flowing? How is it possible that a movement that is characterized by higher-than-average levels of education and that includes so many highly competent scientists seems so often to oppose *any* marginal oil and gas development or infrastructure on the grounds that it contributes to global warming? In part, the explanation is that many Greens indulge in a "supply-side" fantasy: strangle supplies of petroleum and society will be motivated to stop using so much energy and to accelerate the pace of investment in alternatives. It is true that artificially limiting supplies of oil and gas will raise prices, but while higher energy prices may have a temporary dampening effect on demand, they ultimately make possible the exploitation of more expensive carbon-based sources of supply. Many Greens fantasizing about $500-a-barrel oil don't realize that it is a dream they share with big oil.

More fundamentally, the tactic of simply drawing a line in the hydrocarbon supply sand and saying "no more" has been disastrous for the Green movement. It confirms the suspicion of many conservatives that Greens should not have a seat at the table when serious energy-policy decisions are being made. If the Green movement is apt to oppose *all* oil and gas drilling, development, and infrastructure, then why seek its views regarding *which* petroleum developments have more or less impact on surrounding land, water, and ecological resources; why seek or trust its views on *which* petroleum resources have more or less impact on the climate during the multidecade transition to alternatives?

This tension was illustrated in both the long-running debate over permitting petroleum development in the Artic National Wildlife Refuge (ANWR) and the permitting of the Keystone XL pipeline. Each of them illustrates the severe self-imposed handicap that burdens the Green movement's effectiveness. Whether or not to permit drilling in the ANWR was a complex policy question. There were important issues of precedent (i.e., regardless of actual impacts and risks, should previously designated natural areas be open to resource exploitation?), analysis required of the extent to which new drilling technologies would mitigate environmental impacts, and the question of how to weigh America's energy security interests with other priorities. In my view, the Green position was correct, largely because it would have been an unacceptable precedent to allow drilling—whatever its impact—in a place previously designated as natural and set aside for its wilderness values. But an intelligent discussion about ANWR was almost impossible when the gross stupidity of "drill, baby, drill" on the right was matched by the fantasy of "beyond petroleum" on the left.

Nor is intelligent analysis of energy-policy questions aided by the Green movement's habit of making selected issues a litmus test of environmental purity. There is no better example of this than the strange decision by the Green movement to elevate a single oil pipeline to litmus-test status. Opposition to Keystone became a proxy for climate-change orthodoxy, despite the fact that the incremental (compared to conventional crude oil) EPA-estimated 18.7 million metric tons per year of carbon emissions caused by producing and burning the tar sand oils to be transported by Keystone is what the *New York Times* called "an infinitesimal slice" of the global total, and that stopping the pipeline would be highly unlikely to prevent those emissions, because the State Department (in its January 2014 Final Supplemental Environmental Impact Statement) and others concluded that the oil would find its way to markets even if the Keystone XL pipeline is not built. But to many in the movement, even those who admit that the pipeline itself would hardly rank on any list of substantive Green priorities, this is beside the point. As California hedge fund manager and philanthropist Tom Steyer, who is a major funder of the anti-Keystone effort, told the *New York Times*, "The Keystone XL pipeline is a line in the sand that signifies whether our country has the courage, the commitment and the capacity to be a global leader in addressing the challenge of climate change before it's too late."[24] In announcing his administration's decision to deny the Keystone permit, President Obama referred to it as a "symbol" rather than a "serious policy matter," and suggested that he acted principally to avoid undercutting America's "global leadership" on climate change in view of his departure three weeks later for the international climate change conference in Paris.

One final example. Shifting our energy supply mix away from high-carbon-emitting coal and diesel and toward relatively clean natural gas is one of the very few actions realistically available to the United States that would move the needle on greenhouse gas emissions. So just when the Green movement should be cheering that abundant and cheap domestic natural gas has the proven effect of accelerating the replacement of dirty coal-fired power plants (and, potentially, inefficient and carbon-intensive sources like Canadian tar sands), the Sierra Club launched its "Beyond Natural Gas" campaign. Although the campaign exploits popular (and in some cases legitimate) fears about "fracking," the Sierra Club president is at least honest about the actual reason for the campaign: "Fossil fuels have no part in America's energy future—coal, oil and natural gas are literally poisoning us. The emergence of natural gas as a significant part of our energy mix is particularly frightening because it dangerously postpones investment in clean energy at a time when we should be doubling down on wind, solar and energy efficiency."[25] It seems pretty clear that any project to provide needed hydrocarbon fuels—whether relatively clean or relatively dirty, whether involving ill-regulated fracking by undercapitalized fly-by-night wildcatters or tightly regulated fracking by competent and responsible companies, whether threatening to a sensitive and important local ecosystem or relatively benign—all will be opposed by the Sierra Club. And with that overbroad strategy, the Sierra Club, one of the oldest and greatest pillars of the Green movement, gripped by the feverish delusion that a world "beyond petroleum" is at hand, has effectively taken itself out of the game at a time when making exactly those distinctions is vital to protecting public health and the environment. And by doing so it also has deepened the estrangement between the Green movement and the right. Noting that cheap natural gas has already accomplished the greatest reduction in the carbon intensity of electric power generation in recent times, the *Wall Street Journal* editorial page explained to the faithful: "The Sierra Club campaign underscores that the modern green agenda is about far more than clean air and water and protecting wildlife. The real goal is to ban all fossil fuels—regardless of economic cost. It's hard to imagine a campaign that poses a greater threat to the U.S. economy, energy security and American health."[26]

It is 2008. The deepening divide between right and left has driven American politics for years, and the environmental movement has suffered accordingly. Nearing the end of his career, one of the eminent establishment figures of the Green movement, Yale Forestry School dean Gus Speth writes what may be his swan song, the summa in which he shares what he has concluded following a lifetime of thinking deeply about the issues.[27] His main message is that we face a tsunami of environmental collapse and catastrophe caused not only by climate change, but by peak oil, toxics, loss of terrestrial ecosystems, and the attendant loss of biodiversity. The coming catastrophe, he says, is being caused by too many people, too much economic growth, too much consumption, the dominance of the corporation, and modern capitalism "out of control." In his view, the only solution is to effect a radical change in human nature and thereby transform and transcend contemporary capitalism. If we are to attract moderates and conservatives to the Green cause, one of our highest priorities should be to repudiate voices like Speth's and convince Americans that Greens in general don't wish to stop growth; that they accept the capitalist system, value market mechanisms for setting priorities and creating efficiency, and understand that continued development of fossil fuels will be required while we strive for a low- or no-carbon future.

Without meaning to suggest equivalency—either in merit, good faith, or blame for the Great Estrangement—there is a strange symmetry between the poisonous orthodoxy of market fundamentalism within movement conservatism and, within parts of the Green movement, the anticapitalist sentiment and delusion that we can live without fossil fuels now or in the near future. Both are extreme, wildly popular with a base of enthusiastic supporters, and major impediments to broader acceptance of their respective causes. If either side is serious about reengaging with the other to recommence governance and actually influence environmental outcomes, it must cast off this ideological baggage.

THE GREEN MOVEMENT
AT FIFTY

I believe in climate change. I ride my bike everywhere,
I work at a solar company, I buy organic and local
when I can. I am young, liberal, and idealistic. But I'm
not an environmentalist. And I'm not alone.

—BLOG POSTING BY LISA CURTIS,
WWW.GRIST.ORG (MAY 7, 2012)

The over-professionalization, the over-technicalization
of the environmental movement is a decision to work at
the elite level but not the popular level. It's a defensible
strategy. It might have worked. . . . It's just that it didn't.

—BILL MCKIBBEN[1]

The latest report of the Nobel Prize–winning Intergovernmental Panel on Climate Change, released in three phases over 2013 and 2014, was stark: global warming soon will be impossible to address with existing technologies, meaning that the livability of the planet will likely depend on our ability to discover new technologies to scrub carbon from the atmosphere and sequester it.[2] In other words, despite understanding the problem for nearly thirty years, we have failed to act in any meaningful or effective way. The window for meaningful prevention is closing fast, the prospects for meaningful prevention are dim, and we lack the technologies necessary to reverse or adapt. The Kyoto Protocol was not a success and, despite the optimism engendered by the Paris agreement in 2015, the successful implementation of the agreement's nonbinding targets remains highly uncertain. Greens at the end of a twenty-year campaign to secure the planet have been forced to look failure squarely in the face, and are deeply traumatized by the shock.

The long failure of the American Green movement to make any appreciable progress on its global-warming agenda at the national or international level (prior to the Paris agreements reached at the end of 2015), is simple enough to summarize. At the Earth Summit in Rio de Janeiro in 1992, President George H. W. Bush made limited commitments to reduce America's carbon emissions. During the eight years of the Clinton presidency (with the nation's leading climate-change advocate sitting in the vice president's office), no federal action was taken to follow through on these commitments or to reduce American CO_2 emissions. The environmental movement then invested all its hopes in the Kyoto treaty, designed to reduce greenhouse gas emissions below 1990 levels. In 1997 the U.S. Senate, by a vote of 95–0, preemptively rejected the treaty, which was never officially submitted for ratification. The movement's next climate-change priorities were cap-and-trade schemes under the McCain-Lieberman Climate Stewardship Act, which was rejected by the Senate (55–43) in 2003, and the McCain-Lieberman Climate Stewardship and Innovation Act, which failed by a vote of 60–38 in 2005. In October 2007, Senator Lieberman teamed up with Senator John Warner on the Climate Security Act, which failed to make its way to the Senate floor when the required cloture motion attracted only forty-eight votes. Then, with Democrats in control of both houses of Congress and the newly elected president having promised quick action on global warming, the Waxman-Markey cap-and-trade bill passed the House 219–212 in June 2009. But by July 2010 the bill was abandoned when it became apparent that it could not pass the Senate. And that, after two decades of vigorous efforts and the expenditure of over $1 billion by Green NGOs, was that.[3]

The Green movement has never been particularly introspective, but the failure of cap-and-trade in 2010, when conditions for passage were singularly favorable, unleashed a torrent of hand wringing, blame, and scholarly postmortems. Bloomberg journalist (now a senior staffer with EDF) Eric Pooley wrote *The Climate War,* a riveting account of the USCAP partnership and the political saga that resulted in approval of Waxman-Markey by the House. Chief among the scholarly efforts are a pair of papers prepared for a February 2013 symposium at Harvard. One, by journalists Petra Bartosiewicz and Marissa Miley, is *The Too Polite Revolution: Why the Recent Campaign to Pass Comprehensive Climate Legislation in the United States Failed;* the other, by Harvard sociology professor Theda Skocpol, is *Naming the Problem: What It Will Take to Counter Extremism and Engage Americans in the Fight against Global Warming.* Discussion of both papers lit up the blogosphere with a lively debate about who really is to blame for the failure.[4] The term "post-traumatic stress" quite literally applies: the abrupt and complete failure of cap-and-trade in 2010 is one of the great traumas suffered by the modern Green movement in its nearly fifty-year history, and the stress from it is clearly evident more than five years after the event.

Much of the postmortem has focused on the arguments about the proximate causes of the 2008–2010 failure of cap-and-trade, as opposed to its root causes. Some argue that the main cause was the effectiveness of the GOP opposition, which ultimately prevented the needed Republican senators from crossing the aisle to support the bill enacted by the House. Others point to the fact that electric utilities and the fossil-fuels industry far outspent Greens on lobbying and advocacy.[5] A significant number of Greens pin primary blame on President Obama, who chose to pursue health-care reform first, and then, they argue, failed to provide sufficient leadership on climate. Left-of-center Greens fault the USCAP coalition's probusiness strategy and many compromises with carbon producers, and some of the USCAP NGOs point to the failure of the Sierra Club, other left-leaning Green groups, and the green-technology zealots to rally around this historic opportunity. Other analysts cite tactical errors, such as the failure to pursue reconciliation in the Senate, which would have reduced the number of required supporters from sixty to fifty-one, and the complexity of the legislation, the final form of which ran to nearly 1,400 pages. Economic conditions at the time, with high unemployment and the GDP still contracting, also clearly affected the outcome.

What I find most interesting about the dialogue within the Green movement following 2010 is how widely Greens ignored the *root* causes of the failure, including both the fact and implications of the Great Estrangement, and the nature of contemporary environmentalism. I agree with Professor Skocpol, who observed, "[W]hat is striking to me as a political scientist is how few of the post-mortems have looked deeply into the overall political dynamics that preceded and accompanied the USCAP effort. . . . Missing from all these reports was any clear analysis of the larger political context in the United States."[6] That larger political dynamic has two main aspects: the failure to effectively combat conservative antienvironmental extremists and the failure to mobilize the popular support necessary to animate and sustain political action, which was critical.

Interestingly, the causes of failure most discussed inside the movement and by the scholarly analysts omit the reason most often cited by Americans on the street: too much "crying wolf." Greens told the world repeatedly that it needed to act immediately or risk destroying life on Earth as we know it. The most recent episode was the aftermath of the 2007 IPCC Report, when the leader of that effort, Rajendra Pachauri (appointed by George W. Bush) said, "If there's no action before 2012, that's too late."[7] Well, we didn't act by 2012, and if we take Pachauri at face value, then there is nothing to be done. And yet a skeptical public sees Greens continue to hit the reset button and argue again and again that now is the time to act or all is lost. As the director of the American Geophysical Union study of public attitudes described it: "The more we talk about global warming, the [more the] public's concern goes down."[8] And the hit we have taken from being seen to have cried wolf on climate change has profoundly hurt the broader environmental movement, giving the right ammunition to cast into doubt the validity of the entire enterprise of science-based environmental policy making.

So where does the climate trauma of 2010 leave the Green movement? Some thoughtful Greens argue that climate change challenged the American people to think globally, asked them to step away from being free riders, demanded that they trust in sophisticated and abstract science, and rallied them to postpone pleasure and wealth for the good of future generations. In this rather depressing view, the people failed on all counts, showing that humanity is simply not sufficiently evolved to deal with the first planetary-scale crisis. But another school of thought holds that it is the leaders of the Green movement who failed the people. The Greens lost credibility with major parts of the public and tried unsuccessfully to motivate people with a nightmare. The people sensed that many Greens were not only motivated by saving the planet from the ravages of climate change, but also influenced by their hostility toward capitalism and their conviction that limiting economic growth was necessary to save the planet. Of course, neither of these theses is fair or complete, yet both contain important grains of truth and some explanatory power.

Whatever history's ultimate verdict, one thing is clear: the Green movement was not and is not configured to address its greatest challenge. "[N]ot since the 1920s," writes one historian of American environmentalism, "has the movement been so impotent."[9] Although open introspection among Green group leaders is relatively rare, a few of them recently have become more willing to speculate about what has gone wrong. For example, at a meeting in the Pacific Northwest that I attended, the chief executive of a respected environmental organization reminded an audience of environmental leaders that one definition of insanity was doing the same thing over and over and expecting a different result. The Green movement, he said, seemed stuck in a rut, using the same strategies and tactics it had used for forty years, seemingly surprised every time they still didn't work. The unhappy truth is that the movement of professional NGOs that the Earth Day generation of Greens has bequeathed to us is aging, lacks the diversity of the nation it serves, and rests on a base of public support that is broad but perilously shallow. As a result, these Green NGOs are curiously unable to communicate with and engage the constituency necessary to return environmentalism to its earliest configuration as a true mass movement with corresponding political influence.

Although some of my Green movement colleagues will doubtless be offended by certain observations in this chapter, many others will—at least in private—recognize some truths about themselves and their organizations. This portrait of a movement in crisis is offered in a spirit of affection and support. It is not intended to devalue the many achievements of the movement during the past half century. Nonetheless, I fully expect some Greens to direct at this book the special rage that is reserved for the apostate. When other environmental insiders have broken ranks and expressed their concerns in a very public way, they were accused by fellow Greens of arrogance, self-indulgence, patricide, and nihilism, among other things. The Green movement suffers from an overdose of orthodoxy, and I am convinced that questioning that orthodoxy from a place of solidarity with its goals is a good and healthy thing. The fact that the Green movement's enemies may try to use the ideas and criticisms in this chapter against us does not change the fact that for the half-century-old Green movement, introspection and self-criticism are absolutely vital.

The first problem is that most Americans are Green, but just not very much. Environmentalism is securely embedded in wide swaths of American popular culture. It is an accepted part of the school curriculum. Its iconic practices, such as recycling and energy conservation, are a ubiquitous part of our work life and consumer experience. Envi-

ronmentalists often take comfort from polls showing that large percentages of Americans, often in the 70–80 percent range, consider
themselves environmentalists, support the Green movement, or support the goals of protecting our land, water, and air. Eighty-three
percent want more government support for clean energy,[10] 72 percent
believe that global warning should be a priority for government,[11]
and in their personal lives, roughly 70–90 percent "walk the walk"
by engaging in behaviors like recycling and energy conservation.[12]

What these polls do not answer is the question of how much
Americans care, how strong their support for Green causes really
is, or how much it affects their voting. When asked how much they
care about environmental issues, the answers look very different. By
January 2009, the percentage of Americans polled by Pew stating
that the environment was "a top priority" (note: *a*, not *the*, top priority) dropped to 41 percent,[13] and later that year—for the first time
in nearly thirty years—more Americans told Gallup that they were
willing to sacrifice the environment to achieve economic growth
than said they supported protecting the environment at the risk
of curbing economic growth.[14] When asked to rank sixteen issues
in terms of their importance, the environment consistently comes
in *last*, and in polling for the 2014 midterm elections, Gallup again
found that climate change ranked dead last of thirteen issues in a
poll of registered voters.[15]

The persistent shallowness of popular support for the environment is exacerbated by the propensity of the Green movement to
ignore it. Greens too often take false comfort from poll results, focusing primarily on the indicated breadth of support and shrugging off
the low priority given to Green causes. As a result, Greens overestimate their own popularity and, time and again, are surprised and
disappointed when the poll numbers do not translate into political
action. As one environmentalist and historian admitted in 2003, he
had expected for most of his career that "the environment would be
one of the top two or three issues that would decide a presidential

election."[16] Needless to say, it never came close. And this conviction that "most everyone is an environmentalist" has contributed to the movement's continuing belief that when push came to shove people would support the sacrifices necessary to assure sustainability. But after twenty years of trying to get Americans to do just that to ameliorate climate change, it is now pretty clear that they will not, and the Green movement doesn't know what to do about it.

A related problem with the contemporary Green movement is that too many of its adherents are old. Take The Nature Conservancy, the largest, richest, and in many ways most successful Green organization in the world, which ought to be attracting armies of idealistic young people schooled in concern for coral reefs and rain forests. The average age of all its supporters (in 2012): sixty-two. That's right, sixty-two—the age of people who were twenty at the time of the first Earth Day, in 1970. And, even worse, the average age of *new* members was reported to be exactly the same, sixty-two; only 5 percent of the organization's members are under forty.[17] TNC is not alone. Other reports estimate the average age of members of all environmental and conservation groups in America to be fifty-seven.[18]

That the Earth Day generation has failed to attract their children into the Green movement is puzzling. Unlike their parents, many of those children grew up in a world where environmental consciousness was embedded in their homes and schools, and where they learned from an early age about rain forests, coral reefs, and recycling. There is no question that views on environment differ greatly by cohort, with Americans between the ages of eighteen and twenty-nine consistently reporting higher levels of concern about global warming. So why aren't they taking over the Green movement and leading the fight on the environmental problems of the twenty-first century?

Part of the answer has to do with loss of faith in the political process, and part may be attributable to the economic stresses suffered by young people entering the job force after the Great Recession of 2008. As one disaffected young activist put it, "The environmentalism of my grandparents' generation was focused on preserving pristine wilderness, free from human interference. For my parents, environmentalism was all about the legislative victories."[19] It is easy to sympathize with the depth of that generation's cynicism about the ability of politics to bring about solutions to anything, especially given their passionate engagement with that moment of "Yes, we can" optimism in 2008 and the frustrations and disappointments that followed. This particular young activist did not continue and tell us what environmentalism was for her generation; she suggested that young people are attracted by "Green jobs," reminding us that today's youth are as afflicted by economic uncertainty as their elders, and also are searching to align their idealism, such as it is, with their work lives. But as expedient as it is to focus people on the employment-creating consequences of investment in green technologies and alternative energy, we cannot simply redefine the movement as some kind of grand jobs program.[20] Bill McKibben's global warming organization, 350.org, is targeted solidly at college-age and young Greens, but its obsessive focus on a single pipeline project, Keystone XL, hardly shows the way for the Green movement as a whole to reconnect with youth.

The aging of the Green movement matters. Not only is demography destiny, but the failure of Greens to attract the young is a huge political liability. During the critical period when environmentalists were focused on moving Waxman-Markey in the Senate, Chris Miller, adviser to Majority Leader Harry Reid, asked quite reasonably, "Where are all the college students?"[21] However we get there, one thing is clear: failure to rejuvenate will result in the Green movement riding the demographic curve into oblivion.

Closely related to this failure is the Green movement's stubborn inability to increase its diversity. Environmentalism is overwhelmingly white. The problem is hardly new, but it is curiously intractable. In 1990 a group of civil rights leaders wrote to eight of the leading national Green NGOs and accused them of racism in their hiring practices. At the time, not one of the national Green groups had a black or Hispanic person among its top leadership.[22] Go to any environmental conference today (other than one aimed specifically at the environmental-justice movement) and you will see a sea of white middle- and upper-middle-class faces.

This is not a recipe for success in the twenty-first century. The vast majority of America's population growth between now and 2050 will occur among traditional racial minorities, particularly Asians and Hispanics, with whites becoming a minority by 2050. The resulting America will be a post-ethnic and post-racial mélange, drawing strength and economic advantage from its diversity, and finally realizing Walt Whitman's vision of the country as "not merely a nation, but a teeming Nation of nations."[23]

In my experience, Greens suffer genuine angst about the fact that their movement looks more like 1950 than 2050. Mostly people of goodwill and good conscience, they are mortified by their failure to attract, retain, and motivate people of color. And many thoughtful Green leaders also understand that in a country where half the members of the House of Representatives will represent urban and nonwhite districts, lack of diversity will impair their ability to fulfill their missions.

There are some signs that the Green movement may be making the shift to a more diverse base of support. The long effort to foment some sort of national action in response to climate change did succeed in mobilizing a number of nonwhite groups.[24] The Sierra Club has elected its first African-American president. Demographics and social change will facilitate this process. When nonwhites enter the middle class, they can be expected to prioritize health and quality-of-life issues over the concerns of their parents, who may have focused on racial discrimination, access to education, and economic opportunity. Nonwhites are flooding into the suburbs in record numbers, and like their white neighbors will face issues of water quality, energy use, and sprawl. There is every reason to expect that these middle-class and suburban nonwhites will become increasingly Green.

Opening the doors of environmentalism to middle-class and suburban minorities is not enough. To configure itself for the America of 2050, the Green movement must transition from its perceived prioritization of the concerns of the rural and suburban affluent to an authentic dedication to the health of cities, which will provide the "environment" for more than half the population. The Green movement must give voice to urban concerns about the management of density, urban pollution, urban green spaces, access to healthy food, adaptation to climate change, and the host of environmental problems relevant to those who live in cities. If we do, then there is every reason to think that city dwellers of all races will rally to the Green cause. But until we do, the white complexion of the Green movement remains a major hurdle to political effectiveness and success.

———————

Supporter demographics and political effectiveness are closely related problems. In the climate debacle of 2009, Green NGOs came face-to-face with the stark reality that they needed to learn to be more assertive, more deeply engaged in politics, and more skillful in playing the political game. And, most importantly, they learned that correct policy arguments don't lead to victory unless perceived by the political class to be enthusiastically supported by a significant number of motivated voters. In a now infamous private meeting at the White House, Obama chief of staff Rahm Emanuel was secretly tape-recorded blasting the political ineptitude of the Green NGOs, which had failed to deliver the promised Republican votes for cap-and-trade: "They didn't have shit. And folks, they were dicking around for two years. And I had those meetings in my office so it was not that I wasn't listening to them. . . . This is a real big game, and you've got to wear your big-boy pants."[25] Ouch. The Green movement, which could turn out millions for Earth Day in 1970, has lost the ability to mobilize ordinary citizens in support of its most important causes, and thus has lost the political moxie necessary to play the "big game" in Washington.

A wide streak of political reluctance runs through the Green movement, in part arising from the movement's history and aspiration to be above politics, and in part due to legal complications arising from the status of most Green NGOs as public charities. The Green movement has long indulged the hope that the universality of the environmental cause, its roots in objective science, and its widespread popular support would allow it to avoid the political mud pit. Before 1970, none of the American conservation organizations employed full-time lobbyists or endorsed candidates for public office.[26] But in 1970, realizing that the federal government was the arena in which environmental policy would be forged, the leaders of various environmental groups pooled their resources and founded the nonpartisan League of Conservation Voters, the group that, with its various state counterparts, are still the principal vehicles for Green participation in elective politics. But for the other Green NGOs, partisan political activity is strictly off limits, and lobbying activity is limited. Many Greens remember that David Brower's militant campaigns against federal dam projects caused the IRS to take action. When he formed his new group, Friends of the Earth, he made sure that it was a 501(c)(4)—a direct-action social welfare organization—and not a 501(c)(3)—a classic public charity—and thus would be free to take unlimited lobbying and legislative action (and limited political action).

The Green movement is still grappling with a fundamental structural problem. Most of the large Green NGOs remain organized as 501(c)(3) public charities because they believe that they could not achieve the required fund-raising without contributions being deductible for federal tax purposes. As a result, they are prohibited from supporting or opposing specific candidates, and their lobbying (e.g., for or against legislation) is limited to a small percentage of their total activity. This is an enormous problem for organizations that need to serve as the vanguard of a mass political movement, and whose opponents face no such constraints. Some groups, such as the Trust for Public Land, have established their own (c)(4)s, and this is critical if the Green movement is to supplement policy prescriptions with aggressive lobbying and direct political action, as it must. Some Green NGOs have formed affiliated political action committees, which are able to make direct contributions for the purpose of electing or defeating specific candidates. But as a whole, the structure, financial support base, and mentality remain that of a movement dominated by public charities. As Nicholas Lemann wrote in the *New Yorker*, "To turn concern into action requires politics. The science of carbon emissions is there. The politics is not."[27]

All of these problems, demographic and political, arise in part from a failure to communicate. The movement's struggle to tell the environmental story in a manner that ordinary Americans find compelling antedates the climate wars. It dates, I believe, from the very beginning of the modern movement, when the old-fashioned references to "nature" and "conservation" gave way to "environment." I have always believed that "environment"—in stark contrast to "nature"—is a cold abstraction, lacking warmth or any cultural or emotional association. "Environment" is also a passive word that is, in its essence, value neutral. It signifies only the abstract idea of the physical context in which things takes place. Most significant is the problem that the word exists to distinguish between the things that are acting and interacting (principally human beings) and the stage (environment) on which the activity occurs. By enshrining the dichotomy between man and nature, the word opens us to the criticism that when choosing between "it" (the "environment") and "us" (the people), "environmentalists" will of course prefer the object of their affection, at the expense of the rest of us. The word "conservation," in contrast, is based on the verb *conserve*, and carries both a call to activism ("to conserve") and a strong implication of positive value: we conserve only what is useful, good, or beautiful.[28] Even the word "ecology" is preferable to "environment" because, based on the Greek word *oikos*, meaning house, it signifies how life forms interact both with their habitat and with each other.

Other baggage from the earliest days of the modern movement includes a propensity for pessimism. At varying times over the past half century, environmentalists have predicted water rationing in America by 1974, worldwide famine by 1975, food rationing and a pesticide-induced decline of life expectancy to forty-two in America by 1980, and a complete collapse of fishery stocks by 1990. A conservative friend explained to me why she disliked environmentalists: "They make depressing dinner companions." In that flip comment lies a deeper truth. Hopelessness is a major cause of depression, disengagement, and indifference. One climate scientist warned in 2007 that "the discourse of catastrophe is in danger of tipping society onto a negative, depressive and reactionary trajectory."[29] He was prophetic, because it is hard to characterize the course of the climate-change debate since then as anything but "negative, depressive and reactionary."

For too many Greens, the glass is always half empty. In 2002, the EPA announced that two-thirds of America's rivers and half of its lakes had met the Clean Water Act goal of making U.S. waters fishable and swimmable. Most environmental NGOs greeted this news by countering that a third of American rivers were too polluted to fish or swim in, choosing to see the glass as one-third empty, instead of two-thirds full. They missed the opportunity to inspire Americans with the remarkable fact that after a century of treating rivers as open sewers, we had managed in only thirty years to return two-thirds of them to fishable and swimmable condition. That it was achieved by a federal statute administered by a large and imperfect federal bureaucracy could have served as a useful reminder that some problems are big enough and tough enough to require action at the national level, and that not all "command and control" solutions have detrimental economic effects. They should have noted that over that same period the American economy grew nearly threefold in real terms. The habit of pessimism has proven hard to break. And, most importantly, the Green movement at fifty is not yet able to articulate a vision that will inspire and motivate the American people.

Learning how to inspire and motivate, to change hearts and minds, is a core challenge. Shellenberger and Nordhaus were perceptive in their explanation of the Green movement's fundamental failure to change hearts and minds, especially in relation to global warming. Most environmentalists, they argued in 2004, are "children of the enlightenment who believe that they arrived at their identity and politics through a rational and considered process. They expect others in politics should do the same and are constantly surprised and disappointed when they don't."[30] Thanks to psychologists such as Jonathan Haidt, Daniel Kahneman, and Dan Kahan, we now understand that most people do not arrive at their political opinions through a conscious, deliberate, and highly analytical process (what Kahneman calls "System 2" in his book *Thinking, Fast and Slow)*,[31] but in a largely unconscious intuitive fashion ("System 1"), which is heavily influenced by one's community, general world view, and sense of identity—what Kahan calls "motivated reasoning" or "cultural cognition." This helps to explain the roughly one-third of Americans who reject the scientific consensus about global warming. According to Kahan's ideas about the cultural cognition of risk, these people don't reject science, but simply accept the data and choose the experts whose views align most closely with the values and "cultural predispositions" of their community and peer group.[32] So if your worldview (like that of many conservative Republicans) is "hierarchical individualist," Al Gore's PowerPoint slide show is unlikely to change your mind about global warming.[33] When asked what positive advice he would give environmentalists, Kahan replied that the key is "not to use language or modes of communication that convey animosity, contempt, and hostility [because then] the signal that will come through is . . . that our group is under assault."[34] So when the Green movement uses language that signals challenge and disrespect to conservatives (such as the adoption of the term "denier," with all of its Holocaust associations, for those who don't accept the reality of climate change), and this disrespect is amplified and exaggerated by the conservative media, the risk is that conservatives will retreat further into the defensive circle of their group. This partly explains why the Green movement is making little progress with the large segment of the American population that, every so often, delivers control of the White House and/or a house of Congress to the Republican Party.

The Green movement's failure to communicate, or at least to communicate as well as its opponents, was well illustrated during the 2009–2010 fight over cap-and-trade. When Waxman-Markey passed the House, a poll found that only 24 percent of Americans could identify that "cap-and-trade" had something to do with the environment, much less begin to articulate its operation, rationale, or benefits.[35] In contrast, conservative anti-Green strategists brilliantly dubbed it a "light switch tax," a moniker that stuck, and that 100 percent of Americans could understand. Talk radio called it "an Enron-style profiteering scheme, " and "a Ponzi scheme" that would cost the average family $5,400 per year; said one anti–climate-change campaigner, "My guess is we'd cut out things like piano lessons, dance lessons, or Little League or summer camp. . . . The idea of saving for college for your kids—*that's gone*."[36] In contrast, Green NGOs and their USCAP industry partners did extensive polling and came up with the flat tagline: "More jobs. Less pollution. Greater security." The Greens initially claimed that climate legislation would result in

1.9 million new jobs. In response, NRDC's Frances Beinecke was right to complain, "We're not about job creation."[37] When people hear environmentalists talking about jobs they are appropriately skeptical, because they understand that economic growth is not the environmentalists' mission and have already heard a chorus of job-creation claims from advocates of other causes. The Waxman-Markey proponents changed their messaging to national security. Anything, their polling told them, but climate.

———————

By some estimates America in 2015 supports about ten thousand organizations dedicated to conservation and the environment. Some are well-known national and international generalist groups (such as Sierra Club, Environmental Defense Fund, and National Resources Defense Council), but most focus on single parts of nature (e.g., wilderness, rivers, oceans), specific species (fish, ducks, birds, other wildlife), defined constituencies (hunters, anglers, etc.), specialist areas of expertise (science, economics, law, public policy), or a specific geography. Only a country as enamored as ours with voluntary associations, and a people as generous in its support of not-for-profit endeavor, could support a Green independent sector of this depth and breadth. By one estimate, the NGOs represented in the informal club of organizations that refers to itself as "The Green Group" have a combined membership of approximately four million;[38] the sportsmen Green groups participating in the American Wildlife Conservation Partners consortium are estimated to represent six million Americans.[39] The Nature Conservancy alone reports that its membership has now exceeded one million, and the nation's 1,700 land trusts are estimated by the Land Trust Alliance to include about five million individuals. There are no reliable statistics regarding the total number of Americans who legitimately could be considered members of Green NGOs, but one scholar reported a decade-old estimate of twenty-five million.[40]

The entire first generation of American Green NGOs remains alive and active: the Boone and Crockett Club, founded in 1887, Sierra Club (1892), National Audubon (1905), National Wildlife Federation (1936), Izaak Walton League (1922), and The Wilderness Society (1935). Though some of the established groups, including National Wildlife Federation, Audubon, and the Sierra Club, started to look beyond their land, parks, and wilderness agenda to the newly revealed problems of pollution and toxics, most of the older Green groups were slow to ride the new wave of environmental concern in the 1960s and 1970s. Partly as a result, a new generation of Green groups arose and assumed leading positions in the movement: The Nature Conservancy, now the largest Green organization in the world, took its present form in 1951, Environmental Defense Fund in 1967, Friends of the Earth and the League of Conservation Voters in 1969, and Environmental Action and Natural Resources Defense Council in 1970. This new generation of Green groups is, in general, more focused on legislation, regulation, litigation, policy, and politics, and deploys highly professional scientists, economists, lawyers, and lobbyists in the cause of environmental protection.

The newer and older groups often work together, and both are represented in the informal Green Group that seeks to coordinate the efforts of the movement.[41] But there is a fundamental fault line that runs through the field of Green NGOs, separating the groups dominated by outdoor sportsmen from the rest. As we have seen, conservation in America has deep roots in the stewardship sensibility shared by hunters and anglers, and the groups representing them still have large memberships with a complexion far different from their Green brethren. Many of those members are gun owners, residents of rural areas, and Republicans. These wildlife-focused groups are better coordinated than the Green movement as a whole and have their own leadership group called American Wildlife Conservation Partners.[42] These groups generally call themselves "conservationists," not "environmentalists," and the ethic and tone of these groups can be gleaned from the Member's Pledge of the Izaak Walton League: "To strive for the purity of water, clarity of air, and the wise stewardship of the land and its resources; to know the beauty and understanding of nature and the value of wildlife, woodlands and open space: to the preservation of this heritage and to man's sharing in it."[43]

The fault line between the conservation and environment groups rarely manifests itself in public, but is a significant impediment to the movement as a whole effectively representing the full spectrum of the Americans who support elements of the Green agenda. Paul Hansen, the former executive director of the Izaak Walton League, reports that, despite a broad common agenda, "sportsmen and environment groups act as if they have almost nothing to do with each other. . . . At times, they act like enemies." He tells the story of an 2002 effort by Trout Unlimited, Izaak Walton League, Wildlife Management Institute, and Theodore Roosevelt Conservation Partnership to convene a broad group of stakeholders to consider a solution to the long-standing objective, shared by all Green groups, of extending to the roadless areas of the national forests the protections of the National Wilderness Preservation System (in this case, a compromise that would have allowed additional timber harvesting from regrown trees in areas with an existing road network). Hansen reports that nine major Green groups, including the Sierra Club, NRDC, and Earthjustice, boycotted the meeting and pressured others not to attend. I have myself observed a sometimes condescending attitude on the part of the leading national Green NGOs toward these grassroots conservation organizations, perfectly captured by Hansen's anecdote that the head of one prominent Green NGO was "fond of referring to hunters as 'bubbas.'"[44] The opportunity cost of this estrangement is enormous, as the sportsmen and conservation-oriented groups represent the exact constituency that is required to advance the Green agenda in Washington.

Today, the archetype of Green NGO activity is a team of suited experts, perhaps a scientist, an economist, and a policy expert, arriving in the office of a congressman to explain why he or she should support or oppose a particular piece of legislation. The message is largely policy based, delivered earnestly by real experts, although the team would be shrewd enough also to outline the political case for the vote, supported by sophisticated polling. Politicians and regulators generally listen because the leading Green NGOs hire good people, are professionally run, and play the inside game relatively well. On the other side of the NGO house, communications staff push out to the group's members focus-group-honed messages through savvy use of social media and slick print publications, and the NGO development staff pay the bills by cultivating foundations and individual philanthropists, in some cases soliciting smaller retail gifts with campaigns featuring stirring photographs of cuddly or noble animals facing the perils of rising seas and a warming climate. The individuals who are members of this type of NGO are essentially in a passive one-way relationship with the organization, reading materials promulgated by the organization, dispatching emails and letters when mobilized by the NGO for purposes of a campaign, and sending money when required, but they have no real influence on the policies and positions of the organization itself. A member who does not approve of the direction of the organization can quit and withdraw financial support, but that is about all.

What is missing from this picture? What the mature national Green NGO sorely lacks is the bottoms-up energy that animated environmentalism at its inception and during its youth. Adam Rome, who has recently chronicled the first Earth Day of 1970, argues that its astonishing success—twelve to thirteen thousand separate events in which roughly twenty million people participated (far more than the quarter million who came to the Mall for the

1963 civil rights March on Washington, or the roughly two million participating in the 1969 Vietnam Moratorium)—was due largely to Senator Gaylord Nelson's decision to provide only loose coordination at the national level and permit local people in every state to take ownership of their own events.[45]

The main tool used today by Green NGOs to mobilize public interest, action, and funding is the "campaign." The modern pattern, in which environmental activism periodically coalesces around a single-issue campaign, was set in the mid-1950s during a long fight to stop the Echo Park Dam from being built within Dinosaur National Monument, as part of the larger Colorado River Storage Project. That campaign, which was led by the Sierra Club and The Wilderness Society, was joined by 78 national and 236 state organizations.[46] It was the first campaign to engage the tools used ever since: national direct mail, support by cultural figures and celebrities, a relentless media blitz, and even—for those who mistakenly think that Michael Moore invented the genre—a professionally produced motion picture shown all around the country.[47] Recently, the defeat of Trans-Canada's Keystone XL crude oil pipeline became (unfortunately, from a Center Green perspective) the main campaign focus for many Green groups, and—as too often happens—also became a litmus test of one's commitment to fighting climate change, and of environmental credentials more generally. The requirement to keep running on the campaign treadmill has warped priorities and contributed to the Great Estrangement. A Sierra Club letter rallying the troops against the Wise Users read: "We are confronted by a super-financed, anti-environmental juggernaut that is craftily masquerading behind a totally deceitful public relations 'Wise Use' blitz to conceal their profit-driven designs. . . . They will stop at nothing to destroy us and the entire environmental movement." The letter concluded by urging the reader to make an immediate "emergency contribution."[48] All this has come at a cost to the kind of quieter thought leadership and subtlety that is critical to the environment in a way it is for few other areas of public policy. Adam Rome observes that "the professionals on the staffs of the major environmental organizations today are much better at leading campaigns than asking questions. They are adept at marshaling scientific evidence, making legal arguments, framing messages, and assessing environmental costs. They also know how to raise money—the *sine qua non* of not-for-profit advocacy. But they seldom inspire the deep reflection that might make the environmental movement dramatically bigger and stronger."[49] Or, as the Green movement's friend journalist Nicholas Kristof put it, "Some do great work, but others can be the left's equivalents of the neocons: brimming with moral clarity and ideological zeal, but empty of nuance."[50]

Finally, the Green movement at fifty has fractured into numerous subsidiary strains and schools, each with its own recipe for getting the Green movement back on track. We now have Dark Green, Light Green, Bright Green, Neo-Green, Post-Green, Hard Green, and Soft Green.[51] We even have Viridian Green[52]—not to mention "third wave" and "fourth wave" environmentalism[53]—and I have doubtless missed some others.

Broadly speaking, in one corner stand the traditionalists (often called Dark Greens), who still base policies on the idea of resource depletion, have doubts about growth and capitalism, and want to save nature for reasons other than its utility to man. The group sometimes called Bright or Post Greens has stepped away from traditional environmentalism, and instead expressly embraces a pro-growth agenda on the ground that only massive public investments in technology will provide solutions to environmental problems, including climate change.[54] The Environmental Defense Fund is an example of a mainstream NGO that broadly supports the Bright Green approach while not completely eschewing Dark Green. EDF leader Fred Krupp argues that climate calamity now can be avoided only by a "second industrial revolution as sweeping as that effected a century ago by the likes of Thomas Edison, Henry Ford, and John D. Rockefeller."[55] The heroes of this strain of Bright Green are inventors and innovators, and the venture capitalists and other investors who support them. They hope that technology will provide the solution to carbon emissions that political will could not.

Light Greens stand off to the side of the whole debate, turning inward to focus on their own personal behavior and choices. This is an expression of the old Green idea that the way to change the world is through individual action ("think globally, act locally"). The Light Greens, sometimes called Lifestyle Greens, recycle religiously and can be found each Saturday morning driving a Prius to the farmers' market. Marketing professionals refer to them as LOHAS, an acronym for "Lifestyles Of Health And Sustainability." And Dark Greens, especially those focused almost exclusively on global warming, excoriate the Light Greens for indulging in the illusion that changing their light bulbs and remembering to bring their hemp bag to the market will make a difference.[56] The Light Greens are, as one recent Dark Green critic put it, "fiddling with the small stuff while the planet burns."[57]

What should we make of these competing schools of thought? On balance, I believe this diversity is healthy. The environmental movement historically has suffered from an excess of orthodoxy and groupthink. It will be energized and rejuvenated by its willingness to reconsider the basics, an opening on which the possibility of Center Green depends.

———————

None of the challenges faced by the Green movement is insurmountable. Each can be addressed in a way that leaves the core values of the movement intact, does not require capitulation to the aberrations of market fundamentalism, and allows environmentalism to move forward with new vigor and wisdom. A specific program for reform of the Green movement, expressed as a "Decalogue for Green Groups," is set out below as the third step in Getting to Green. But the required reform of Green NGOs will not be effective unless two predicates are satisfied: reconnecting a reasonable number of moderates and conservatives to the values of conservation, and reconstructing the case for environmentalism on a basis that puts people first.

GETTING TO GREEN, STEP ONE

Reconnecting Conservatives with Conservation

Nothing is more conservative than conservation.

—RUSSELL KIRK

I n March 2005, an editorial columnist for *The Economist* wrote, "The Greening of conservatism is a revolution waiting to happen." It is now a decade since *The Economist* made this pronouncement, and we are still waiting for the revolution.

Ask a typical American what conservatives stand for, and she or he will probably say that conservatives oppose abortion, gun control, gay marriage, tax increases, and environmental regulation, and they disagree with laws keeping religion out of the public sphere. But these are merely policy positions, and not ideological precepts or fundamental principles. Opposition to tax increases, for example, is not a basic conservative value, but only the application of a conservative's more fundamental beliefs (in this case, a preference for limited government, together with hostility to the equalizing tendency of the left) to a particular question of policy. The false idea that conservatives must support a fixed agenda of policy positions is what I call "programmatic conservatism." It ends inevitably in the litmus-test mentality, under which adherence to a fixed agenda (e.g., opposition to abortion, gun control, gay marriage, tax increases, and environmental regulation) and a fixed set of factual beliefs (e.g., that global warming is a "hoax") becomes the definitional test for an ideology. The result may be a surge in political success as a movement coalesces around popular positions, but in time this sort of stubborn adherence to policy over principle inevitably ends in disaster, as culture and politics move on, and so-called conservatives, clinging to an incoherent and antiquated agenda, lose both intellectual leadership and political power.

The more dynamic version of American conservatism, eclipsed since the mid-1990s but with roots deep in American history and the broader history of conservative thought, defines itself with reference to permanent ideological preferences, to be applied flexibly as culture and politics change over time. This is what I refer to as "principled conservatism." As Russell Kirk put it, "[C]onservatives inherit from Burke a talent for re-expressing their convictions to fit the time."[1] This is a talent that lies largely dormant among conservatives in contemporary America.

The triumph of programmatic conservatism over principled conservatism lies at the heart of the strange durability of market fundamentalism and its contribution to the Great Estrangement. Opposition to regulation of carbon emissions from power plants, enhanced auto emission standards, endangered-species protection, green energy innovation, zoning, and other Green priorities became core programmatic tenets of movement conservatism. Some of these positions were grounded in principled concerns about the growth of government and/or the use of regulatory tools when private market solutions were available. But many of these conservative positions on environmental issues are deeply at odds with core conservative values. I believe that reconnecting twenty-first-century American conservatives with the permanent enduring principles of the conservative frame of mind will *compel* the principled conservative to embrace a vigorous ethic of stewardship for the natural world.

So what are the enduring core principles of American conservatism? To answer this question, I needed a guide who was well versed in the American conservative tradition and reflected both the libertarian and traditionalist wings of the conservative movement.[2] My authority also needed to antedate the rise of the new right, so as to represent the long tradition of mainstream conservatism in America, and not its current political manifestation. I found my guide in Cornell professor Clinton Rossiter, whose 1955 book *Conservatism in America* carefully analyzes what American conservatism is. He outlines the core elements of conservative ideology that, in his view, reflect the particularly American fusion of libertarianism (with its emphasis on the primacy of individual liberty) and traditionalism (the conservatism with its roots in Edmund Burke that rests on the value of cultural continuity).

There was a time when European conservatism meant, in essence, defense of a status quo that was based on hierarchy and tradition coupled with a rather pessimistic view of human nature and deep skepticism toward reform. In America, a revolutionary society, this brand of European conservatism morphed into a homegrown brand of Burkean conservatism, which does not involve outright hostility to change but emphasizes prudence in the approach to it ("Prudence is not only the first in rank of the virtues political and moral, but she is the director, the regulator, the standard of them all," writes Burke).[3] For the American conservative, Rossiter observes, this is a discriminating defense of the social order against change and reform. The conservative knows that change is the rule of life, but he insists that it be "sure-footed . . . and respectful of the past"[4] To assure that change is "sure-footed," the conservative adopts an approach of prudence, or cautious respect for continuity, which leads to a preference for evolution over revolution.

In this sense, conservatism is not some kind of blanket preference for the past, blind adherence to tradition, or resistance to progress. Instead, conservatives respect social norms—things like manners and our sense of what behaviors are or are not virtuous—as a type of guide that has evolved in response to human reason and the interests of society. Social norms, in this view, reflect the cumulative adjustment to human nature and human society over a long period of time and thus are owed some deference.

The American conservative understands that the building and maintenance of civilization is a continuing project. The conservative looks beyond the utilitarian expedient needs of the present, always conscious of the foundation laid by our ancestors, and of our deep responsibility to our descendants. This intergenerational perspective is at the heart of Burkean conservatism. As Burke wrote in his *Reflections on the Revolution in France*, "[O]ne of the first and most leading principles on which the commonwealth and the laws are consecrated, is lest the temporary possessors and life-renters in it, unmindful of what they have received from their ancestors, or of what is due to the posterity, should act as if they were the entire masters; that they should not think it amongst their rights to cut off the entail, or commit waste on the inheritance . . . hazarding to leave to those who come after them, a ruin instead of a habitation. . . ."[5]

This is the most fundamental premise of principled conservatism— the idea, in fact, that gave conservatism its name—and is at the same time the essential ethic of the environmental movement.[6] We are not the "entire masters" of the Earth, entitled to "commit waste on the inheritance." We must not leave to those who come after a planet that is "a ruin instead of a habitation." The principle that gave conservatism its name is the same one that gave conservation its name, and is the principle that most powerfully pushes its adherents into the Green camp. The principled conservative has an obligation to prudently husband all of a society's resources: the civic capital that consists of the society's institutions and laws, the national wealth and productive capacity that is its economic capital, and its natural resources. The conservative takes the long view of society and believes he or she has a duty to limit present consumption with a view to the interests of future generations. Looked at this way, there is nothing remotely conservative about saving a few bucks now by dumping carbon into the atmosphere or garbage into the ocean, and leaving future generations to deal with the consequences.

So deeply and strongly does this principle resonate in conservative thinking that it sometimes demands to be given voice, even in politically inexpedient circumstances. In 1985, looking for political cover amid mounting criticism of his administration's policies regarding public lands, President Reagan appointed the President's Commission on Americans Outdoors, packed with business interests and reliable conservatives, to make recommendations. Two years later, to the surprise and consternation of the administration, the Commission issued its report, commenting in words easily recognized as an outbreak of principled conservatism, that we were "robbing future generations of the heritage which is their birthright. We are selling the backyard to buy the groceries. . . ."[7] Burke would have been pleased.

———————

The primacy of individual liberty is the core idea of libertarianism. The high value attached to individual liberty in turn informs a conservative's ideas about property rights, markets, and limited government. There is no country in the world where the values of personal and economic freedom are more deeply or widely held.

The main animating dynamism in American conservatism is the tension between liberty, with its emphasis on personal and economic freedom, and traditionalism, with its dedication to the preservation and continuity of the collective culture. This tension is apparent in the contemporary politics of the right, where conservative Christians seek to impose their brand of morality on their fellow

Americans—through their antipathy to abortion, stem cell research, contraception, homosexuality, and the like—and where the libertarian wing of the right is horrified by the infringement of personal freedom that would result. The balance point between these two values shifts as the relative influence of the libertarians and traditionalists fluctuates.

Regardless of where that balance point rests at any particular time, both sides share a fundamental conviction: that the generous measure of freedom and liberty afforded the citizen in a democracy entails a similarly broad weight of personal responsibility. To a conservative, a person cannot have rights without duties, or enjoy personal freedom without personal responsibility. To Russell Kirk, they are inseparable: "Every right is married to a duty; every freedom owes a corresponding responsibility. . . ."[8] Theodore Roosevelt sounded this theme in a prophetic speech in 1886 to the citizens of Dickinson, in what was then the Dakota territory, when he said "[A]s you already know your rights and privileges so well, I am going to ask you to excuse me if I say a few words to you about your duties. Much has been given to us, and so much will surely be expected from us; and we must take heed to use aright the gifts entrusted to our care." Even modern theocentric conservative theorists like William Harbour endorse this idea as fundamental: "Conservatism distrusts talk about freedom that gives exclusive stress to notions of rights and the claims that individuals make against society while it ignores the notion of responsibility."[9] And yet the 2012 Republican Platform sums up its section on environment with the words, "The most powerful environmental policy is liberty . . . ," with no acknowledgment of the restraint or responsibility that is its necessary twin.

Responsibility in the conservative tradition has always implied restraint, in both the personal and economic spheres. As Burke put it, "Men are qualified for civil liberty in exact proportion to their disposition to put moral chains upon their own appetites. . . ."[10] Given the uniquely American emphasis on economic freedom, liberty here has implied in large part the freedom to pursue individual gratification through production and consumption. For American conservatives, Burke's "moral chains upon [our] appetites" obviously mandate limits on that production and consumption, limits drawn when that pursuit of gain threatens the common good, including the health of the planet and interests of future generations. This appears, however, to be far from obvious to America's contemporary "movement" conservatives, who too often seem to celebrate the gross excesses of our material culture, and the selfish and reckless character of our material appetites.

Responsibility, discipline, and self-restraint involve another idea to which conservatives attach much importance: that individuals should be accountable for the consequences of their actions. Individual liberty, including an individual's rights in property, does not imply the right to impinge without consequence on the liberties of others. As Richard Nixon argued in the 1970 State of the Union speech, "[W]e are no more free to contaminate [air and water] than we are free to throw garbage in our neighbor's yard." This means, among many other things, that one should be responsible for the damage caused to others and their property. This is the basis of the law of tort, and also of a value system in which the morally responsible person forbears the taking of a free lunch, even if it is offered. To the theoretical economist, the hypothetical rational economic actor always will be a free rider if afforded the opportunity; but the principled conservative, indeed any moral person, ought to willingly assume responsibility for the consequences of his or her actions, and thus voluntarily forbear from opportunities to benefit from "negative externalities" like pollution, which should be seen as an abuse of freedom.

The conservative's ideological convictions regarding responsibility, discipline, and self-restraint powerfully align conservatism with the goals of the environmental movement, and provide clues to how to end the Great Estrangement. After all, what is the Green movement if not a call for individuals and societies to recognize that freedom comes with responsibility, and act accordingly? The Whig politician and early American conservationist George Perkins Marsh wrote in 1864 that humanity's "power to transform the natural world should entail a commensurate sense of responsibility."[11] The "land ethic" advocated by Aldo Leopold eighty-five years later was little more than the assumption by individuals of responsibility for the health of the land under their care. Greens and conservatives alike call for our rights of property and economic freedom to be exercised within a framework of discipline and restraint in which we fairly pay the true costs of our present consumption, and act not merely as economic animals, but as free moral agents cognizant of this higher duty. The naturalist Edwin Way Teale, writing in 1953, captured perfectly this intersection between conservatism, democracy, and conservation: "The long fight to save wild beauty represents democracy at its best. It requires citizens to practice the hardest of virtues—self-restraint."[12]

To an American conservative, the protection of an individual's rights in property is not only mandated by the deeper value of individual liberty, but is seen as a necessary condition for achieving many other social goods. A stable, strong, and effective regime for the establishment and protection of private rights in property is the foundation not only of a capitalist economic system, but also of a just and free society. But conservatives also have long understood that private property as an institution cannot be maintained without a culture of stewardship and responsibility that reins in our natural appetites for exploitation and excess. Russell Kirk was prescient when he warned in 1953 that without the restraints of duty and stewardship, Americans would "treat this world . . . as if it were their private property, to be consumed for their sensual gratification; and thus they will destroy in their lust for enjoyment the property of future generations, of their own contemporaries, and indeed their very own capital. . . ."[13]

The American right has abandoned principled conservative views about property. In its place, "property" has become a dumbed-down talisman invoked to resist almost any socially motivated limitation on a citizen's use of her or his assets. Movement conservatism hosts a powerful group of "property rights" advocates opposed to the sorts of land use regulation that have been an accepted feature of capitalism for centuries and are noncontroversial features of market economies around the world. The fundamentalist view of property presents a grave threat to the very rights it seems to worship. To say that people have the "right" to use their land in a way that impinges on their neighbors' rights in their own property is incoherent and simply invites anarchy. And private ownership of property is a social system that only can be defended if individual property can be subject to communitarian priorities like public health and safety. Tell a community that your "rights" from ownership of a piece of land defeat, totally and absolutely, any limitation on use (such as zoning or environmental regulation) for public purposes, and those rights become inconsistent with virtually any form of social or political organization.

Just as the survival of private property rights ultimately depends on boundaries to those rights that appropriately balance private ends with social interests, so conservatives have long believed that free markets depend on boundaries to the sphere of human life in which the pursuit of profit is the governing principle. Traditionalist conservatism never indulged in the uncritical worship of "free enterprise" that is the hallmark of contemporary market fundamentalism. This sort of market fetishism can lead to only one place—what George Will called "an anarchy of self-interestedness," in which the mercantile interests of big business and their owners are not only admitted to the political sphere (as in the Supreme Court's deeply flawed *Citizens United* decision), but made the touchstone for correct policy. Any conservative walking the planet before 1970, not to mention most conservatives walking the planet today in the UK, Europe, and elsewhere, would be appalled by a "conservatism" that embraces unlimited acquisitiveness and sociopathic greed.

What's the alternative? Rossiter explains that the American conservative "does not for a moment deny the prominence of the profit motive, [but] he insists that it be recognized for the selfish thing it is and be kept within reasonable, socially imposed limits."[14] Barry Goldwater was clear what this meant when it came to the contest between business and nature: "While I am a great believer in the free enterprise system and all that it entails, I am an even stronger believer in the right of our people to live in a clean and pollution-free environment."[15] American movement conservatives have lost sight of the necessity for limits and become strangely comfortable with the sorts of greed and excess that have, for centuries, shocked the traditional conservative. It sounds as if Edmund Burke was peeking ahead at twenty-first-century America when he warned in 1757 that "[t]he great Error of our Nature is, not to know where to stop, not to be satisfied with any reasonable Acquirement; not to compound with our Condition; but to lose all we have gained by an insatiable Pursuit after more."[16]

This sound instinctive conservative revulsion with the "insatiable pursuit after more" is what makes old-school conservatives much more likely than today's Tea Party Republicans to be skeptical about claims by business that market capitalism forbids any attempt to limit their activities, and thus that virtually all environmental regulation is "socialistic" and will "kill jobs." The history of such claims made by regulated industries between 1970 and 1990 demonstrates that industry consistently exaggerated the impact of proposed environmental regulation on both employment and profits.[17] Principled conservatism requires conservatives to insist that businesses, like individuals, take full responsibility for the costs and impacts of their actions. If proposed regulations are impractical, unreasonably costly, or otherwise ill conceived, then affected corporations should engage in the debate on those grounds. If the best they can come up with is whining that environmental standards are "socialistic" or will "kill jobs," their arguments should be greeted with skepticism.

Finally, a conservative defender of property, capitalism, and markets should be alert to those situations where markets fail to produce an efficient result, and should support arrangements designed to correct those failures and allow markets to function properly. So, for example, faced with a situation where there is zero price attached to the emission of pollution, the principled conservative advocates some kind of governmental intervention to set a price that recognizes the costs of those emissions to others, present and future. Once a price is set, then the market can once again work its magic, and the market, not the government, can determine the economically optimal present level of the pollution. So it should be no surprise that the list of conservative economists favoring a carbon tax as the most efficient response to CO_2 pollution is a long one: Martin Feldstein (chief economist to Ronald Reagan), Michael Boskin (chief economist to George H. W. Bush), Greg Mankiw (chief economist to George W. Bush), Kevin Hassett (American Enterprise Institute), Arthur Laffer (a member of Ronald Reagan's Economic Policy Advisory Board), George Shultz (Republican Secretary of Treasury and State), and Gary Becker (Nobel Prize–winning Chicago School economist).[18] And the position of today's GOP? When former House Speaker John Boehner's spokesman was asked if the Speaker would *ever* support a carbon tax to curb carbon pollution and lower the deficit, his one-word answer was "No."[19]

A preference for government that is limited, diffused, and balanced is another one of the core principles of American conservatism. Lincoln explained it with admirable simplicity: "The legitimate object of government is to do for a community of people, whatever they need to have done, but cannot do at all, or cannot so well do for themselves, in their separate and individual capacities." By "limited," the conservative does not necessarily mean small, but instead means limited to the scope of activity that is necessary to be conducted by government, and cannot be conducted more efficiently by other social institutions. This means that government can serve many purposes, but should rarely substitute for other institutions—such as family and other instruments of civil society—that traditionally have performed necessary social functions, and can continue to do so. The conservative also is alert to government's predilection for inefficiency and overreach. This means that those in positions of power must be restrained by constitutional limits, and that power itself should be diffused throughout various layers of governmental authority, and limited in each case by checks and balances, as is the case under the U.S. Constitution.

The current view of Tea Party conservatives that virtually all government action is "socialistic" and all regulation an intrusion on economic freedom is a complete aberration from these conservative values and traditions. When this line of thinking arose in the 1980s, thoughtful conservative commentators like George Will were horrified, calling it "decayed Jeffersonianism characterized by a frivolous hostility toward the state," and arguing that true conservatives have never believed that large government is an *"inherently* liberal device."[20] This sort of deviation from a more traditional understanding of the roles of government and private sector is not only a betrayal of conservative principles, it is hazardous to the very survival of conservatism. "If all government action is automatically dismissed as quasi-socialist," argued conservative commentator David Brooks, "then there is no need to think. A pall of dogmatism will settle over the right."[21]

The principled conservative therefore should not oppose any

new government action on the ground that government should be reducing its role in American life, but instead should ask whether the goal of that proposed action can be achieved more effectively by nongovernmental institutions. In the environmental field, this means figuring out which governmental interventions are appropriate and which are not. For intelligent conservatives such as William F. Buckley, environmental protection did not present a difficult case. In 1970 he wrote, "I take it as axiomatic that no one has the right to pollute the air I breathe, or the water I drink, and that the latitudinarian habits of a society whose frontier was always bigger than any of us, have finally caught up with us, generating a common revulsion. It is overdue for government to assert its responsibility in these matters."[22] Richard Nixon did just that, declaring that "because there are no local or State boundaries to the problems of our environment, the Federal Government must play an active, positive role. We can and will set standards. We can and will exercise leadership."

Not surprisingly, the conservative's commitment to the market has much to teach about the appropriate nature of government intervention in environmental matters. Market economics teaches us that it is legitimate for the government to intervene in free markets to correct market failures, such as the failure of markets to price pollution and other externalities. Market economics also provides guidance for determining how far that intervention should go: as long as the value of social benefits to cleaning up a river (e.g., in terms of restored fisheries, increased human health, aesthetic enjoyment, and recreation) exceeds the cost of compliance (whether borne by the polluter or the government itself), the intervention is proper.[23] Critically, this cost-benefit approach provides only general guidance, and in certain circumstances other tests may be more appropriate to determine the limits of the intervention (for example, where compliance costs are relatively low, simply insisting on the use of best available technologies, or, where the external impacts are high, ignoring costs altogether and prohibiting externalities that have a material and detrimental impact on human health and safety). And finally, the market can tell us how to allocate the cost and burdens of compliance most efficiently (as in cap-and-trade, which skews emissions reduction to emitters that can achieve such reductions most cheaply). Conservatives may come to market-based solutions for environmental problems as an ideological preference, but even the most liberal Greens will frequently join them on the pragmatic grounds that such solutions work. When water meters are installed, people invest in having their leaks fixed and become the more careful consumers of water that Greens wish them to be. In this case, the market-based solution is preferred because it works.[24]

Of course there still will be ample ground for disagreement between right and left about identifying where significant market failures have occurred and what intervention is necessary. We will disagree about the pricing of costs and benefits, and about where cost-benefit analysis should apply (e.g., carbon) and where it shouldn't (persistent toxics demonstrated to cause cancer and other fatal diseases, even in small amounts). But in order to have even these arguments the right and left need to be on the same page, the right abandoning its habit of dismissing any government intervention as quasi-socialistic, and the left agreeing to look first (but not exclusively) to the market for economically sound and efficient solutions.

———————————

The traditionalist branch of American conservatism has always held that political problems are essentially moral problems, and that social norms ultimately should be based on some stable and stabilizing transcendent order.[25] For a traditional conservative, the moral always trumps the material. For much of American history, and again in the past three decades, that transcendent order has been provided by religion. Mainstream Protestantism provided American conservatives with a stable value system that emphasized integrity, thrift, hard work, education, and personal responsibility, and that proved powerfully conducive to the economic and political development of the nation.

When mainstream Protestantism was hijacked by evangelical extremism and a more severe Calvinist strain of fundamentalism started to replace it as the "mortar" of the conservative movement, the very idea of a society based on a moral foundation began to be undermined. This is because instead of integrity, thrift, hard work, education, and responsibility the new Protestants insisted on the counterfactual of the Bible's literal truth, and emphasized sexual purity, abstinence, and strict compliance with the Old Testament. These preferences, although shared by a dynamic and growing group of evangelicals and other conservative Christians, left moderate Christians and principled conservatives of other (or no) religions, unable to support the new transcendent order.

The fact remains that *some* transcendent moral order is an essential element of principled conservatism, and virtually all conservatives are comfortable with appealing to moral (as opposed to religious) reasoning to inform issues of public policy. Virtually all Greens share with conservatives a conviction that there is a moral dimension to environmental issues that informs, and in some cases trumps, a purely utilitarian or economic calculus. Building on this shared conviction is a key element of Getting to Green.

Here is a simple thought experiment. Imagine that you are sitting on your front porch reading the paper on a Sunday morning. A car drives up the street and stops at the stop sign. You see the driver take a last sip from his can of soda, toss the empty can out the car window onto the lawn in front of your house, and drive off. This is no big deal: no one is harmed, and the cost and effort of picking up the soda can is trivial. Yet you would almost certainly be offended and disturbed, probably to an extent out of proportion to the act itself. Why?

Any homeowner probably would feel a sense of intrusion into his or her space because throwing the can onto someone's lawn is a type of trespass, and one might also perceive it as a type of indirect assault, or at least a gesture of disrespect. There also would be an aesthetic reaction, as the crushed can on the lawn would be ugly. But I don't think that these factors adequately explain how unsettled the person on the porch would likely feel. I think the littering victim would see this as a thoughtless, vulgar, and at root aggressively antisocial act, and be reminded, at least subconsciously, of the tenuousness of the social fabric. We all know intuitively that we rely on people to suppress their selfishness to the minimum degree required to live in society, and that when this restraint breaks down, the chasm awaits. The homeowner knows the driver has deliberately done something he knew was wrong.

This little thought experiment demonstrates to me that our reaction to pollution, like littering, is fundamentally a moral one: we know right from wrong, and we know that messing up the planet shared by all of us—either thoughtlessly, or deliberately for convenience or profit—is wrong. We know sociopathic behavior when we see it. But while we see jerks throwing soda cans out of their car windows, we don't see the coal-fired generating plant in Ohio injecting tons of particulates and carbon into the atmosphere from its 700-foot smokestack. The environmental movement should harness this sort of intuitive moral indignation, this insistence on neighborly behavior, which is shared by right and left. I believe that Paul Hansen had it right when he called conservation "a neighborly vision; it asks how we can live together without hurting each other."[26]

In the moral case for environmental stewardship Greens and conservatives will find common ground, and it provides a promising point of entry for conservatives to reengage with the environmental movement.

Conservatives, of course, do not have a monopoly on patriotism. But many conservatives are motivated by a deep love of country. Flag burning, for example, is largely tolerated by the left as an act of free speech, but generates considerable ire on the right, which sees it as an open and notorious act of disrespect to the nation and, they believe, to those who have sacrificed to build and protect it. Why, I wonder, do the same conservatives who abhor flag burning not take equal offense at open and notorious acts of desecration to the physical fabric of the nation itself? The flag is only a symbol, and flag burning is a symbolic act, the equivalent of speech.[27] But pollution of our rivers, clear cutting of old-growth forests, building shopping malls on Civil War battle sites, and destroying iconic landscapes with development—all of these constitute actual physical destruction, motivated not by self-expression, but by profit.

If a company burned an American flag at each of its factories once a week because doing so would increase its profits by 2 percent, would most conservatives find that a more or less reprehensible act than burning the flag as an act of political speech to protest a government policy? Desecrating the flag for money, most conservatives would agree, is the more egregious act. There is no doubt that history treats the traitor motivated by ideology much more kindly than the person who sells out his country for money. And yet every day American businesses lawfully exploit opportunities to impose external costs on others, and by doing so destroy ecologically critical lands, devastate fish stocks, discharge greenhouse gases, mar historical landscapes—that is, they desecrate for profit the very fabric of the country, our patrimony. Why don't the patriots who defend the flag defend the land for which it stands? I have found it deeply ironic, and occasionally offensive, that in recent years right-wing groups like the Tea Party have used images of amber waves of grain and majestic purple mountains as patriotic symbols, yet they oppose most attempts to protect and preserve these symbols in the real world.

The connection between patriotism and conservation has long roots in conservative and Republican thinking. In 1908, in his speech to the National Governors Conference, President Theodore Roosevelt called the conservation of natural resources "the patriotic duty of insuring the safety and continuance of the nation."[28] Even Ronald Reagan seemed to get it, writing in 1986, "A strong nation is one that is loved by its people and, as Edmund Burke put it, for a country to be loved it ought to be lovely."[29]

There are some more recent signs that the patriotic instinct may still work its magic and motivate even those corners of the new right most hostile to environmentalism to take better care of the physical fabric of the country. A conservative group, the George C. Marshall Institute, sought to reconnect patriotism with feelings for the natural world. In a 2001 report they wrote, "Many of us feel a 'poetry of place' about the sites we care about—from prosaic woodlots to awesome peaks, from familiar city streets to grand natural vistas. This poetry of place is not mere sentiment; it connects our private concerns with a larger public good."[30] Some years later Newt Gingrich argued, "Anti-environmental politicians are out of step with the American people as concern for the environment is widely acknowledged as an important component of a patriotic worldview."[31] In this he was correct. A 2012 bipartisan poll found that four out of five Americans of all political viewpoints (89 percent of Democrats, and 79 percent of each of Independents, Republicans, and Tea Party Republicans) agreed with the statement that "conserving our country's natural resources—our land, air and water—is patriotic."[32] The key challenge will be to convert these sentiments into active political support for at least some parts of the Green agenda.

Although it is true that patriotism should motivate conservatives to be more Green, conservatives also should recognize that the beauty and health of the physical fabric of the country—if it can be sustained—can serve as a vigorous wellspring for the patriotic sentiment that conservatives value. It is no accident that America's most popular patriotic anthem, topping the actual national anthem in the affection of the citizenry, celebrates "America the Beautiful." Countless people over two centuries have been led to love of country through love of the land, an ingredient vital for national sentiment in a country of immigrants.

—————————

Reconnecting contemporary conservatives with the traditions and values of their chosen ideology will expose the aberrational nature of market fundamentalism and motivate many of them to embrace a vigorous ethic of stewardship for the natural world. This is the foundational step in ending the Great Estrangement and reestablishing a functioning bipartisan consensus on at least some environmental priorities.

9

IS CONSERVATIVE
ENVIRONMENTALISM
REALLY POSSIBLE?

My brother is a right-wing environmentalist. I don't
understand why his head hasn't exploded from all
that cognitive dissonance.

—ANONYMOUS COMMENT ON A
GLOBAL WARMING BLOG, 2008

The argument that conservative ideology demands an ethic of
environmental stewardship is logical and compelling. But,
you might well be thinking, logic and principle don't always
determine outcomes. Dislodging the anti-Green convictions of the
Tea Party and resurrecting the conservative environmentalist model
of the 1970s seems like a heavy lift. Haven't previous attempts to
make this argument to rank-and-file conservatives failed? Didn't
GOP politicians get badly burned when flirting with the idea of
"right-wing environmentalism"? What makes me think that reconnecting conservatives with conservation is a realistic prospect now?

These are important questions, and the answers begin with a
look at previous attempts to reconcile conservatives and Greens.
These attempts, by both thinkers and political activists, are not, I
admit, promising. Previous advocates of right-wing environmentalism tended to be highly idiosyncratic and were not well received
by their fellow conservatives. One of the earliest, Gordon Durnil,

a longtime conservative Republican Party official in Indiana who was appointed by the first President Bush to the International Joint Commission, an intergovernmental body established by Canada and the United States to look after the Great Lakes, wrote *The Making of a Conservative Environmentalist*. This conservative pro-business stalwart discovered the scary effects of persistent toxics, was rather naively surprised when industry ignored the science and stubbornly resisted limits on emissions,[1] and proceeded to champion total bans on emissions to the Great Lakes of the worst chemicals. Predictably, the hard right had no tolerance for his attempt at moderation. In a review, Matthew Carolan wrote: "Mr. Durnil makes occasional genuflections to the free market, limited government, and traditional values, but . . . Mr. Durnil's policy prescriptions . . . are right out of the Greenpeace playbook."[2]

During the 1990s, a number of "free-market environmentalists" with strong libertarian streaks conducted research and wrote a great deal about market solutions to environmental problems. Chief among these was Terry Anderson, a fellow of the Hoover Institution and professor at Montana State College, who also served as president of the Property and Environment Research Center (PERC), a think tank in Bozeman, Montana. His influential book, *Free Market Environmentalism*, was first published in 1991. PERC's mission statement sounded many of the right notes: "We believe environmental quality can be achieved by managing our resources based on property rights, private initiative and voluntary activity. Free market environmentalism offers a genuine alternative to excessive government control and regulation."[3] Many of Anderson's ideas are sound. His work provided an important early voice advocating that markets and conservation are not necessarily incompatible, and showed that in the case of certain environmental problems, a property-rights-based solution proved more effective than regulation (a compelling example being the granting of property rights in fishing quotas). PERC and its ilk are afflicted with a strong ideological purity and a tendency to believe that any market solution is superior to any regulatory one. PERC continues today, running an "Enviropreneur" institute and publishing policy reports and case studies that illustrate the possibilities of property- and market-based solutions to environmental problems.

In the spirit of the time, attorney Peter Huber in 1999 wrote the polemical *Hard Green: Saving the Environment from the Environmentalists, a Conservative Manifesto,* an idiosyncratic defense of the sort of robust big-picture conservation practiced by Theodore Roosevelt. Sarcastic in style and deeply unfair to environmental science, the book in some ways presaged the hard right's later attacks on climate science, without meaningfully helping conservatives reconnect with the older conservation tradition. Much more serious and analytical— but alas equally ineffective—was the effort two years later by Texas Tech professor John R. E. Bliese, hopefully titled *The Greening of Conservative America.*[4] Carrying lots of ideological baggage, Professor Bliese nonetheless helpfully lays out the case that conservative political philosophy virtually mandates support for resource conservation and environmental protection, and takes aim at what he refers to as various "myths," such as the notion that environmental protection necessarily is "bad for business" or involves infringement of property rights. He endorses the customary conservative solutions of "free-market environmentalism." There is little evidence that Republicans or conservatives paid any attention to his book.

In contrast, former *National Review* journalist Rod Dreher's 2006 *Crunchy Cons* did manage to start a conversation by spotlighting the growing group of Republicans whose passion for various Green causes put them at odds with the emerging GOP anti-Green consensus—a group he refers to in the book's subtitle as "Birkenstocked Burkeans, gun-loving organic gardeners, evangelical free-range farmers, hip homeschooling mamas, right-wing nature lovers and their diverse tribe of countercultural conservatives."[5] The book is important in highlighting the already significant group of GOP voters who may subscribe to the conservative agenda on abortion, taxes, and "family values," but are already living model Green lives that are faithful to their love of nature and deep feeling of responsibility for the planet. Dreher is appropriately savage in his criticism of the "prideful philistinism" of his comrades on the right and their fetishistic worship of big business and markets, which, he believes, is at the heart of their strange betrayal of a conservative philosophy requiring restraints and limits on our material appetites. I know from discussions with fellow Greens at the time *Crunchy Cons* was published that many of them were intrigued by the book and motivated to reach out to Dreher's Birkenstocked Burkeans as a promising bridge to the right. But only two years later came the election of 2008, and soon after the Tea Party tide swamped Dreher's countercGETURALS, who again went silent.

Also caught in that that tsunami of disgruntled Tea Partiers was the usually more astute Newt Gingrich. A year after *Crunchy Cons*, Gingrich surprised most everyone with his *Contract with the Earth*, cowritten with zoologist Terry Maple. Gingrich called for "green conservatism," which he described as "a positive, entrepreneurial, market-based, solutions-oriented, mainstream environmental movement conducive to a pragmatic, nonpartisan public policy."[6] The book seemed heartfelt in its embrace of environmental goals, especially the preservation of biodiversity (Gingrich was founding chair of a local chapter of the Georgia Conservancy and had a track record of conservation work in Georgia and elsewhere). He called for sound science, green leadership by business and philanthropy, and the reorientation of the regulatory model toward public-private partnerships. In February 2007 Gingrich said on PBS's *Frontline* he "would strongly support" a cap-and-trade scheme for carbon emissions (provided it was combined with a tax incentive program), and in 2008 appeared with Nancy Pelosi in an ad stating that the "country must take action to address climate change."

Illustrating just how intolerable those views had become only a short while later, Gingrich stated that this had been "the dumbest single thing I've done in the last few years,"[7] and published a second book titled *Drill Here, Drill Now, Pay Less*.[8] Gingrich advocated *elimination* of the Environmental Protection Agency in the platform for his 2012 presidential primary bid. Being a right-wing environmentalist simply was not an option for a candidate in the GOP's presidential primary system in 2012, and many of the good ideas in Gingrich's 2007 book, such as federal loan guarantees and other incentives for green technology and alternative energy, now have been thoroughly repudiated by the GOP.

Although crushed by broader trends, these outbreaks of Green conservatism suggest that the conservation instinct survives in the hearts of many Republicans. From time to time, that instinct is expressed in organized political action. Reacting to the party's embrace of the extremes of the Wise Use agenda in the 1980s and early 1990s, Republicans led by a Republican county commissioner from Illinois, Martha Marks, organized Republicans for Environmental Protection, now known as ConservAmerica. Its slogan: "Conservation is conservative." ConservAmerica is genuinely dedicated to the Green agenda. In 2001 Martha Marks appeared at a press conference with the Sierra Club and other Green groups and publicly opposed Gale Norton as President Bush's choice to lead the Department of the Interior. In 2004, they courageously declined to endorse President Bush for reelection, stating that his administration "has compiled a deliberately anti-environmental, anti-conservation record that will result in lasting damage to public health and to America's natural heritage."[9] In 2005 they attempted, with some success, to persuade GOP congressmen to oppose the opening of the Arctic National Wildlife Refuge to drilling. The Republicans at ConservAmerica are convinced they can persuade a large number of Republicans and independents to break with the GOP's antienvironmentalism. In 2010 they went right to the source of the problem, placing advertisements on the Rush Limbaugh and Glenn Beck radio broadcasts in selected markets, asking the faithful, "What would Reagan do about climate change?" and then reminding listeners

that it was Reagan who advocated and negotiated the Montreal Protocol as a solution to the emerging hole in the ozone layer. And their
website, www.climateconservative.org, launched by their formerly
affiliated 501(c)(3), Conservatives for Responsible Stewardship, presents a clear roadmap for conservatives wishing to reconsider their
opinions about climate change. Unfortunately, these organizations
are small: prior to 2014, the (c)(3) and (c)(4) together spent less than
a half-million dollars each year.[10] ConservAmerica is not alone, and
recently has been joined by a number of other start-up GOP Green
groups, not surprisingly focused on young people. One, Young Conservatives for Energy Reform, aims to stimulate grassroots conservative backing for alternative energy, clean-air regulation, and the
fight against climate change.[11]

Few NGOs outside of the sportsmen's groups have tried to cross the
great divide and engage conservatives in Green causes. Environmental
Defense Fund is an exception. Under its longtime leader Fred Krupp,
EDF assembled a coalition of corporations with major carbon foot-
prints to work together to develop carbon legislation that could win
the support of both the Green movement and business. To EDF's great
credit, it engaged companies such as BP America, Duke Energy, and
General Electric, created the coordinating group U.S. Climate Action
Partnership (USCAP), and succeeded in gaining the group's endorsement for the cap-and-trade legislation passed by the House in the sum-
mer of 2009. Unfortunately, the coalition, like the legislation itself,
started to fall apart immediately thereafter.[12] And in 2012, National
Audubon Society (which has said that 40 percent of its members identify as "moderate to conservative")[13] reached out to conservatives by
partnering with ConservAmerica to found the American Eagle Com-
pact (tag line: "Because Conservation Doesn't Have a Party"), which
ConservAmerica reports added 55,000 new members to Audubon,
mostly red state conservatives. But the campaign apparently petered
out after a couple of months, and (as of the time of this writing) no
post has appeared on the campaign's blog since December 2012.

Where does this leave us today? Antienvironmentalism is not simply a passing fad on the right. Like the conviction that all abortion is murder, it has become part of the conservative identity, a marker of community and virtual article of faith. As Republican presidential candidate Jon Huntsman Jr. put it in 2014, "So obtuse has become the party's dialogue on climate change that it's now been reduced to believing or not believing, as if it were a religious mantra."[14] As a result, proenvironment Republicans have a hard time at the ballot box, and many of them have retired rather than risk humiliating primary defeats. Green Republicans are frequently accused of being "RINOs" (Republicans In Name Only) and some of the dwindling number of incumbent Green Republicans observe that they could not be elected if running for the first time today. One GOP congressman, an intended "yes" on Waxman-Markey, changed his vote when Rush Limbaugh mentioned his impending apostasy on the radio, and his Capitol Hill phones were jammed for days with an outpouring of fury. Many Republican legislators inclined to support Green causes report that they are too frightened to say anything publicly for fear of suffering the same fate or worse.

It does not seem to be a propitious time to suggest reconnecting conservatives with their conservation roots. But I believe that the prospects to do exactly this are better now than at any time in the past quarter century. First, millions of Republican voters—roughly 60 percent of them—say they are *not* members or supporters of the Tea Party.[15] We don't hear much from these moderate conservatives, because they are deeply overshadowed by what one commentator called "an imbalance of passion" when compared to movement conservatives.[16] Nonetheless, they are there. This vanguard of moderate conservatives holds the key to convincing others on the right to reembrace their proconservation heritage as the GOP inevitably shifts to a more sustainable position on the political spectrum. Political scientists Jacob Hacker and Paul Pierson argued in 2005 that the Republican "revolution" knocked the GOP "off center" to a set of extremist policy positions that are not in the economic interests of the GOP rank and file (as argued a year earlier by Thomas Frank in *What's the Matter with Kansas?*) and are far to the right of American public opinion as a whole. Hacker and Pierson were prescient, in view of the 2012 election, in arguing that "Republicans have built up formidable floodwalls against electoral tides," but would face bigger and bigger storms in the future, against which even those formidable floodwalls would not hold.[17]

There is every reason to think that this moderate vanguard, which will recover its voice when the influence of the Tea Party finally abates, will support a moderate Green agenda. This is illustrated by late 2013 polling by Pew, which shows that 61 percent (only slightly below the both-party national average of 67 percent) of *non*–Tea Party Republicans say there is solid evidence for global warming (compared to only 25 percent of Tea Partiers).[18] This is a remarkable difference, and a strong indicator of what will happen when the extreme right returns to the noisy but impotent fringe where it has festered for most of America's history. A Republican micro-targeting firm recently predicted that each district now under GOP control contains an average of 25,000 to 30,000 active Republican voters who prioritize conservation and environmental protection (numbers often above the margin of victory in swing districts),[19] a group which some pollsters have told the party could start to affect House races.[20] And the *New York Times* has reported that a cadre of GOP congressional staffers, mostly under the age of forty, have started to push their bosses to move away from the climate denial posture.[21]

Who are these GOP voters who prioritize conservation? Many of them are hunters, fishermen, ranchers, farmers, and other people whose livelihood or primary recreation is deeply connected with the natural world. About 15 million Americans hunt each year, 30–50 million people fish, and 290 million visit a national park. There is no "imbalance of passion" here, as the broad community of what is somewhat anachronistically still called "sportsmen" cares deeply about America's land, waters, and the creatures on and in them. Of this group, about 4 million belong to a national sportsmen's or conservation organization, and tens of millions of others belong to local organizations. For over a century, their passion for nature has translated into exactly the sort of activism that the movement needs. And, most importantly, it is a group that transcends partisan boundaries. According to one study, 35 percent of hunters self-identify as Republican, 21 percent as Democrat, and 28 percent as Independent.[22] This is a strong base from which a Green voice can emerge from the right.

On the ideological, as opposed to party-affiliation, dimension, about 35 percent of Americans currently self-identify as "moderate." In recent years, a shrinking number of Republicans (only two in ten in 2011) told Gallup their political views are "very conservative." The thirst of moderates and moderate conservatives for an alternative is reflected by the strong support among Republicans for the No Labels movement, founded in 2010 by a group of political insiders from both parties and now headed by Jon Huntsman Jr. and Joe Lieberman. Although not explicitly centrist, the thrust of the No Labels movement has been to promote pragmatic problem solving by changing the structures and incentives that have driven legislators toward partisan posturing instead of governing.

In addition, prior to the 2008 election we had a short-lived sneak peak at how the Green movement might begin to make common cause with Republicans. John McCain and Newt Gingrich, two very different types of conservative, both recognized the problem of climate change and supported—for a time—a bipartisan effort to reduce carbon loading of the atmosphere. Climate change was one of the McCain campaign's top priorities. The GOP's presidential candidate was dismissive of voices on the right urging inaction on the grounds of uncertainty: "I'm a proud conservative and I reject that kind of live-for-today, 'me generation,' attitude."[23] Arnold Schwarzenegger, Charlie Crist, and other GOP governors signed climate bills in their states and joined with fellow governors in suing the federal government over climate change. A strong group

of moderate GOP congressmen served as models for a different generation of GOP lawmakers. This group included Rep. Sherwood Boehlert
in New York, senators Susan Collins and Olympia Snowe from Maine,
and virtually the entire GOP delegation from Connecticut, including
Christopher Shays, Nancy Johnson, and Rob Simmons. Unfortunately,
Congress has been hemorrhaging these moderate conservatives during
recent years due to gerrymandered districting and actual or threatened
primary challenges from the right, and most of these salutary role models are gone.[24] Although the promising events of 2007 were swamped by
the politics of the moment, they give us a good idea of what could happen if the GOP finally emerges from the insidious spell of the Tea Party.

On a different front, the emergence of a Green strain of Christian
evangelicals raises the question of whether religiosity might serve as
a possible bridge between environmentalists and the right.[25] After all,
The Economist asked in 2005, "What could be more Godly than good
stewardship of the environment? (Just consult Genesis 2:15)."[26] Greens
were cheered when evangelicals became interested in mercury pollution because of its effect on the "unborn," and asked, "What would
Jesus drive?" when considering whether the large SUV was a morally
responsible choice of vehicle.[27] Then, in 2006, eighty-six of the country's leading evangelical pastors broke with the Bush administration
to sign on to the "Evangelical Climate Initiative." The group's October
2007 press release declared, "Human activity is increasing greenhouse
gases in the atmosphere, and the impacts on God's creation and his
people will be tragic. To ignore this is unthinkable. To grasp the problem with faith and courage, and with the wind of American ingenuity
and goodness at our back, is morally right and, in our view, faithful to
our Creator God."[28] Not surprisingly the highest-profile evangelicals
leading the political project of the Christian right—including Jerry Fal-
well, Pat Robertson, and James Dobson—called on the group to retract
its statement of support for climate-change action, but they refused.
Today, groups like Evangelical Environment Network and Evangelical
Climate Initiative, mostly marching under the banner of "creation

care," carry on pro-Green work within an evangelical community that remains divided on the question of climate and environment.[29] The "creation care" evangelicals were joined by a growing number of American Catholics, many influenced by a 2009 encyclical by Pope Benedict XVI stating, "The environment is God's gift to everyone, and in our use of it we have a responsibility toward the poor, toward future generations, and toward humanity as a whole."[30] In July 2014, when the EPA held hearings on its proposed rule to limit carbon pollution from power plants, more than two dozen faith leaders, many of them from traditionally progressive congregations and traditions, but including some conservative and evangelical Christians, testified in support.[31]

Then, with his May 2015 encyclical letter, *Laudato Si': On Care for Our Common Home*, Pope Francis forcefully asserted the moral case for environmental stewardship and climate action, and created a profound crisis for the American religious right. I believe that many of the 23 percent of Americans who are Roman Catholics, together with millions of other believers of all sorts, will be moved by the Pope's beautifully crafted and persuasive message to see climate change and environment as moral issues. In their initial response, movement conservatives largely ignored the climate change parts of the Pope's letter, and instead dismissed it as a broadside attack on capitalism and the market economy. GOP presidential candidates had a tougher time sidestepping the awkwardness. Conservative Catholic GOP presidential candidate Rick Santorum told a radio interviewer, "The church has gotten it wrong a few times on science, and I think we probably are better off leaving science to the scientists and focusing on what we're good at, which is theology and morality."[32] Jeb Bush commented cryptically, "I don't think we should politicize our faith," and Rick Perry reiterated his skepticism about man-caused climate change.[33]

Greens should welcome this growing environmental sensibility among America's religious citizens, particularly when based on the sorts of nonsectarian moral and ethical arguments advanced by Pope Francis. I remain skeptical, however, about overreliance on the American evangelical enthusiasm for "creation care" as a bridge to the right, as the appeal to the Judeo-Christian concept of man's dominion over nature does not accord with our ecological understanding of man as planted firmly within, and not over, the rest of "creation." Nonetheless, the vast religious community in America presents a promising target, and we need to make it possible for them to support Green causes. As one evangelical wrote: "[M]any of us who love the natural world . . . feel we face an almost impossible either-or predicament. Voting for proenvironmental candidates usually means voting for a package of other policies that we will never swallow."[34] Reconnecting conservatives to conservation requires giving them candidates of both parties who have commitments to the Green agenda, including some who share their conservative views on social and other issues. GOP primary voters are there waiting for these candidates, should the GOP ever reform itself sufficiently to allow them on the ballot.

Ironically, the prospects for a revival of right-wing environmentalism have been boosted by a backlash within the GOP to the fever of irrationality that has infected their party. Many Republicans are horrified by the GOP's reckless flirtation with default and recession in pursuit of quixotic goals. Greens have a historic opportunity to ride this wave of backlash to reconnect with conservatives. This is exactly what is advocated by John G. Taft, the descendant of multiple generations of prominent Republicans, who calls for a return to the GOP's "brand promise": "The Republican Party is (or should be) the Stewardship Party. The Republican brand is (or should be) about responsible behavior."[35] A brave group of eleven House Republicans, led by New York State Representative Chris Gibson, embraced this injunction by introducing, one week before Pope Francis addressed a joint session of Congress, House Resolution 424, which calls on the House to address climate change, "including mitigation efforts and efforts to balance human activities that have been found to have an impact" on climate, stating that "it is a conservative principle to protect, conserve, and be good stewards of our environment." It was reported that Gibson and his co-sponsors were prompted to act by a coalition of faith and Green groups that calls itself the Call to Conscience on Climate Disruption (CCCD).

There is an emerging sense that many more GOP politicians are ready to reclaim a sensible position on climate change and environment, just as soon as the price—in terms of fundraising impact and the threat of being "primaried" from the right—is not too high. Eduardo Porter, writing in the *New York Times*, reported Senator Sheldon Whitehouse's belief that there are "eight, 10, maybe 12 Republicans in the Senate" waiting to breakout from the GOP's anti-Green orthodoxy. "When the moment comes," the Senator opined, "they could all jump together."

But even with GOP self-interest pointing to a rapprochement between environment and conservatism, many Greens with whom I have discussed this fear that right-wing views on climate and the environment may be qualitatively different from other political positions (immigration, for example) and thus more difficult to dislodge. This time, they fear, the party rank-and-file is less well educated, accustomed to a faith-based way of knowing, and trapped in a new media and Internet bubble that constantly reinforces their beliefs, all of which make it far more difficult for a critical mass of conservatives to surrender their hostility to environmentalism. I agree. Thanks to advances in cognitive psychology, we now understand that people are programmed to welcome facts that fit their preexisting convictions. People feel good when such confirming facts present themselves and feel bad when facts challenge those convictions. Our aversion to dissonance between cherished beliefs and contradictory facts is very high, and we are prepared to pay a high cognitive price (in terms of rationalization, selective bias in admitting and processing information, refusal to consider alternatives, irrationality, and willful blindness) to avoid that kind of dissonance.[36] We may be quick to call out hypocrisy in others, but find it remarkably easy to ignore in ourselves. These essential psychological characteristics are reinforced by the well-understood hazard of "groupthink," with its social pressures to conform, to which even the mentally tough are acutely sensitive. And

those pressures increase when the belief is not simply a shared opinion, but a marker of identity for the person and his or her membership
in the group. If anti-Green convictions are an essential part of what it
is to be a conservative, then for individual conservatives to change their
own minds about the environment requires nothing less than a willingness to surrender, at least in part, their identity (e.g., as a Christian, a
conservative, a Republican, or a patriotic American).

These psychological insights teach us that such a change in views
is difficult, but it is not impossible. One inspiring example is six-term
GOP congressman from South Carolina Bob Inglis, who traveled to
the Great Barrier Reef and to Antarctica, spent time with climate scientists, and changed his mind about the reality of climate change—a
change which cost him his seat in Congress, but launched him on a
courageous campaign to convince conservatives to support carbon
pricing.[37] Over the longer term, whole communities are capable of profound changes in course, as illustrated by the switch in allegiance by
southern conservatives from Democrat to Republican over the thirty
years between 1964 and 1994, and the widespread embrace in a single generation of integration and civil rights. More recently, in an
even shorter period of time, moderates changed their minds about
marriage equality. Of course the full explanation for each of these is
different, but they had in common the leadership of prominent figures within the group. Social scientists who studied this phenomenon
in relation to possible paths to ending the Great Estrangement concluded that "[t]his political polarization is unlikely to reverse course
without a noticeable convergence of support of environmental protection among political elites . . . with prominent conservative figures and Republican Party leaders becoming less anti-environmental
in their public statements and voting records."[38] Thus, an end to the
Great Estrangement, like these other shifts, requires at least a few conservative leaders, like Bob Inglis, to conclude that the transition will
advance the interests of conservatives or Republicans generally, and
publicly embrace openness to at least part of the Green agenda. Even a

subtle shift in "elite" opinion can create a safe place for individuals to reconnect with conservation without fear of apostasy.

The final reason for thinking that a revival of conservative environmentalism is possible in the United States is the modernization of conservatism in the United Kingdom, which shows that a shift toward Green is possible and can be a salutary strategy for electoral success. Asserting leadership on Green issues was an important part of David Cameron's effort to move his party to the center right and make it more attractive to young and socially liberal voters. Tories supported a Green Investment Bank with an investment of £3.8 billion, with the goals of achieving a reduction in U.K. greenhouse gas emissions of 34 percent by 2020 and at least 80 percent by 2050; ensuring that 15 percent of all energy consumed in the UK is generated from green sources by 2020; and achieving a significant reduction in waste going to landfills. This initiative has a distinctly conservative flavor: it operates independently of the government, has been designed to leverage £15 billion in private funding, and operates on a "double bottom line" principle of profitability plus achieving its Green goals. The bank was created following enactment of the U.K. Climate Change Act of 2008, which mandated reductions in carbon emissions and increased use of renewable energy sources. Interestingly, the parliamentary committee on climate change, which advocated the creation of the bank and these other initiatives, was established on a nonpartisan basis.

Walter Lippmann wrote that "the notion that political beliefs are logically determined collapses like a pricked balloon" once you consider the biographical and human factors of the people who hold those beliefs.[39] If we can acknowledge and work with these human factors, challenging the particular belief without challenging people's deeper value systems and identities, then there is a real prospect that certain strongly held counterfactuals, like climate-change denial, will themselves pop like a pricked balloon and assume their proper role as a historic aberration. It won't be easy, but each of the three steps of Getting to Green involves, one way or another, this core idea of changing particular beliefs on environmental issues without challenging (and indeed, working with) these deeper value systems. Step One calls for a direct appeal to the deeper values of conservatives and a reminder of how those values mandate planetary stewardship. Step Two calls for Greens to adjust the philosophical case for conservation to make it more resonant with the values of conservatives, and to undercut the criticism that Greens put nature before people. Step Three calls on the Green movement to reform itself, in part to become a more congenial home for conservatives, without compromising any of its core values. The three steps constitute a mutually reinforcing virtuous circle, with steps two and three making the first step—reconnecting conservatives with conservation—possible.

Even if you are skeptical about the potential success of the enterprise of reconnecting a critical mass of conservatives to the environmental movement, I hope I have at least persuaded you that we have no choice but to try. Every historian who has looked at the history of the Green movement in America has reached the same conclusion: the Green agenda advances when and only when supported by a bipartisan consensus sufficient to break through partisan gridlock and produce action. One historian's articulation is typical of those with a historical perspective: "The call for environmentalists to embrace progressive ideologies over bridge-building with Republican moderates overlook[s] the success the movement enjoyed when it had bipartisan appeal. While the far right is likely beyond reconciliation, it is doubtful that the [Green] movement could ever rebuild a political majority without appealing to GOP centrists."[40]

———————

Undeniably, the greening of the GOP would be a good thing for the environment. It also could be a good thing for the Republican Party. By 2015, only 27 percent of Americans polled thought the Republicans would do a better job than the Democrats in protecting the environment.[41] As *The Economist* put it in a fruitless attempt to persuade President George W. Bush to tack Green, "The current monopoly of [environmentalism] by the Democrats is a . . . disaster. . . . The greening of conservatism is a revolution waiting to happen."[42] Even Karl Rove, writing in *Newsweek* after the party's losses in 2008, argued that Republicans need a "market-oriented 'green' agenda that's true to our principles."[43] I have no doubt that leading figures in the GOP establishment pondering the electoral map for 2016 are keenly aware that swing states like Colorado, Iowa, Virginia, and Wisconsin host large groups of Green voters.[44]

An appreciation for nature and a renewed dedication to its stewardship might also help the Republican Party recover some of its traditional connection with Burke's "unbought grace of life." Many thoughtful conservatives believe this departure from Burkean sensibility has resulted in what longtime *National Review* editor Jeffrey Hart called the "mark of yahooism . . . prominent in Republicanism today." By "yahooism" he means exactly the sort of market fundamentalism that precipitated the Great Estrangement, where markets become "a kind of utopianism [that] maximizes ordinary human imperfection, unleashing greed, short views, and the resulting barbarism."[45] Forging real connections with nature and shouldering the duty to defend our children's inheritance against the predations of market fundamentalism would surely help cure the "yahooism" that, in the long run, all thoughtful Republicans know will prove deeply damaging to the party's standing with the American people. And even in the short term, the usefulness of environmental ridicule to mobilize the ultraconservative base may be outweighed by its tendency to repel swing voters. In the 2014 midterm elections, the GOP criticisms of Democratic positions on climate change and energy were encapsulated by a slogan accusing the president of a "war on coal." But how many voters outside of Wyoming, West Virginia, Kentucky, and Pennsylvania care about coal? Is positioning the other party as "anticoal" really a national winner in the long run, when coal has no meaning or relevance to ordinary voters outside of coal country, and many of those same voters are now personally experiencing the impacts of climate change?

Interestingly, both Greens and Democrats seem to understand that the greening of conservatism would be good for the GOP, and therein lies a problem. Because it has been an article of faith for Greens for a quarter century that Democrats in general are better for the environment, many of them regard the prospect of a conservative re-embrace of conservation with deep skepticism, fearing that it would make the Republican Party more competitive in national politics. This is of course a weirdly circular bit of illogic, since if the GOP recovers some of its traditional leadership on the environment, then continuous Democratic ascendancy is no longer necessary to advance the Green agenda. More importantly, I have to ask fellow Greens who might indulge in this sort of thinking to carefully distinguish between ideology and politics: ideology looks for acceptance of its ideas; politics looks for power. The Green movement is fundamentally an ideology, a set of values and ideas about the importance of farsighted stewardship of our natural environment, and not a political movement in a quest for power. As a movement of ideas, we should welcome anyone, right or left, who accepts our ideas, regardless of the political consequences. I don't think any serious Green could argue that a return to the days when proenvironmental policies were considered good politics *by both parties* would not be a good thing for the movement and the planet.

GETTING TO GREEN, STEP TWO

A Philosophy That Puts People First

> [T]he great majority of men live like bats, but in
> twilight, and know and feel the philosophy of their
> age only by its reflections and refractions.
>
> —SAMUEL COLERIDGE, *ESSAYS ON HIS OWN TIMES*

As Coleridge suggested, most of us know environmental philosophy only indirectly, by its "reflections and refractions" in the rhetoric around environmental policy. Few Greens, whether ordinary citizens or those working as professionals in environment-related fields, spend much time worrying about the "why" of caring for the natural world. And yet the reflections and refractions are there, dictated by the deeper philosophical premises that sit, often unseen, behind the environmental debates of the day. Ideas matter. Change the way we think about nature, or change the way we think about man in nature, and then the political rhetoric and arguments—and the outcomes of those arguments—will change as well.

When a previously successful political movement becomes stalled, the explanation often lies in the limits of its underlying core idea or philosophy. For the first wave of Green projects (the basic cleanup of water and air in the 1970s and 1980s), the benefits were self-evident, so little weight was put on an intellectual or moral narrative that explained why it was the right thing to do. For the second wave of Green issues, however, the case for the Green agenda was not so obvious, and the public quite reasonably asked exactly why the snail darter or spotted owl had to be "saved" at the cost of a needed highway or valued local jobs. The quality and coherence of the answers to these questions, and particularly the manner in which the answers dealt with the apparent tension between the interests of nature and the interests of people, became a key factor in determining the success of the Green agenda.

So how strong and coherent is the case for environmentalism? The Green movement has long been troubled by a fundamental conflict: is our reason for saving nature utilitarian (that is, because of its usefulness to man), or is nature worth saving for its own sake? Closely allied to the question of *why* we should care for nature is the question of *how* we come to the conviction that doing so is the right thing to do. Our movement's prophets, a pantheon including Aldo Leopold, Wallace Stegner, and Henry David Thoreau, were in love with nature and based their ethics and environmentalism largely on this love. They wrote freely of beauty and spiritual transcendence. On the other hand, the modern movement tends to be vaguely embarrassed by this legacy and instead has gravitated toward science, which is regarded as a firmer foundation for a movement that seeks to change the world. Since the 1980s, Greens have told us that climate change is all about science. The case for preventing loss of biodiversity and the elimination of persistent toxics is presented in the same way. So which is it? Are we scientists or poets?

When it comes to finding a sound philosophical basis for environmentalism, we do not start from a promising place. For the past forty years, the answer to "why save nature?"—at least when provided by the academy and most of those practicing in the new field of "environmental philosophy"[1]—consisted of a set of justifications for Green action commonly referred to as "deep ecology."[2] The core idea of environmental ethics, according the introduction to a standard college text, can be explained as follows: "[P]rogress could be made in ending the ecological crisis by challenging anthropocentric ethical norms and extending moral considerability to nonhuman beings."[3] In other words, turn three thousand years of thinking on its head and adopt an ethical system in which plants and animals have the same moral entitlements as humans.[4]

Originally coined in the 1970s by the Norwegian philosopher Arne Naess, the term "deep ecology" has been applied to many different strands of environmental philosophy. I use it in its broadest sense, which encompasses two essential ideas: that the goals of environmentalism are almost entirely nonutilitarian and thus can be justified without reference to human benefit, and that achieving those goals requires a major paradigm shift, whether in human nature, the nature of capitalism, social organization, the nation-state system, or the like.

This philosophy was given expression as a legal approach to environmental issues by a 1972 law review article titled "Should Trees Have Standing? Toward Legal Rights for Natural Objects."[5] Its author noted the gradual evolution of our conception of what entities deserve to be treated by the law as if they held entitlements—which came eventually to include children, women, and corporations—and offered the proposition that it was now time to extend rights, with the legal and operational consequences implied by that status, to "natural objects" and indeed the environment as a whole. The "trees have rights" way of thinking is one strain of a much broader and more widely accepted type of antianthropocentrism. The antianthropocentrists seek to shift the touchstone of human interests to nature itself. The "biocentric" or "ecocentric" advocates (Leopold, Naess, E. O. Wilson) mostly agree that, as Leopold puts it, "A thing is right when it tends to preserve the integrity, stability, and beauty of the biotic community. It is wrong when it tends otherwise."[6]

Leopold was right, and indeed prophetic, in teaching that environmental decisions have a moral dimension. But Leopold—and those who followed him in elaborating the nonanthropocentric approach—went too far in taking man out of the moral equation, and erred in replacing one absolutist framework (all revolves around the utilitarian interest of man) with another one (all revolves around the "biotic community"). They are right that ethics need to be a big part of the conversation about environmental policy, but wrong in proposing a deceptively simple answer.[7] The right answer is more complex, with humans remaining at the center of moral considerability, but humans correctly understood as being deeply embedded within the natural world, dependent on it for health, wealth, and happiness, and as having a profound moral responsibility for the stewardship of nature.

This core project of deep ecology, to extend rights to animals and plants that may at times balance or trump the rights of humans, has made the Green movement vulnerable to a number of politically devastating accusations. The first is that Greens care more about plants and animals than fellow humans. Close behind is the often-heard claim that, by advocating an alternative morality with nature at its core, environmentalism is a sort of competing religion inconsistent with the human-centered moral systems of the traditional monotheistic faiths. GOP presidential candidate Rick Santorum was fond of saying that some environmentalists care more about animals than people; the accusation that Greens put the interests of nature before the interests of humans echoes widely and loudly around the right.[8] The preoccupation of some Greens with population control, and even Green fantasies about a postindustrial world with a significantly reduced human population, contribute to this vulnerability.[9]

Right-wing critics are not the only ones to detect that Green values can appear indifferent to human needs. Testifying in support of the spotted owl, the chief scientist of The Nature Conservancy gazed at the loggers and their families in the back of the room and experienced an epiphany: as described by the New Yorker, the scientist realized that "if you saw nature as having unlimited and unquantifiable rights and humans as having none, you turned environmentalism into a form of class warfare."[10]

Deep ecology has failed the movement for two other reasons. First, its argument that the planet cannot be saved without changing human nature is a loser. Aldo Leopold, the seminal theorist of a "land ethic," wrote privately to his friend Doug Wade, a naturalist at Dartmouth College, "Nothing can be done without creating a new kind of people."[11] Many others since have indulged in the same wishful thinking. Gus Speth, in a throwback to Charles Reich's *The Greening of America*, devotes a chapter to calling for "A New Consciousness," requiring a radical change in the human heart.[12] And yet the clear lesson of history is that humankind is stubbornly constant in both its virtues and its vices. I have no argument with the proposition that a better world, including environmental nirvana, would follow the introduction of new people, in whom wisdom, foresight, charity, and love largely prevailed over ignorance, myopia, and avarice. But just as political utopians of all persuasions have learned to work with what they have, so must environmentalists. Andrei Sakharov, from the perspective of the gulag in 1975, wrote that "the reality of the contemporary world is complex with many planes. It is a fantastic mix of tragedy, irreparable misfortune, apathy, prejudices and ignorance, plus dynamism, selflessness, hope and intelligence." This great truth could have been uttered in 975, and it will be true in 2175. We had better get used to it. If we build an environmental ethic that requires a new man, if we accept that ecological systems cannot function with a dominant species in which avarice and ignorance are in a perpetual struggle with selflessness and wisdom, then we had better get ourselves a new planet.

The final failing of deep ecology is its willingness to stray far from the objective anchor of science. A common right-wing accusation against Greens is that they are "sentimental," meaning that their policies are dictated more by emotion and preference (often class preference) than sound science and the rational balancing of all relevant considerations. This accusation is rarely merited. Most mainstream Green NGOs are dedicated to science, and labor in good faith to ensure that Green positions are based on sound science. But certain strains of deep ecology do devalue science relative to humanistic factors, and seek to base environmentalism almost exclusively on the rather softer and more subjective foundation of human emotion. But when powerful economic interests, and public values such as jobs and housing, are arrayed against nature, nature's defenders have a hard time if their arguments are based primarily on purely subjective factors. To be clear: Getting to Green requires connecting with people emotionally and harnessing the power of stories and relationships, but we must not confuse the *tools* the Green movement uses to motivate citizens with the proper bases for difficult decisions that are at once environmental, economic, and political. It is rarely sufficient to say we should preserve a forest rather than build housing because we love the forest. The environmental case always must be based, at least in part, on a utilitarian argument referring, when relevant, to scientific and/or economic analysis that is as objective and informed as we can make it. Every time the Green movement is tempted to dismiss the need for a scientific basis and instead appeals solely to sentiment, the right is able to frame the Green agenda as nothing more than a "preference." You prefer hiking a quiet forest trail; we prefer riding our snowmobiles and ATVs. You prefer a meadow; we prefer housing. Nothing more than feelings.

If deep ecology doesn't provide a solid foundation for environmentalism to move forward, then what will? The answer must start with some fresh thinking about what we mean by nature, and address the problem identified by Nietzsche, who complained that when we think and talk about nature, "we . . . forget ourselves in it." The most common way of using the word "nature" is simply to signify all those things in the world that would be here if humans were not. This model of the world without man is closely related to religious ideas regarding the separateness of man and nature. As *The Catholic Encyclopedia* explains, "From a theological point of view the distinctions between nature and person . . . are of primary importance."[13] This idea is the foundation for the traditional Christian view, highly influential in evangelical circles today in the United States, that God created a static and perfect natural world in which unity, order, and harmony are assured due to the wisdom and perfection of the creator. God then created man, unlike the rest of the creatures, in his image, with a divine mandate for dominion over the rest of the world.[14] Moreover, man's presence in the world is only temporary, pending the end of the world, pursuant to various eschatological beliefs. The "dominion" model lifts man out of nature, and posits that nature exists for our use. Nature is bountiful, and man may drink the milk and eat the honey without remorse, in full confidence that the natural world exists for his sustenance and pleasure.

This model has several shortcomings. The first is that its validity was demolished in the nineteenth century by Charles Darwin. We now know that nature is a dynamically evolving web of life, not the static order of a divine designer. And man is as much a product of the evolutionary forces of natural selection as any other creature. We do not sit apart, but exist in complex interdependency with each other, with the other forms of life, and with the whole terrestrial ecosystem. Morever, the theology behind the popular dominion model is highly suspect. Pope Francis in his 2015 encyclical letter on the environment went out of his way to expressly reject the idea: "This is not a correct interpretation of the Bible as understood by the Church," he wrote. Instead, the Pope observed, "Nature cannot be regarded as something separate from ourselves or as a mere setting in which we live. We are part of nature, included in it and thus in constant interaction with it."[15]

Rejection of the supernatural notion of man having dominion over nature does not imply rejection of our deep sense that something permanent and unchanging lies "behind" our empirical experience of nature. Philosophers once taught that nature has two fundamental aspects: creat*ed* nature and creat*ing* nature, the former being the material (and temporary) form we see when we look at the natural world at any point in time, and the later being the animating dynamic creative force that brings physical nature into being and which, unlike the natural world, is unchanging.[16] Of course, to religious thinkers the animating force of creat*ing* nature was God, and they believed that the distinction between God and his work is what allows us to gain insight into the divine through the study of nature.[17] This distinction can be uncoupled from its theological origins to allow secularists to articulate what most of us feel instinctively: that the physical forms of nature are animated and given their power by some underlying force.[18] Our sense of the "eternal," which generations of poets and philosophers have reported from deep contact with nature, comes not from the physical forms we encounter (modern man knows that forests, species, and even mountains are transient), but from the forces that control and govern all of this change, which are themselves unchanging. American transcendentalists felt this deeply and used immersion into created nature to transcend it.

So if God-the-creator is not the animating force behind the natural world, then what is? Of course, post-Darwin, we know that evolution and natural selection form the rule book that governs the rise and fall of species, including man. Our study of biology has led us beyond the superficial sense of the "balance" of nature to an understanding of the complex web of relationships and interdependencies that drive biotic systems. We now see "behind" material nature more clearly than ever before: species may come and go, great forests may rise and fall, but the animating force—the software, the rules of the game, the relationships that govern the constant change experienced by biotic systems—these indeed are awesome, magnificent, and permanent.[19] And, perhaps most importantly, we now understand that technological man has stepped out of the material world and has one foot on the creating side of the divide. Suddenly, having passed a tipping point in only the blink of a geological or evolutionary eye, it is *human* agency that is awesome in its power and global in its reach. We now have the power to change the world—whether through nuclear holocaust, genetic engineering, our relentless seeding of the world with insidious toxins, or our having inadvertently reengineered our atmosphere—and it is nature itself that has proved to be fragile, frequently a victim, and in need of our care. During the Enlightenment, mankind started the long and difficult intellectual journey to wrest control of his destiny from God. During the modern era, mankind succeeded, crossing the threshold to Mount Olympus and joining the world of the creators. With great power comes great responsibility, and the case for environmentalism is firmly anchored in the moral implications of our species having acquired powers that once were the exclusive province of the gods.

Given the abandonment of the supernatural model of God-privileged man sitting outside of nature, it is curious that the animating paradigm for environmentalism has, for most of its history, been the idea of wilderness, or nature without man. When European civilization was presented with a "new world" of unimaginable scope and richness, the idea of pristine nature received a powerful boost. And it was in the New World where a secular and peculiarly American model for nature as "world without man" achieved its clearest expression. In 1851 Thoreau started to say, in his lecture "Walking," that "in wildness is the preservation of the world," and over a century later, in 1964, a bipartisan Congress enacted the Wilderness Act, protecting those places "where the earth and its community of life are untram-

meled by man, where man himself is a visitor who does not remain."
That is what the wilderness model is, and under that model, keeping
that wilderness wild is what environmentalism is all about.

In my opinion, Thoreau was wrong; the preservation of the world
lies not in the wildness of wilderness, but in the health and resiliency of the places where human beings live. There are three basic
problems with the Green movement's long obsession with wilderness: little real wilderness is left on the planet, the wilderness model
carries the false premise that nature exists in a state of unchanging
harmony, and thus the wilderness ethic tells us little about how to
care for the planet we have now.

It has been a long time since significant portions of the planet
were truly unaffected by human activity. Even Paleolithic man may
have had a profound effect on the environment through his use of
fire, and he is now thought to have played an important role in the
extermination of the larger animals that survived the last Ice Age.[20]
By the time of Greek civilization, writers rarely made a distinction
between man-affected landscape and the wild, but instead focused
on the distinction between the agrarian and the urban. Today, wilderness as pristine nature untouched by man has few examples on
this planet. Those startling photographs of the earth at night tell
the story of the global spread of human population. The fascinating "human footprint map" produced by the Wildlife Conservation
Society demonstrates that 83 percent of the earth's surface has been
directly affected by human activity.[21] Many scientists now argue that
Earth has entered a new geological era called the "anthropocene,"
the defining feature of which is the global phenomenon of human
influence on nature.

This science supports the argument of Bill McKibben that we have
experienced the "end of nature," in that there is now no corner of the
Earth—not the most remote corner of the Congo or unexplored Ant-
arctic valley—that remains free of human impact.[22] Mankind proved

to be a great migrator, ultimately occupying every continent other than Antarctica, and our technologies (including hundreds of chemical compounds unknown to the plants and animals that evolved in their absence) amplified the impact of our lives on the biosphere to levels previously achieved only by geophysical and climactic forces. Today, there is no nature apart from man, and "wilderness" must be understood as a relative term, referring to places relatively less affected by human life than others. We may long for Arcadia, but it doesn't exist.

The second problem with the wilderness model is its implied message that the world in the absence of man is in some important sense unchanging. Human beings are largely blind to what scientists call "deep time," in which continents drift, ice ages come and go, and species rise and fall, sometimes dramatically through mass extinction events and sometimes slowly through mutation and natural selection. Our brains, and the culture they have created, create powerful presumptions that nature is and should be static, and that the "balance" of the moment is the "natural" state of the geologic and biotic system, from which any variation is deviant and "unnatural." When a forest is ravaged by fire or a mountain is destroyed by a volcanic eruption, we tend to perceive this as "damage" to the environment, simply because it changes the status quo. But we now know better. In his book *Discordant Harmonies: A New Ecology for the 21st Century*, Daniel Botkin gives the illuminating example of Kirtland's warbler, a songbird in Michigan, whose population declined precipitously despite the fact that well-intentioned managers had suppressed the periodic forest fires that had devastated its jack-pine habitat.[23] It turned out that the fires did not destroy but *created* the habitat required by the birds. So the managers reversed course, undertook a prescribed burn, and then let the natural cycle of burn and regeneration occur without human intervention. Kirtland's warblers are now recovering, dependent, as so many creatures are, not on a static environment, but on a cycle of constant change. In order to deal sensibly with the most difficult issues of planetary steward-ship, such as when to intervene in forest fires and how to deal with anthropomorphic climate change, we need to become comfortable with a mental model of nature that is highly dynamic and complex.

Finally, the wilderness ethic calls on us to preserve pristine natu-ral systems, but one thing is missing: man. The interconnectedness and interdependence between nature and human life is missing, because man is missing. All the wilderness ethic tells us is how to treat the few remaining places where man isn't. But for the Green movement in the twenty-first century, we need an environmental philosophy that informs our responsibilities to the places where peo-ple are. The emerging science of "reconciliation ecology" is teach-ing us the importance of encouraging biodiversity and creating healthy biotic systems in the places where people live. It is based on the premise that increasing habitat for other forms of life is a prime objective. Even if that habitat is human-dominated and far from pristine, it still can play a powerful role in avoiding extinctions and increasing species diversity. Reconciliation ecologists such as Michael Rosenzweig investigate how we can reconcile human use of place with the retention of biodiversity. He explores strategies such as changing agricultural practices (e.g., moving toward shade-grown coffee plantations, allowing weeds to grow among crops, and leaving significant amounts of fallow land adjacent to farmed fields) and the greening of urban planning (e.g., restoring urban rivers and rede-signing urban and suburban green spaces to replace lawn with more productive wildlife habitat).[24]

The wilderness ethic, like its progeny, the deep-ecology preference for saving nature for its own sake, also has contributed to the percep-tion that Greens care only about pristine nature, and are indifferent to the places where people live. Adam Werbach, the former Sierra Club leader now viewed by some as an apostate, blames this for much of the movement's political failure: "[O]ver the years, ordinary Americans have sensed it, the media has amplified it, and . . . the keenest conservatives saw an opportunity to exploit it."[25]

Many traditional environmentalists feel threatened by any critique of the wilderness ethic, which is usually accompanied by openness to the idea of human management of relatively natural areas. They quite understandably worry that any dilution of a hands-off approach to the wild will be the thin edge of a wedge exploited by powerful economic interests determined to reopen wild areas to logging, mining, and other forms of exploitation. They also argue that our understanding of ecosystems remains too primitive to support interventions that are likely to be successful. And of course most environmentalists, myself included, hold a deep personal attachment to the idea of wild places, and are loath to embrace anything that might be seen to devalue them.

As global warming has accelerated the pace of observable change in protected areas, the stewards of our wilderness face difficult choices in the field. Should those protecting our ancient sequoias be permitted to water them if necessary for the trees to survive a protracted drought? Should exotic invasives be left alone to wreak devastation on "wilderness" areas? Does it change our answer if the drought is caused by man's greenhouse gas emissions and the invasive plants escaped from suburban backyards? The debates over these questions among conservation biologists have escalated steadily, and often turn on the question of whether the wilderness model still provides appropriate guidance to those grappling with these practical questions.[26] Although an increasing number of scientists believe that it does not, the wilderness model remains deeply embedded in the worldview of many who have devoted their lives to the protection of our wildest places from the depredations of man. The reaction of one prominent conservation biologist is typical: "Conservationists and citizens alike ought to be alarmed by a scheme that replaces wild places and national parks with domesticated landscapes containing only nonthreatening, convenient plants and animals." He went on to accuse the critics of the wilderness model of painting traditional environmentalism as a "dysfunctional, antihuman anachronism."[27]

I believe that the defenders of the wilderness model protest too much. The "slippery slope" argument ignores the ability of policy makers and land stewards to discriminate between science-based interventions intended to increase the health and resiliency of relatively wild places, and exploitation of resources for economic gain. Allowing a forest ranger to save a giant sequoia by providing supplemental water during a drought hardly opens the door to the cutting of those trees for timber. And the argument that we simply know too little to intervene successfully argues not for paralysis, but for caution. When a human being is suffering from a poorly understood disease, the doctor does her or his best, and we would never accept ignorance as an excuse for inaction.

Most fundamentally, those who call on the movement to transcend the wilderness ethic recognize that our most wild places are physically, ecologically, and spiritually precious, increasingly rare, and worthy of our protection. As Aldo Leopold pointed out, wilderness "can shrink but cannot grow."[28] All environmentalists should work to thwart any attempt to weaken the protections on wilderness that has already been saved (and thus were right to oppose drilling in the Arctic National Wildlife Refuge), and should work tirelessly to protect our few areas of surviving wild lands from encroachment and development. But this is not enough. Nature includes the places where people are, and thus the wilderness *ethic* does not tell us what to do with the 83 percent of the planet that is not wilderness. Howard Zahniser, who campaigned tirelessly for the Wilderness Act, argued that "we should be guardians, not gardeners." But fifty years later, the authors of the Wildlife Conservation Society human-footprint analysis concluded that "[t]he global extent of the human footprint suggests that humans are stewards of nature, whether we like it or not."[29]

A worldview in which man sees himself as firmly embedded within nature need not result in a loss of that sense of caring that flowed from man's standing apart from nature, where "dominion over" implied at least some "responsibility for." Instead, the sense that man stands deeply interconnected with and dependent on nature should lead to a deepening of the moral imperative to consider the impact of one's actions on the natural world. Michael Pollan developed an apt metaphor that captures both the illusions of the wilderness ethic and the sense of stewardship that grows out of a deep sense of man's connections with the natural world. In *Second Nature*,[30] he reminds us that the garden is a place where we have long experience with the issues of man in nature, and asks us to consider as our model the gardener, who knows that not all interventions in the natural world are harmful, embeds himself deeply in a place, and assumes stewardship responsibility for the health, beauty, and resilience of a piece of the natural world.[31]

The gardener metaphor addresses two of the primary shortcomings of the wilderness model: the illusion of a harmonious "natural" state that should be preserved, and the idea that our highly imperfect understanding of nature makes it too dangerous to intervene. Wilderness preservationists and many old-style Greens, for example, frequently cite non-native plant life as an "unnatural" scourge, with the idea that ecosystems should be "restored" to some "natural" past. To the gardener, this is nonsense. The gardener knows how dynamic plant life is, with species moving about as habitat changes through fire, flood, and climate change, and as seeds and spoors transit the earth on the wind and the bodies of birds. One recent study of the eighteenth-century North American plant surveys conducted by the Swedish botanist Peter Kalm revealed that most of the European weeds we consider non-native were already well established in New York and New Jersey as early as 1750. The gardener does not look for some hypothetical past time when the eco-system was wholly native and natural, but instead asks only whether the mix of plants is healthy, sustainable, and resilient. A thuggish weed unfriendly to diversity, even if all-American, will be eradicated. A well-behaved visitor from abroad, well suited to soil and climate here, will be embraced and nurtured, diversifying and thus strengthening the quality of the biotic system under the gardener's care.

This comfort with change is made possible not by some hubris-tic conviction that the gardener is sufficiently knowledgeable and skilled to reliably direct it, but by a highly tuned sense of the gar-dener's limits. No gardener feels in control. Plants rarely behave as they should, weather is never as expected, insects are both vital pollinators and fatal scourges, trees die, soil floods, and any illusion harbored by beginning gardeners that they can manage the chaos is quickly dashed. But gardeners do not give up. Ignorance and diffi-culty are not excuses for inaction. There are victories as well as comic failures, and each adds to gardeners' closeness to the place under their care and determination to do the right thing by the pieces of land they occupy.

Once you start to look at the relationship between humans and nature through the prism of the gardener metaphor, a powerful moral imperative to the stewardship of nature is revealed. Unlike other animals, humans have the capacity to understand, even if imperfectly, the impacts of our actions on our environment. We have the technology to intervene in nature on virtually all scales relevant to life on earth. And we have free will, and brains that are hardwired to exercise that will in a morally responsible way. The bird that fouls its nest is not the subject of moral opprobrium, but when modern humans do it, they most certainly are.

The gardener model is simple to understand and explain. It does not require the intermediation of science, or depend on rhetoric or ideas that divide right and left. David Rothenberg put it well: "[W]e will evolve into a species that just chooses to shepherd the rest of the world; taking care of the rest of the world; fitting into the world."[32] *Fitting in* and *taking care*. Man does not need to be outside of nature to take care of it. Fitting in does not mean being passive. Once we know that our decisions affect the natural world, there is no system of ethics under which we are not required to consider the impact of those decisions on our fellow humans, both now, and those who will follow us. I don't know of any conservative who would not sign up to be a conservationist under this model. Aldo Leopold put it beautifully: "I have read many definitions of what is a conservationist, and written not a few myself, but I suspect that the best one is written not with a pen, but with an axe. It is a matter of what a man thinks about while chopping, or while deciding what to chop. A conservationist is one who is humbly aware that with each stroke he is writing his signature upon the face of the land."[33]

Adopting the gardener model—where man is integrally connected to a dynamic biotic system for which he, as the only rational actor with technology, has a unique responsibility—helps remove much of the long-standing confusion over the foundation for environmental ethics and policy. *The Economist* made the analogy to a dance, where "man and nature are entwined in a dynamic dance of development, scarcity, degradation, innovation and substitution," and man is in the lead, making the choices, and correcting his steps as learns more and more about his partner. [34] As explored in the final part of this chapter, under the gardener model both the utilitarian and moral cases for conservation become redefined in a way in which they are no longer in conflict, and the imperative for conservation becomes coherent, sustainable, and compelling whether you approach it with the sensibility of either the right or the left.[35]

———————

So why save nature? Is there an answer that is coherent, understandable, and persuasive to Americans at both ends of the ideological spectrum? Forty-six years after the first Earth Day we find the Green movement still engaged in the tedious argument about whether nature should be saved for its own sake, as opposed to for what it can do for, and means to, man.[36] As we have seen, the intrinsic-value position is held by virtually all schools of deep ecology, and its language is used by many mainstream Greens.[37] This debate, echoing the original tension between the "conservation" of Theodore Roosevelt and Gifford Pinchot, and the "preservation" of the Sierra Club and John Muir, animates a lively debate among conservation scientists today. In 2013, a distinguished group of conservation biologists, including Michael Soulé and E. O. Wilson, went public in their criticism of The Nature Conservancy's chief scientist, Peter Kareiva, who had questioned whether there was a scientific basis for the intrinsic-value position. These critics called Kareiva's arguments "wrongheaded, counterproductive, and ethically dubious," and criticized The Nature Conservancy as "an organization formerly, and heroically, dedicated to conserving *nature*, and not merely *natural resources* for people."[38]

I do not find this debate illuminating and believe that its very terms are stacked against the political success of environmentalism: a purely utilitarian anthropocentric argument is almost universally recognized as being too narrow, but the intrinsic-value position opens us to the politically fatal accusation that the Green movement is indifferent to human welfare. Many sophisticated NGOs are now careful to avoid the question, and particularly any implication that man is not part of the equation. Even Audubon, whose mission revolves around birds, adopted a mission statement in 2012 stating that its goal of habitat conservation is "for the benefit of humanity and the earth's biological diversity."[39] Why argue? Saving nature benefits all living things, including humanity, which depend on healthy biotic systems.

The false argument around whether we are saving nature "for man" or "for its own sake" is not the only element of potentially harmful philosophical confusion among Greens. We also argue about whether our case for conservation should be driven by morality vs. science, NIMBYism vs. a high-minded global outlook, and whether there is any role in modern environmentalism for the seemingly archaic value of aesthetics. These are not matters on which we need to disagree. The best answer to "why save nature" is "all of the above." Our personal motivations may depend more on one than another, but it is critical that the Green movement acknowledge all of them as valid, and welcome those—particularly our compatriots on the right—who come to environmentalism through any one of them. In the Center Green approach I advocate in this book, the philosophical foundation for environmentalism is unapologetically human-centered and nonideological. It rests on five principal pillars: utility, morality, aesthetics, place-based ethics, and the pursuit of happiness.

The best utilitarian argument for environmental health is simple: without a healthy environment, neither human life nor the economy can flourish or be sustained. Senator Gaylord Nelson, the Democrat from Wisconsin who had the idea that led to the first Earth Day in 1970, got this right when he argued that "[t]he economy is a wholly owned subsidiary of the environment, not the other way around."[40] It's a neat formulation, as a corporation and its subsidiaries are not opponents; the interests of one are generally aligned with the others and they work together for mutual benefit. It's telling that Senator Nelson, often associated with the more radical sort of environmentalism of the early 1970s, was unabashed in making the economic case for saving nature.

Nonetheless, this type of utilitarian thinking continues to make many Greens uncomfortable. We must get over it. Of course nature has utilitarian value. Resources like copper and oil are, ultimately, limited and are (pending technological changes that render them superfluous) material resources that will be valued by the marketplace. We now also understand that nature provides a wide range of "ecosystem services" (such as the role of wetlands in buffering flood waters).[41] A widely cited analysis from 1997 estimated the value of the average annual global output of natural systems at $33 trillion, greater at the time than the estimated annual economic output of humanity.[42] The U.N.'s Millennium Ecosystem Assessment concludes that 60 percent (fifteen out of twenty-four) of these valuable primary ecosystem services are "being degraded or used unsustainably."[43] This alone surely provides a sufficient answer to "why save nature?" But "sufficient" does not imply exclusive or complete, and Greens attached to the intrinsic-value proposition must stop behaving as if it does, and as if any utilitarian argument somehow undercuts the deeper value of nature. Admitting that we will sometimes protect natural systems because of their value to humans and the economy does not mean that the same natural systems cannot at the same time make a powerful claim on our moral or aesthetic sensibilities. It in no way diminishes our affection or even the claim to moral considerability to admit that something also is useful. Many in the art world believe deeply in the intrinsic worth of great art, and see the millions paid at auction as validating, not somehow undercutting, that intrinsic value. For many of us, our motivation for planetary stewardship may be based on a disinterested sense of responsibility. We can be in love with the rain forest, we can believe and act as if it has worth that cannot be measured and priced by the market, and at the same time measure its value as a source of medicine and a powerful carbon sink, and make the economic case for government and business to invest in its protection.

———————————

Utility may be the first pillar of the philosophical case for environmentalism, but the moral pillar stands just behind, and may in the long run prove the stronger of the two. Today, however, there remain several objections to an open embrace of moral reasoning as a justification for environmentalism. Some environmentalists argue that this distracts from the primary role of science in environmental policy. These environmentalists "tend to see values as a distraction from 'the real issues'—environmental problems like global warming."[44] They see much of the values-based enthusiasm for the natural world as thinly veiled sentimentality and subjective preference, which they fear will fail if challenged by more tangible values, such as jobs and economic growth. There are some good reasons for this skepticism. Too often, like the conversation of someone who has read too many self-help books, Green values talk can be dominated by cliché rather than analysis, permitting the right to pounce on every unsupported assertion of intrinsic value as evidence that the entire Green agenda is nothing more than a "preference," and an "elitist" one at that. You think that "nature" has "intrinsic value," we think that there are no higher intrinsic values than personal and economic liberty.

These conflicts—both within the Green movement itself and between Greens and the right—must be resolved in order for the Green movement to move forward. That resolution is not complicated. To function in the real world of economics and politics, the utilitarian case for nature needs to remain part of the Green playbook. But the utilitarian case is not enough. As Jonathan Haidt, who has done a great deal to explain the psychology of morality, explains, "the most important lesson I have learned in my twenty years of research on morality is that nearly all people are morally motivated."[45] And politics, contemporary psychology reveals, is mainly about people coming together in joint pursuit of a moral vision. So Greens must get comfortable with making the moral case for environmentalism, and learn to make it without relying exclusively on assertions of the intrinsic value of nature, without devaluing utilitarian arguments, and without undermining the critical role of sound science in environmental policy making. Getting this right is a necessary condition to reconnecting conservatives to the cause of conservation.

Religious leaders are, of course, completely comfortable with moral argument. Pope Francis's 2015 encyclical sees ecological concern as integral to human responsibility, morality, and conscience: "Human ecology is inseparable from the notion of the common good, a central and unifying principle of social ethics."[46] The Pope is not alone. Leaders of other religions, including the Ecumenical Patriarch Bartholomew, known as the "Green Patriarch," also preach that the environmental question has a moral dimension. Bartholomew argues that "[a]ll of us—individuals, institutions, and industries alike—bear responsibility; all of us are accountable for ignoring the global consequences of environmental exploitation."[47]

While the leadership of these religious figures is commendable and useful, the key to getting the Green movement comfortable with a moral case for environmental stewardship lies in crafting an argument that is not based on the received wisdom of a particular religious tradition, but on secular moral philosophy. And that philosophy needs to be one that is not grounded in the deep-ecology strain reviewed above (which takes human beings out of the center of the moral equation), but on traditional anthropocentric morality that asks how human beings in a human society ought to behave, and answers it with the tools of reason and deep insight into human nature.

So where does this leave Greens trying to make a secular moral case for environmentalism by appealing to something a bit more solid than metaphysical notions about the intrinsic value of nature or religious authority? Traditional secular moral philosophy offers a rich menu of approaches, most of which can be applied to make meaningful statements about right and wrong conduct in relation to the environment. These include a wide range of theories about what constitutes inherently good conduct, like Kant's imperative that we should follow the rules that we would like applied to other people when determining how those people should act in ways that affect us. They include classical and modern arguments about the sources and nature of personal virtue, and all sorts of consequentialist approaches, which measure the rightness or wrongness of the action by its results (such as the actor's pleasure, the goals of a social group, or the achievement of other ends). There can be no doubt, as Gregory Kaebnick observed in his recent exploration of the subject, *Humans in Nature*, that "the debate about environmental protection . . . can be handled by means of relatively traditional moral concepts, without invoking the idea that nature is intrinsically valuable."[48]

In my opinion, invocations of virtuous behavior and good character provide the best foundation for a public conversation about conservation that will both feel authentic to the left and be compelling to the right. Ordinary people of good faith and good sense do not require a philosophical case for why virtuous conduct is right; they simply accept that politeness, prudence, temperance, truth, justice, generosity, compassion, humility, responsibility, self-discipline, courage, and the like are reliable guides to correct conduct, personal contentment, and a well-functioning society. These values have been found by modern science to be nearly universal.[49] The champion for recourse to the widely held virtues in making the moral case for conservation is the American philosopher Thomas E. Hill, who sees a strong connection between the traditional virtues (humility, gratitude, self-discipline, etc.) and caring for nature, and also between indifference to nature and characteristics, such as ignorance and self-importance, that have long been regarded as vices.[50]

Is there any doubt that whatever scientific models tell us about when and how the climate will be affected, the injection into the atmosphere of large quantities of greenhouse gases is not consistent with the virtue of prudence? Does a person of compassion and self-discipline appropriate to himself a disproportionate amount of a limited resource, in disregard of the interest of the following generations? Does a polite and generous person clear-cut a forest and foul a stream that gives pleasure to his neighbors to earn a few bucks? Every Green, including the most liberal of us, knows the answer and is deeply moved by our sense of what humility, compassion, and courage require of us. The left can make these arguments with authenticity and conviction. And if they do, they will be speaking a language with which their compatriots on the right are completely comfortable.[51] The belief that there is such a thing as good character and that it requires much of us as individuals is a deeply American value, shared by right and left. Dr. Martin Luther King Jr. did not want his children judged by the color of their skin, but he accepted that they should be judged by "the content of their character." The right, too often mistaking an embrace of secularism and rejection of sexual taboo for abjuration of values, needs to hear this kind of moral energy from the Green movement. This character- and virtue-based flavor of moral judgment is not only expedient given the political realities of the present moment, but will be a more profound and durable foundation for environmentalism than mere sentiment or metaphysical assertions of nature's value.

––––––––––

Place-based ethics is another powerful force that should be enlisted in the cause of providing a philosophical foundation for the Green movement. Place-based ethics tell us to protect the places we love, to care about places loved by others, and to nurture our feelings of responsibility for nature not by abstract or metaphysical thinking, but by cultivating a strong connection with a *particular* place. The longtime headmaster of Deerfield Academy and one of the most influential educators of the twentieth century, Frank Boyden, famously instructed his students in values and ethics through the admonition, "Look to the hills, boys." People relate to nature specifically, not generally. When they forge a real connection, it is not to the idea of nature, but to one or more places that they know intimately. Sometimes this affection for place is tied to family, and sometimes it is linked to the connection forged with a place, like a farm or a ranch, that provides one's livelihood. Peter Forbes, who writes movingly about the way people become motivated to care for land, quotes some ranchers in northwestern Colorado: "We feel a life-long responsibility to the land. . . . This land is us, so we take much better care of it."[52] This connection to place is not only found in rural areas, it flourishes in the neighborhoods of our cities. Only in our most alienating suburbs—perhaps because as Gertrude Stein famously said "there is no there there"—are these sorts of connections scarce.

Where they do exist, these connections to place are very nearly synonymous with the ethical instinct to protect them. The postenvironmentalists are wrong in their disdain for NIMBYism, which they argue fails to make the necessary distinctions regarding conservation priorities, leaving "environmentalists largely unable to distinguish among places like the Arctic National Wildlife Refuge, Nantucket Sound, and a couple of acres at the end of a cul-de-sac that nobody got around to developing twenty years ago."[53] This is an odd objection, as simply acknowledging the tremendous value the two acres on the cul-de-sac has to the people there (as, perhaps, their sole remaining access to a bit of nature, or the last bit of habitat supporting birdlife in the neighborhood) in no way devalues, replaces, or precludes vigorous science-based prioritization of protection of globally significant lands. They also analogize place-driven ethics to preference claims based on race or ethnicity, calling it a "prejudice of place," which they find both "conservative and undemocratic."[54] Far from being "undemocratic," allowing that the two acres of woods at the end of the street may be precious to the people there *is* profoundly democratic. If the people on the street organize themselves and raise the money to protect the woods, are they not more likely to believe that grassroots activism can make a difference, and more likely to connect with and support a broader environmental agenda? What these critics miss entirely is that the attachment to place fosters an ethic of caring and stewardship that makes us more empathetic to and supportive of the NIMBY claims of others. Instead of an atomizing effect characterized by clashing claims for preference, love of place fosters a collective sense of mutual responsibility, which is more firmly grounded, more sustainable, and ultimately more powerful politically than the more universal and abstract enthusiasms on which the postenvironmentalists would have us rely.

———————

The contemporary attitude toward the beautiful—what I see as the fourth pillar of the case for taking care of nature—represents a sharp break from prior generations. Beauty, like truth and goodness, was for most of human history an accepted measure of worth. From my grandparents' generation back, no one would have found it embarrassing or awkward to praise a thing for its beauty or to express the view that it was wrong to destroy a thing because it was beautiful. As late as 1965, Lyndon Johnson believed it sufficiently important to be the subject of a presidential message, arguing to the nation that "[b]eauty is not an easy thing to measure. It does not show up in the gross national product, in a weekly paycheck, or in the profit-and-loss statements. But these things are not ends in themselves. They are a road to satisfaction and pleasure and the good life. Beauty makes its own direct contribution to these final ends. Therefore it is one of the most important components of our true national income, not to be left out simply because statisticians cannot calculate its worth."[55]

Shortly after President Johnson delivered that message, the relativist tendency of modernism annihilated aesthetic judgment. Popular sentiment now doubts that there is any objective standard for beauty; it is, after all, in the eye of the beholder. Whereas previous generations were trained in discernment and aesthetic judgment, we have taught our children only tolerant observation. Nor do we hold beauty high in our esteem as a useful thing, compared, for example, to justice, truth, or compassion. Indeed, an appreciation for beauty is often regarded as superficial, elitist, and even unwholesome. Would you wish to be regarded as an aesthete?

This decline in aesthetic judgment has had disastrous consequences for the environment. Long before the words *environment* or *ecology* were used with their present meanings, conservation in America and around the world was grounded in the love of beauty. The same year Johnson gave his message on natural beauty, Congress passed the Highway Beautification Bill into law, and First Lady "Lady Bird" Johnson organized twenty citizens—including Laurance Rockefeller and Katharine Graham—to serve as the "First Lady's Committee for a More Beautiful Capital." There was nothing embarrassing about the promotion of beauty, and it was instrumental in raising support for the environmental movement as a whole.

Beauty, if not exactly a moral value, is certainly not a purely utilitarian one either, and is a perfect example of what Burke called the "unbought grace of life." Beautiful things are valued for their intrinsic quality of beauty, and they also are useful. Individually, they give us pleasure and inspiration, and collectively they ennoble the society that produces and celebrates them. Beauty often draws us into a thing or a place, and then opens the door to deeper observation and more profound understanding. Pope Francis argued in his 2015 encyclical that "[b]y learning to see and appreciate beauty, we learn to reject self-interested pragmatism. If someone has not learned to stop and admire something beautiful, we should not be surprised if he or she treats everything as an object to be used and abused without scruple."[56] And we share a universal cultural tradition in which relatively unspoiled nature is held to be beautiful per se. For all these reasons, beauty still has the capacity to be a powerful motivator for the protection of nature, and should not be ignored by Greens. If nothing more, Greens should tell the truth when their care for a thing or a place is grounded in part on its beauty. Yes, make the scientific case. Engage the utilitarians on their terms and talk about

taxes and jobs. But don't think that it makes you less of an environmentalist to be honest about the thing you so often feel most deeply:
the place is beautiful.

I feel unable to end this exploration of reasons why we should care for
the natural world without making the simple point that both nature
itself, and the caring for it, makes us happy. Beauty and love of place
explain this in part, but are not sufficient to explain the unique emotional state that is induced by exposure to the natural world. And
here I also do not mean the various types of transcendence and spiritual experience induced by nature, although they can be part of it
too. Nor do I mean only the connection, perhaps evolutionary, that
humans feel with other forms of life, which E. O. Wilson and others
call biophilia.[57] I mean something more simple: an appetite to be outside. A feeling of coming home when we come to a relatively natural
place. Profound contentment, akin to that we feel when sitting in
front of the fire, where 200,000 years of experience have imprinted a
deep genetic signal that associates the fire with safety and comfort.
If we are feeling troubled, hurt, or angry, we know that simple exposure to trees, plants, rocks, water, and animals, in almost any con-
ceivable combination, makes us feel better. Nature makes us happy.[58]

The partisans in the wars between science and morality, and
between anthropocentric utilitarianism and intrinsic-value theory,
will doubtless argue that my "all of the above" approach is a copout.
I don't think so. The Green movement wants to save the planet, so
why should we care if supporters want to join us because they believe
it is the right thing to do, or because they think that environmental

protection is cheaper than trashing the planet now and cleaning it up later, or because they are lovers of natural beauty?

In this chapter I have called for three fundamental changes in the way the Green movement makes the case for environmental protection: First, we should broadly repudiate deep ecology and its notion that plants and animals deserve the same moral consideration as people, and commit ourselves to being a movement that puts people first and is perceived to do so. Second, while maintaining our work to preserve relatively wild areas, we must escape the thinking and rhetoric of "man outside of nature," and talk more about "the environment" as a place where people are, and a thing of which people are an integral part. And finally, while continuing our hard-hitting arguments based on science and economics, we must become comfortable with making the aesthetic, place-based, and moral cases for conservation, appealing to virtues such as prudence, responsibility, humility, generosity, courage, and patriotism.

GETTING TO GREEN, STEP THREE

Reforming the Green Movement

Each of the three steps to Getting to Green facilitates the others. They are deeply synergistic and together constitute a mutually reinforcing virtuous circle that will slowly but surely demolish the barriers to advancing the Green agenda. Step Three looks at the architecture, culture, and technology of the Green movement itself and calls for modest reforms designed not only to throw off self-imposed shackles on our effectiveness, but also to advance the other two steps by making environmentalism a more congenial home for conservatives and coalescing around a vision that puts people first. I propose a concise blueprint for the required reforms I call a Decalogue for Greens—ten commandments that apply both to environmental NGOs and to environmentalists individually.

First Commandment: Tell the Truth, Admit Uncertainty, and Be Humble

The first commandment calls on Greens to forgo the temptation to justify exaggeration or outright falsehood on the basis that righteous and urgent ends—including saving the world from climate apocalypse—justify any means. Even if it renders them less effective, fund-raising appeals and PR campaigns should stick to the facts. Leaders of NGOs should rein in their marketing, communications, and development professionals, who too often have been schooled in partisan political battles where the anchor of truth has been abandoned in favor of assertions that poll well. Greens must hold themselves to a higher standard, because their essential role is to convince a skeptical population that environmental problems exist and are serious enough to deserve their attention. Politicians (who benefit from low expectations) can bounce back from loss of credibility, but Green NGOs have found that loss of credibility severely compromises their ability to function. The practitioners of so-called environmental psychology have long studied the question of how Green institutions can be more effective. One the clearest findings: environmental leaders and institutions can only be effective if they can maintain the people's trust.[1]

The credibility crisis from which the Green movement suffers cannot be blamed solely on the misinformation campaigns of climate deniers and other critics. Green NGOs themselves have contributed to the climate of skepticism through their long practice of indulging in alarmist predictions, exaggerations, and misleading claims that Nicholas Kristof, a friend of the Green movement, compared to car alarms, which after a while become just an irritating background noise.[2] Paul Ehrlich set an early template for apocalyptic rhetoric by famously declaring in 1968 that "The battle to feed all of humanity is over. In the 1970s and 1980s hundreds of millions of people will starve to death."[3] In the 1970s Green groups predicted that the Trans-Alaska Pipeline System would devastate the caribou herd. Instead, the massive pipeline was built and the herd has quintupled. A national NGO fund-raising letter in 2014 asserted that the Keystone XL pipeline would, among other things, "destroy the boreal forest," rather an extraordinary feat for a single oil pipeline.

The chief scientist of The Nature Conservancy tells a story from the late 1990s, when he was a senior ecologist at the National Marine Fisheries Service and completed a report showing that dams on a number of salmon runs were *not* a cause of declines in salmon population. This didn't stop a coalition of environmental groups from running a full-page advertisement in the *New York Times* claiming that failure to remove the dams would result in extinction of the Chinook salmon in the Snake River by 2017. "I knew that was garbage, scientific garbage," the scientist explained. "I knew the data. I knew market-capture stuff. They made that statement up. And I knew it wasn't true."[4]

When the climate-change debate began in earnest, Green NGOs already were perceived by the public as having apocalyptic tendencies and being prone to exaggeration for effect. This skepticism was compounded when the Green movement succumbed to the temptation to suggest, overtly or indirectly, that individual heat waves or droughts should be taken by the public as evidence of global warning, when of course it is only global average temperatures that are warming, and the particular weather at any particular spot at any particular time is evidence of nothing. What goes around comes around. At virtually the same moment when President Obama declared in his 2014 State of the Union address that "climate change is a fact," snow started to fall over the Capitol and the temperatures in Washington that night plunged to 13 degrees. Climate deniers took to the web to launch a fusillade of mockery.[5] The tragedy is that millions of Americans, having heard their local newscaster point to an unusually hot day as evidence of global warming, happily accepted that one really cold winter meant that global warming didn't exist, or was over.

A corollary of the first commandment regarding truth telling is that uncertainty is okay. Human understanding of nature is incomplete and imperfect. This is one of the few unassailable truths in which Greens can have total confidence. For example, earlier Green movement projections about American greenhouse gas emissions in the absence of treaties or legislation, although based on reasonable assumptions, turned out to be quite wrong. Scientists understandably failed to anticipate either the Great Recession starting in 2008 or the number of dirty coal plants forced to shut down in the face of the natural gas boom. These factors together resulted in America's carbon emissions declining by 7.7 percent between 2006 and 2011 (more than in any other country in the world, according to the International Energy Agency).[6]

Admitting this sort of uncertainty does not mean that the resulting messages will be weak or ineffective. A little creative effort can result in communications that are both accurate and compelling. For example, Yale economist William Nordhaus compares climate outcomes to the spin of a roulette wheel, where the precise outcome cannot be known, but the odds clearly compel investment in prevention and mitigation.[7] An analysis that embraces the reality of uncertainty and argues on the basis of probability and risk tolerance can be as compelling a call for action as the more conventional argument that a specified scary outcome will inevitably result from our failure to act.

In addition to their reluctance to admit uncertainty, too many Greens too often come across to the general public as smugly confident: here is the problem, and here is the solution. Self-righteousness is not only unattractive as a matter of style, but is a barrier to widespread public engagement and thus deeply damaging to successful outcomes. Instead of smug righteousness, our model should be Aldo Leopold's woodsman, knowing that he has made and will continue to make mistakes, changing his behavior as his understanding of the land and his effect on it grows, but always earnestly dedicated to "writing [a] signature on the face of land" that is as respectful and graceful as he then knows how to make it.

A careful dedication to both scrupulous truthfulness and genuine humility would go a long way to putting the Green movement on the sound footing it needs to meet the challenges that lie ahead.

Second Commandment: Be Hopeful and Articulate a Positive Vision

Over a decade ago, the directors (of which I was one) of a regional environmental organization met with a direct-mail consultant who presented the letter he proposed we mail to thousands of residents. *"Your children are being POISONED,"* it read. *"The air you breathe and water your drink are THREATENED. Special interests conspire to ROB YOU of your quality of life."* It went on in this breathless vein. The consultant, a leading expert whom we were paying handsomely, cowed most of the directors into uncomfortable acquiescence. After a while, one of our group suggested that we might note that the Hudson Valley was still beautiful and thus worth saving. Another suggested we note the remarkable ecological recovery of the Hudson River over the previous twenty years. The consultant looked at them as if they were idiots and explained patiently that if our objective was to raise money we had to "scare the bejeezus out of them." If our short-term objective was to maximize the number of $15 contributions sent in response to direct mail, "scaring the bejeezus" might be the right approach. But if our objective is to deepen support for the Green agenda and motivate a broad spectrum of citizens, we need to stop trying to scare them, and start projecting a message of hope. Don Melnick, an environmental biologist at Columbia University, put it this way: "We need to bury the notion that the biological world is going to collapse and we're all going to be extinct. That's nonsense, and it can make people feel the situation is hopeless. We can't have people asking, 'So why should we bother?'"[8]

Ted Nordhaus and Michael Shellenberger struck a chord with

most Greens when they observed that Martin Luther King Jr. said "I have a dream" and propelled a movement that took us from segregation to an African-American president in forty years, while the Green movement has been saying "I have a nightmare" and forty years on is stuck in a rut. We need a dream that inspires and motivates Americans of all political persuasions, and that dream cannot be the traditional Green call for limits and sacrifice to avoid disaster. If we are to reconnect environmentalism with a significant number of conservatives and deepen the commitment of all Americans to the cause, a positive vision is critical.

Above all, that vision should be hopeful. The hope I am advocating is different from the unrealistically utopian hope that even the gloomiest Greens sometimes serve up, such as the suggestion that it will all come right when we let go of greed, abandon capitalism, or discard anthropocentric ethics. The hope I am advocating is not utopian; it is grounded in actual accomplishments and achievable within a time frame to which people can relate. For example, a river-based NGO obeying this commandment would not base its messaging on a nightmare of fish extinctions and growing non-point-source pollution, but would educate people about how the prior generation took an open sewer and turned it back into a swimmable river in twenty years, and how peoples' efforts now can make it even cleaner and better in just another decade or two. The International Union for Conservation of Nature (IUCN) adopted this approach when, after publishing for fifty years the alarming "Red List" of species threatened with extinction, it chose in 2014 to begin publishing a "Green List" of well-managed protected habitats that are contributing to the recovery of endangered species and ecosystems.

A hopeful vision, to be effective, must paint a clear picture of the destination. What exactly does success look like? The destination must appear compelling and desirable to ordinary Americans, who also must believe that it is achievable.[9] Unfortunately, "the vision thing" has been as troubling to the Green movement as it was to the first President Bush. We can paint a vivid picture of swamped coastal cities, violent storms, dead oceans, and mass extinctions. But if people support the Green agenda, then what? What *reward* follows the sacrifices?

It's not that hard. Once we get comfortable that our movement is one that puts people first, then the answers are obvious: Our vision is of a planet that allows humans to flourish. Our vision is of a future of revolutionary improvements to human health and longevity resulting from both the absence of disease-causing toxins from the environment and remarkable improvements in medicine. Our vision is of generations of children—whether urban, suburban, or rural—for whom the medical, mental, and imaginative benefits of exposure to nature are restored as an essential part of childhood. Our vision is of healthy and vibrant cities, reinvented to deeply integrate the experience of green spaces into urban life and to achieve sustainable symbiosis with the communities that surround them and the resources needed to sustain them. And our vision is of a human civilization lifted up, brought together, and ennobled by having saved and cared for all the other life forms with which we share the planet.

Third Commandment: Compromise and Incrementalism Are Okay

Bill Clinton recently said of the U.S. Constitution, "[I]t ought to be subtitled: 'Let's make a deal.'"[10] He's right. But the Green movement has for decades been led by policy experts who are confident that their policies present the best solutions to environmental issues and who often are unwilling to consider alternatives, or accept incremental progress when a comprehensive solution is not possible. Green advocates have appeared to many to prefer confrontation to compromise, and Green colleagues are often harsh in criticizing others who accept partial solutions or show willingness to deviate from the movement's ask in order to show some progress.[11]

Even after the fact, Green orthodoxy often paints landmark compromises as failures. David Brower, longtime head of the Sierra Club, came to regret the deal that saved Dinosaur National Monument because it involved a compromise that permitted a single dam at the spectacular Glen Canyon.[12] Rejection of compromise is deeply embedded in the DNA of the more radical part of the movement. Earth First!, for example, has as its slogan "No compromise in the defense of Mother Earth." And although the rest of the movement does not share the approach of these more radical groups, their rhetoric echoes in the consciences of mainstream Greens. As a result, among Greens purity too often is prized above pragmatism. The former president of the Izaak Walton League complains bitterly about some of his colleagues in the Green movement, where, he says, "people often want to be viewed as the most holy defender of the faith, rather than the most effective at making progress."[13]

The Green movement has had a particular problem accepting incrementalism, although recent history is filled with examples, such as the gradual tightening of fuel efficiency and auto emissions standards, that are successful models of exactly this approach. In some cases opposition to incremental gain is strategically sound, or is simply a tactic designed to improve and broaden the scope of a law or rule. But when it results in positive legislation or regulation being stalled or killed, with no realistic hope of anything better replacing it, then it is a mistake. When motivated by pure politics, such as the desire to deny the Republicans an environmental victory, then it is a betrayal of our environmental mission for partisan gain.

Greens also sometimes seem to take pride in spewing out "big thinking" without regard to its political feasibility. Gus Speth, for example, wrote, "If someone says these proposals are impractical, or politically naïve, then I would respond that we need impractical answers."[14] These habits—reluctance to compromise, distrust of incrementalism, and insufficient attention to pragmatism—have contributed to the movement's failures and resulted in missed opportunities to make at least some progress on climate change. Any well-managed organization should insist that results define success. If the perfect policy is dead on arrival as a political matter, then compromise. The environmental movement is funded by its supporters to make a difference in the environment. So figure out what is achievable and go for that, even if it means you are negotiating with yourself, compromising before you sit down at the table with the other side, or "thinking small," all of which have been cardinal sins in many NGO cultures. Incremental progress is progress, and progress is what is urgently needed.

Many Green NGOs already have taken these criticisms to heart. The country is filled with Green leaders who manage for results and not rhetoric, and have the courage to accept incremental solutions, forge genuine partnerships with their peers, and accept compromise. A notable example is Ned Sullivan, a former commissioner of the environment for the State of Maine, who now leads Scenic Hudson, one of the country's most respected regional environmental groups. He has relentlessly focused on outcomes and created a culture in which the best possible deal with a developer, polluter, or government authority is preferred over a worse result whose only advantage is sparing the organization from having to sully itself with compromise.

Fourth Commandment:
Accept the Imperative of Growth

William McDonough, coauthor of an influential book calling for a rethinking of the conventions of our material culture, *Cradle to Cradle*, put the fourth commandment pretty clearly: "The growth/

no-growth argument is specious. Growth is good. The question is how do you want to grow."[15]

The Green movement must finally repudiate the so-called IPAT formula discussed in chapter 6. There is no doubt that an increasing population is positively correlated with environmental impact. But it is now equally clear that affluence is a mixed bag, increasing demand for energy and materials, but at the same time providing resources to protect the environment and expanding the class of people free from material needs and thus more likely to prioritize saving nature. And, most fundamentally, we now understand that technological advance should not be viewed by Greens primarily as contributing to environmental harm (as it was during the industrialization of the American economy), but instead should be seen as providing the means to mitigate environmental impact, and, in the view of many Bright Greens, as our only hope for avoiding planetary disaster. Should anyone be surprised that twenty-first-century Americans have failed to maintain their enthusiasm for a movement that has preached against both wealth and technology?

The environmental movement must adapt both its policies and its language to acknowledge that humankind for the foreseeable future will and should pursue economic growth as the main means to alleviate poverty and satisfy the aspirations of millions of people for the dream of middle-class comfort. We should banish the language of scarcity and the dark warnings about the consequences of affluence. Instead, the Green movement should be talking about the *kind* of growth and affluence to which the world should aspire—an affluence that brings the health and happiness that only careful stewardship of nature will allow. We can advance environmental agendas by linking them in an authentic nontrivial way to growth and employment (i.e., something more than a superficial promise of "green jobs"). Franklin Roosevelt did this brilliantly to create broad support for his conservation programs among working-class voters.[16]

This commandment does not require capitulation to arguments against specific Green policies on the ground that they limit economic activity. It does not mean that Greens should accept a hierarchy where short-term economic needs trump sustainability. What the fourth commandment asks is that we deny our opponents the ammunition to paint the Green movement as being opposed to affluence or indifferent to poverty, a place from which we cannot hope to garner the popular and political support to achieve our goals.

Fifth Commandment: Accept Capitalism

Although the Green movement largely has come to terms with the capitalist system and the need to work within the framework of market economics, a mix of old-school Greens and new radicals such as Naomi Klein provide fresh provocation to conservatives who believe that the Green menace, like the Red, is fundamentally hostile to a market economy. One of the Green movement's highest priorities should be to repudiate the idea that planetary salvation requires that we transcend capitalism—because it is spectacularly bad politics, and because it is wrong. This means being careful not to entangle the environmental message with the messages of thoughtful progressives who are asking tough questions about unfettered market capitalism.

The responsible core of the Green movement has a good track record of openness to market-based mechanisms (like cap-and-trade), and the movement hosts a vigorous subculture of free-market environmentalism focused on the promotion of market-based solutions. Nonetheless, environmentalists must still work hard to overcome the perception developed over decades that they know only the mantra of "mandate, regulate, and litigate." This means embracing market-based solutions not only as a compromise when regulatory mandates are unachievable, but recognizing that there are various situations—like the hugely successful cap-and-trade system for sulfur, or the use of owned quotas to eliminate overfishing—where a market-based mechanism will do a better job, and do it more efficiently.

Prices and markets can help us set priorities and be more efficient. But while the market can be your friend, it must not be your master. I do not accept the premise, suggested by some on the right, that free-market environmentalism is always superior to what they call "political environmentalism." Markets do not always on their own tell us what is worth saving. Many economists agree that the willingness of consumers to pay for environmental goods and services is not the correct measure of their value;[17] indeed the task of the Green movement is not only to correct market failures where nature is not correctly valued, but to save those things, like beauty, which cannot be priced.[18]

So there are two critical corollaries to the fifth commandment. First, don't fall into the trap of fetishizing markets or market solutions. Second, never talk about the calculus of the market as if it were the only calculation that matters. It is almost always appropriate, per the seventh commandment, to combine the language of the market with the language of morality and values.

Sixth Commandment: Business Is Not the Enemy

During the formative years of the Green movement, the principal enemy was the free-riding, polluting, and regulation-resisting corporate sector. During this period the movement acquired an antibusiness reputation. This needs to change. Greens of course still need to criticize and litigate against corporate miscreants, but engagement with business is more likely to advance Green goals than generalized bashing of business, and can play an important role in reconnecting conservatives with conservation. This view is shared by many of the movement's supportive critics. Jared Diamond's opinion, for example, is that "if environmentalists aren't willing to engage with big businesses, which are the most powerful forces in the modern world, it won't be possible to solve the world's environmental problems."[19]

Of course, engagement requires openness on both sides. Individual businesses can set powerful examples of enlightened environmental leadership. When they do this, even imperfectly, they must be encouraged. But when it comes to the efforts of business, environmental groups have a tendency to see the glass as half empty. Too often when a company makes a start by, say, reducing its greenhouse gas emissions by 10 percent, the response from the environmental community is, "Not enough." An executive vice president of Southern Company, a major utility, commented, "If tomorrow we announced we were shutting down 25% of our plants to put in new, high-tech scrubbing devices, the headline would be, 'Why not the other 75%?' We don't get credit for what we've done, or for what we're going to do."[20]

Many environmentalists remain wary of corporate partnerships and corporate support. Wariness is understandable, as no Green group wants to be accused of "greenwashing" (lending its name and a Green patina to a corporate product or practice that is not truly sustainable) or to seem to be pulling its punches as the result of corporate contributions. But many Green NGOs have learned to do corporate engagement well, and there are many models to follow. The Environmental Defense Fund, for example, has been deeply engaged with the corporate community for years, since working with McDonald's in the 1990s to eliminate Styrofoam clamshell packaging, and many other companies since then, including Walmart, FedEx, and DuPont. EDF has long understood that the global footprint of a multinational corporation, and the ability of companies like Walmart to leverage change in their vast network of suppliers, allows Green organizations to achieve impact at a scale that would be impossible without these types of partnerships. Another example is NRDC, which has a partnership with Walmart and H&M to incentivize the

Chinese textile manufacturers that are their suppliers to reduce pollution. In all these cases, Green NGOs have chosen to work with corporations when doing so can further the NGO's mission, but view themselves as remaining free to criticize their corporate partners when their practices fall short. This is the model to follow.

A corollary to the sixth commandment is that Greens need to be clearer about their expectations of conduct by business, particularly about what it means for businesses to function more sustainably. I believe the movement would do well to unite behind the principles first advocated in the late 1990s by Paul Hawken, Amory Lovins, and L. Hunter Lovins, and outlined in their book *Natural Capitalism, Creating the Next Industrial Revolution.*[21] Despite the passage of more than fifteen years, their principles of "natural capitalism" are still the best framework for making business more sustainable. The first calls on business to increase radically the efficiency with which it uses all resources, which would slow the depletion of those resources, decrease pollution, and decrease corporate costs. The second suggests that companies should mimic biological systems by eliminating waste that involves disposal costs, in favor of outputs that can serve as inputs for some other system or function and thus can be sold, and produce revenues, for the disposing enterprise (an example would be a manufacturing plant selling its excess steam or heat output to a neighboring electric cogeneration facility). The first two of these principles are unequivocally "win-win," meaning they describe corporate conduct that would both increase profits as well as protect the environment. The third principle is more complicated: it calls for businesses to account for and reinvest in the "natural capital" on which they depend. Take, for example, a piece of unfragmented rain forest that serves as habitat for pollinator bees that increase the yield of an adjoining coffee plantation. The plantation gets the benefits, but doesn't book the costs of the pollinators (mainly the costs of preserving their forest habitat). The third principle calls for the coffee plantation to invest in (or pay the government or others who protect) the unfragmented rain forest that supports the pollinating bees.[22]

If Greens unite around these three principles—making resource use more efficient, opposing hidden subsidies, and insisting that all costs be accounted for fully—they are making capitalism stronger in the short term and more sustainable in the long term. In this they should find common cause with conservatives.

Another valuable framework for Green advocacy in relation to business conduct lies in the realm of risk management. Well-managed corporations are proficient at identifying and quantifying risks that could affect their businesses, and then working to mitigate those risks where economic to do so. This risk orientation could make certain corporations natural allies of environmentalists, whose essential mission also is to focus decision makers on long-term risks and how to mitigate their impact. The potential for this synergy was demonstrated in June 2014 when a bipartisan array of sophisticated businessmen, including former treasury secretaries George Shultz, Robert Rubin, and Henry Paulson, joined with Michael Bloomberg and billionaire climate crusader Thomas Steyer in publishing the "Risky Business Report," outlining—in the language of risk assessment, with which business is most comfortable—the potential impact of climate change on U.S. business and the economy.[23] The report examines climate-change impact on a much more granular basis than is typical, focusing on specific industries and regions, and attempting to quantify the potential costs and losses, discounting various risks for probability and time. If the risk analysis is credible, then most well-run businesses will follow whatever the economics suggest, i.e., by investing in loss prevention or mitigation if the costs of those steps are less than the discounted present value of the probability-adjusted amount of the prospective loss.

The sixth commandment requires that we stop the bashing of business in general as the cause of environmental problems, praise businesses and industries when they do the right thing, and criticize them when they don't. It asks that Greens partner with corporations when there is an authentic basis for mutual benefit, urge companies to achieve sustainability by adopting the three principles of "natural capitalism," and find creative ways to provide corporations with the credible data and analysis needed to make economically sound decisions with respect to future environmental risks.

Seventh Commandment:
Make the Moral Case for Conservation

In 2012 a Stanford psychologist and Berkeley sociologist published a paper, "The Moral Roots of Environmental Attitudes," outlining the results of their research into environmental polarization. Their study confirmed that morality plays a critical role in the development of attitudes in relation to environmental issues, and that moral appeals can be a powerful lever in convincing people to change those attitudes.[24] As they explained in the *New York Times,* "[P]ro-environmental messages specifically targeting conservative values could close the moral gap and persuade conservatives to join the environmental cause."[25] The authors noted that the moral messages most compelling to conservatives, such as those revolving around patriotism, respect for authority, sanctity, and purity, were those least used in the Green movement messaging that they studied.

Conservatives tend to see most public policy issues as having a moral dimension. Tapping into this moral sensibility is one of the few things that might overcome the virulence of the anti-Green convictions planted in conservative minds by the Great Estrangement. As a result, Greens must get comfortable with making the moral case for environmentalism, and must learn to make it better. What does this commandment require? We must commit ourselves to being a movement that puts people first and is perceived to do so. This means sweating the small things and taking scrupulous care in communications. Some Green organizations, for example, no longer use photographs of natural places without people in them. And while continuing our hard-hitting arguments based on science and economics, we must supplement those arguments in almost every case with the moral case for our policies and become comfortable and proficient in the language of moral reasoning. Greens should avoid provocative soft claims about the intrinsic value of nature, and instead appeal to easily understood virtues such as prudence, responsibility, humility, generosity, courage, and patriotism.

Eighth Commandment:
Avoid Mission Creep

Stick closely to the environmental mission that you exist to support, leave the rest of the progressive agenda to others, but don't hesitate to partner with others when there is an authentic basis for partnership and cooperation will serve to advance your own agenda.

This commandment flies directly in the face of an influential strain of Green thinking that calls on Greens to align with and support the broader progressive movement, typified by Gus Speth's admonition that "the first watchword of the new environmental politics is 'broaden the agenda' . . ."[26] And what is that agenda? According to Speth, it is the agenda of "the international social movement for change—which refers to itself as 'the irresistible rise of global anti-capitalism'—[a movement for] peace, social justice, community, ecology, feminism—a movement of movements. . . ."[27] This strain of thinking will result in the permanent alienation of moderates and conservatives from the Green cause, needlessly entrench the hyperpartisan divide over Green issues, and be a disaster for the planet. Millions of moderate and conservative Americans stand ready to support and work for critical elements of the Green agenda, but tell them they need to sign up for your positions on income inequality, or indeed the entirety of the global anticapitalism agenda, and you will lose them. I guarantee that you will lose me. Close focus on a specific, well-defined mission is the tried-and-true model for achieving social change. Greens advocating for the merging of environmentalism into a broad progressive agenda ignore the powerful historical examples of successful single-issue organizations and movements, such as those dedicated to female suffrage, civil rights for African-Americans, labor rights, and others.

The corollary to this commandment is that avoiding mission creep in your own organization does not preclude, and may even advance, the strategic imperative of seeking nontraditional partners from outside the environmental movement. Many Green groups have teamed up with others, for example, the Blue/Green Alliance of the Sierra Club and the United Steelworkers, which now has attracted other Green NGOs and labor unions. A Green group working on toxins might team up with a breast cancer advocacy group such as Breast Cancer Action, which is focused on the connection between environmental toxins and breast cancer—an authentic partnership although the two organizations have different missions. Such a partnership does not require the environmental group to be in the breast cancer "business," or the members of the breast cancer group to be comfortable with supporting a broad environmental agenda. Indeed, the partnership probably would not be advanced by mission creep on either side; with their separate missions, the organizations are not competitors and do not have overlapping and potentially nonaligned positions on issues.[28]

Ninth Commandment:
Connect and Mobilize

The failure to advance carbon cap-and-trade in 2010 brought us face-to-face with the Green movement's lack of political capital, which in turn resulted at least in part from the shallowness of public support for environmentalism. This was not from lack of effort, which included the three-year campaign by Al Gore's Alliance for Climate

Protection, designed to organize and energize ten million grassroots activists in support of carbon legislation. But the efforts were largely ineffective, and some scholars claim that failure to engage a mass grassroots constituency is now emblematic of the Green movement, sharply distinguishing it from other successful social movements, including those opposing the war in Vietnam and supporting civil rights. Thoughtful Green insiders are urging a change in course.

Manipulative messaging based on polling and focus groups results in shallow public opinions. This means those opinions are easily dislodged by the next well-crafted message to come along, and are not deep enough to motivate the political mobilization that is necessary. On the other hand, if Greens listen, connect, and engage, then at least some of the people will develop a more authentic attachment to the issues. The odds are higher that they will care (as opposed to just saying they care), and care enough to act.

The ninth commandment calls on the Green movement to transform itself from a movement whose most obvious manifestation is the hundreds of scientists, lawyers, and lobbyists sitting inside the Beltway (what one scholar called "bodiless heads")[29] to a truly national network of millions of committed and passionate local citizens, rooted in their local places, as diverse as America, who fully understand the political dimension of their cause and who engage regularly with their representative and senators. Statewide and national Green NGOs should have networked and empowered local chapters in which their members can interact in person. Research by political analysts has shown that "federated structures" (where local and state chapters are in the lead, loosely coordinated by a national headquarters) are the best way to advance political agendas.

The campaign to mobilize millions of grassroots foot soldiers for the environment must not be left to the more militant forces on the left, and it must not focus exclusively on global warming. We need to take the passion and commitment of 350.org, which has been largely misdirected to the symbolic campaign against Keystone XL, and spread it to other parts of the Green movement. By harvesting the passion that exists, in red states and blue states, on issues as diverse as water quality, food quality, wildlife, farmland preservation, and recycling, we can ignite voters to whom moderate and even conservative Republican politicians will listen and ensure that there are Green activists in every "safe" GOP congressional district. And, most critically, there should be no expectation that all our supporters must accept the entirety of the Green agenda, or any particular prescription for what to do in response to climate change.

Tenth Commandment: Embrace Cities

Today, over 80 percent of Americans live in cities. The depopulation of our cities with the rise of suburbia has now reversed itself, with millennials, families, and even retirees returning to urban centers in what Columbia professor and architect Vishaan Chakrabarti calls a "historic urban reordering."[30] According to Chakrabarti, 90 percent of our gross domestic product and 86 percent of American jobs are generated in cities, which make up only 3 percent of the land area of the continental United States.[31] How have cities been viewed by Greens? William Cronon, a leading historian of the movement, has observed that environmentalists all too often have viewed "the city as fallen, corrupt, polluted, unnatural," an example of what results when Green prescriptions are not followed.[32] For far too long, the whole subject of cities as ecosystems, together with the ecological aspects of the "transects" that run from city center through suburbia and into rural areas, have been marginalized by both conservation science and urban planning.[33] This must change for two basic reasons.

First, the ability of America to absorb the projected increase in population in a sustainable manner depends largely on our ability to accommodate new Americans in healthy and livable cities. America's population is slated to grow by 100 million people by mid-century.[34]

If climate change is the sword of Damocles that will hang over our heads during the second half of the twenty-first century, this demographic fact poses a similar threat for the first half. Simply put, if these new people spread themselves over the landscape in exactly the same way in which the growing population did during the second half of the twentieth century, we would lose more than two million acres of land every year to sprawling development, with severe environmental consequences. The good news is that it doesn't have to happen, and we know exactly how to prevent it: attract most of those new Americans to live in cities by making those cities healthy, livable, verdant, and vibrant.

The second reason the Green movement needs to embrace cities is to gain the attention and support of urban populations. To gain the support of the 80 percent of Americans who live in cities, we must appeal to their interests. Environmentalists, should they turn their sights to the ecology of cities, have a great deal to contribute to the project of accommodating density within an urban framework that is sustainable, healthy, and pleasing. But we also must do a far better job than we have to date in helping urbanites to understand and appreciate the services provided to them by healthy ecosystems in and around their cities, including clean water, fresh air, local food, and the buffering of floodwaters. The division between urban planning and rural conservation must be demolished, since the areas around cities provide these ecosystem services, and the cities and their countrysides are necessary partners in the search for sustainability.

The tenth commandment calls on Greens to recruit city dwellers into a diverse and national community of stewardship uniting urban, suburban, and rural citizens in common cause. A number of Green NGOs, most prominently The Trust for Public Land, are already ramping up their urban efforts. The Nature Conservancy's chief scientist wrote recently, "Conservation is facing a crisis of irrelevance—it is an enterprise that is not urgent to most people. If conservation is to build the support it needs, it must energize young urban dwellers, who now make up most of the world. The best way to get city people to care about conservation is to do conservation where they live, so that nature is seen as relevant and connected to modern life."[35] Lewis Mumford, in his 1961 *The City in History,* wrote that cities are "a symbol of the possible." Cities will both enable and inspire an invigorated Green movement in the twenty-first century.

─────────────

When Moses brought the original Decalogue down from Mount Sinai, most of the injunctions in the new rule book would have been familiar to the people of Israel and many of the commandments were already widely obeyed. So it is here. Many of my "commandments" for the Green movement are followed, in varying degrees, by environmental NGOs. Many individual Green movement leaders are passionate and articulate advocates for certain of these ideas— some, like EDF's Fred Krupp, for decades. I offer the codification of this modest reform agenda in the hope that it will be a useful checklist for leaders and members of Green NGOs, especially those who have decided to pursue a strategy of outreach to Republicans and conservatives. If that strategy is to succeed, at the level of either the national movement or individual organizations, Greens must get their own house in order first. This Green decalogue is a way to start.

A MODEL FOR CENTER GREEN

The Land Trust Movement in America

The late Senator Daniel Patrick Moynihan said, "The central conservative truth is that it is culture, not politics, that determines the success of a society. The central liberal truth is that politics can change a culture and save it from itself." Partisan politics is largely responsible for creating the culture where hostility to environmentalism took root, and thus political leadership, particularly on the right, is now required to restore a culture of conservation.[1] To "change [the] culture and save it from itself" we must refresh the core conservative belief that each of us has a moral duty not to steal from the commons or our common future, either by use of resources we haven't paid for or by the imposition of costs on future generations. Promotion of this common conviction should not be a heavy lift, as the values that are its source already are embedded deeply in America's civil, religious, and political culture. It will require a reinvigorated Green movement that can articulate these values in a compelling way and inspire Americans to embrace them. It also will require political leaders willing to feed the public's hunger for bipartisan action and effective government by advancing a moderate but meaningful Green agenda designed to appeal to the mass of nonpartisan Americans. This moderate but meaningful agenda, a path forward through the paralyzing eddies of the hyperpartisan vortex, is what I refer to as Center Green.

A key to understanding Center Green is to understand what it is not. First, it is not ideologically centrist. It is not ideological at all, but looks both to right and left for pragmatic solutions that would be acceptable to both sides. Center Green is not a new paradigm or a specific initiative like the Breakthrough Institute's ambitious "Apollo Project."[2] I am not proposing, as many of the Post-Greens do, to "look beyond the issue categories of the past and embrace a grand new vision for the future."[3] The Green movement has had a propensity to propose ever-grander and more comprehensive solutions, exactly the kinds of revolutionary nonincremental change that traditionalist conservatives so distrust. Time and time again we have seen conservatives run the other way when told that climate change mandates the rapid implementation of a "grand new vision." In contrast, Center Green is a modest change in approach rooted in the way America is, and not a utopian vision of what it could become. It is, above all, pragmatic and nonideological; policy is measured not by whether it is the optimum solution, but by the two-part test of whether it would make a meaningful contribution to an environmental problem and whether it is achievable politically.

To those who say that making common cause between liberals and conservatives will be too difficult in practice, I point to one corner of the Green movement where liberals and conservatives already work happily together in 1,700 Green organizations in forty-nine states. What is this proven working model of Center Green?

———————

Here's a quiz: What environmental legislation was supported by the National Rifle Association, the National Cattlemen's Beef Association, the Environmental Defense Fund, The Nature Conservancy and sixty-one other groups? What environmental tax incentive appeared in both President Bush's FY2009 budget and President Obama's FY2010 budget? What environmental legislation in the 112th Congress—by some measures the most partisan in history—attracted a bipartisan coalition of 339 senators and representatives, and was cosponsored by the majority of both Republicans and Democrats in the House of Representatives? What tax bill had more cosponsors than any other tax bill in the 113th Congress? What is one of the very few things that President Obama and the House Republicans came together to support in 2014? The answer to all of these questions is the same: legislation providing a tax incentive for farmers, ranchers, and other property owners to conserve their lands through the donation of a conservation easement to a land trust or governmental organization. And therein lies a story.

Over the same quarter century when environmentalism as a whole was crippled by the Great Estrangement, one part of the Green movement—land conservation—grew rapidly, enjoyed victories at the ballot box and in state legislatures around the country, received bipartisan support in Congress, attracted grassroots enthusiasm in both the red and blue parts of the country, and achieved its goals with greater success than even its staunchest proponents had dared to imagine. In the thirty years between 1980 and 2010, land groups permanently protected about fifty million acres of conservation lands, about the same area as is protected by the entire National Park Service, and equal to the land areas of the states of Pennsylvania, Maryland, New Jersey, Delaware, and Connecticut combined. The organizations responsible for this success, land trusts, grew from only a handful in 1980 to about 1,700 today. How did this happen, and what lessons does the story hold for the Green movement today?

The land, water, and air that make up the environment on this planet are all essential for human life, and the quality of each is closely correlated to human health and quality of life. The modern environmental movement has been associated in the public mind mainly with only two of the three: protection of the quality of water and air. But from the origins of the Republic to well into the twentieth century conservation focused primarily on land, the home place of humans. Americans did not need scientists to explain the scarcity and thus preciousness of the land. Will Rogers put it succinctly— "Buy land, they ain't making any more of the stuff"—and everyone understood exactly what he meant. Issues of the allocation and use of land were core political issues from the earliest days of European settlement. And a core strain of that political conversation has been the question of whether all land should be regarded as a commercial commodity to be allocated and used solely in accordance with the dictates of the market, or whether some land should be treated differently and set aside for the public benefit. In 1634, for example, Bostonians (at least the male heads of household who had the vote) voted to tax themselves to fund the purchase of the Boston Common—valuable urban land that would be dedicated to providing the community with shared benefits, initially military training and common pasturage, and eventually recreation.

For most of our history, this instinct to set aside land for the public benefit was given its main expression by governmental action to acquire land for the public, such as the bold decision to carve out the heart of Manhattan to create Central Park, and the equally farsighted move to protect Yosemite as a state park in 1864, Yellowstone as a national park in 1872, and the other national parks that followed. America's vast stock of federal lands other than parks resulted from the unique history of our national expansion westward. The federal government acquired title to frontier lands from the original thirteen colonies as well as original title to the massive areas purchased from Spain, France, and others. Even today, vast tracts of land in the West (typically 20–40 percent of a western state, and over 60 percent of Idaho, Utah, and Nevada) are maintained in public ownership, principally through the federal Bureau of Land Management and U.S. Forest Service. Much of that land is leased to ranchers and otherwise exploited by private enterprise for its timber and mineral resources, and thus is not managed primarily for conservation purposes. Even so, the extensive federal holdings of land in the west led to public frustration at having to deal with a distant bureaucracy as landlord and regulator, which frustration then morphed into ideological antipathy to public ownership and became a contributing cause of the Great Estrangement.

Although public land conservation was caught up in the ideological tempest of the Great Estrangement, its far-less-well-known little sister, private land conservation, was left largely unscathed. Fittingly, private land conservation in America started with our great proponent of agrarian virtue and limited government, Thomas Jefferson. In 1774, Jefferson acted alone to preserve one of the great natural features of the Commonwealth of Virginia, the so-called Natural Bridge. He purchased the land for the primary purpose of protecting this unique landscape feature and during his life brought many visitors to admire it. In 1815, when pressured to sell the property, Jefferson declined, explaining: "I view it in some degree as a public trust, and would on no consideration permit the bridge to be injured, defaced or masked from public view."[4] As in so many things, Jefferson was prescient, and his idea of private land held "as a public trust" would come, two centuries later, to animate a vigorous private land conservation movement that itself served as a "natural bridge" between twenty-first-century Jeffersonian skeptics of big government and the left-tilting environmental movement as a whole.

In 1890 a descendant of one of the Boston "freemen" who had voted in 1634 to establish the Boston Common, Charles Eliot, wrote a letter to *Garden and Forest* magazine proposing the creation of a new statewide nonprofit organization that would be empowered by the state legislature to hold land free of taxes for the public to enjoy "just as a Public Library holds books and an Art Museum holds pictures." The legislature acted the following year, and the nation's first land trust, The Trustees of Reservations, was born, with its charter stating as its mission "acquiring and holding, maintaining and opening to the public . . . beautiful and historical places . . . within the Commonwealth."

The essential features of Charles Eliot's idea characterize the land trust movement today. As a supplement to state and local government action, Eliot envisioned that public-spirited citizens would mobilize private funds to protect precious lands for public benefit, in return for which they would be exempt from taxation. Today's Trustees of Reservations mission statement, which is similar to that of land trusts generally, is remarkably similar to its first charter, the principal change being the addition of a reference to ecological value: "The Trustees of Reservations preserve, for public use and enjoyment, properties of exceptional scenic, historic, and ecological value in Massachusetts."

The land trust movement grew steadily but slowly over the seventy years following the founding of The Trustees of Reservations, to approximately 130 land trusts by 1960.[5] But it wasn't until 1970 that the real hero of this story—an obscure legal instrument known as the "conservation easement"—started to receive the approval of state legislatures, and the private land conservation movement took off. It is not surprising that the modern land conservation movement took flight during the bipartisan environmental consensus of the 1970s. What is surprising—and most important—is that private land conservation, almost fifty years later, still enjoys the bipartisan embrace that the rest of the environmental movement has lost.

In the first year of law school students learn that ownership of land is not a single thing, but really a collection of different rights, usually explained by the metaphor of a "bundle of sticks." If I buy land "in fee simple" (the normal form of land ownership), I ordinarily acquire the whole bundle. But as owner I might decide to sell the right to cut the trees in my back woodlot, so out goes one stick. I might transfer to my neighbor the right to build his driveway across part of my land—out goes another stick. And then the town comes along and asks to build a well on my land and have an unlimited right to withdraw water from the aquifer: the price is good, so there goes another stick. The first-year law students get it: ownership of land is not one right, but a group of rights, many of which can be separately sold or transferred. Once the "bundle of sticks" metaphor is understood, the conservation easement is easy to grasp: the owner of a ranch can choose to transfer the right, say, to subdivide it for residential development and retain all the other "sticks," including the right to own, occupy, and use the land as a ranch. The transferred "stick" is a conservation easement, and it usually is held by a land trust, whose main job is to enforce it for the benefit of the public. For example, if twenty years later one of the owner's children, now the owner of the property, sought to subdivide the ranch and sell it to a developer, the land trust would have the right, and the duty, to take legal action to stop the transaction, since it—and not the heir— owns the right to subdivide and develop.

The creation of an easement for purposes of conservation was not known to the common law, and as a result the early efforts to use this tool to protect land were plagued by legal problems and uncertainty. As a result of these issues, most early land trusts, such as The Trustees of Reservations, simply purchased the land it wished to protect "in fee" (the whole "bundle of sticks"). This started to change in 1959 when a farsighted polymath named William H. Whyte, coiner of the term "groupthink" and author of the influential work on corporate culture, *The Organization Man,* wrote "Securing Open Space for Urban America: Conservation Easements," a pamphlet explaining and promoting the easement as a tool for conservation.[6] That same year, California led the way with the first legislation authorizing counties and cities to acquire "lesser interests" in land. Connecticut, Illinois, and Maryland soon followed suit. A decade later Massachusetts and Montana extended the idea to authorize private conservation entities to hold easements, and more than a dozen other states followed. The real breakthrough came in 1981, when the National Conference of Commissioners on Uniform State Laws, a nongovernmental body that provides model legislation for states, promulgated the Uniform Conservation Easement Act (UCEA). Within a few years, twenty-nine states had adopted the UCEA or a tailored statute to similar effect. Each statute was intended to address legal issues that had plagued conservation easements under common law and established a high degree of certainty for donors and recipients alike regarding the validity and enforceability of the easements. Today, every state except Wyoming has specific legislation providing a legal framework for private land conservation.

In parallel with the process of putting conservation easements on a firm legal footing, the tax treatment of donated conservation easements required clarification. As a general matter the charitable contribution of cash or property to certain tax-exempt organizations is deductible from income for federal income tax purposes, but the IRS took the view that to get a deduction for a donation of property, the donor must have donated his entire interest—the whole "bundle of sticks"—and not a partial interest like a conservation easement. Following a couple of incremental steps by the IRS, in 1980 Congress adopted Section 170(h) of the Internal Revenue Code, which provides that permanent easements for qualifying conservation purposes that are donated to qualified charitable organizations like land trusts would be treated like most other charitable donations, i.e., be deductible from income. So now, when the rancher donates the development rights to the ranch, an appraiser would calculate the value of the full "bundle of sticks" before the donation and the value of the remaining rights after the development rights stick had been donated to the land trust, and the difference is deemed to be the value of the "stick" that was donated, deductible as a charitable donation to the land trust. This basic tax benefit was complemented by a federal estate tax deduction starting in 1997 and by a variety of state tax credit programs, and in some cases partial relief from local property taxes.

The establishment of the conservation easement as a reliable conservation instrument, together with treating easement donations substantially the same as other charitable donations of property, led to the explosive growth of the land trust movement. From a base of about 130 land trusts in 1965, the number more than doubled by 1975 and grew to around 400 by the time federal tax deductibility was clearly available in 1981. Between 1981 and 2005, the number of land trusts grew at an annual rate of about 6 percent. The most recent "census" by the Land Trust Alliance reports 1,699 land trusts serving every state except North Dakota. They are estimated to have about five million members.[7]

What is the secret of the land trusts' success? And why has this corner of the environmental movement been able to retain the bipartisan support that the whole Green movement previously enjoyed? Most importantly, what lessons from the land conservation movement's success might help other Green NGOs reconnect conservatives with conservation?

Private land conservation's success in retaining right wing support cannot be attributed to its being uncontroversial, so like motherhood and apple pie as to sit unmolested, safely apart from the partisan wars. Like public land conservation, which gave rise to the Wise Use movement and even today fuels right-wing antipathy to environmentalism, private land conservation also results in land being placed permanently out of reach of drilling, mining, and other forms of environmentally harmful resource exploitation. It frustrates those who have most to gain from real estate development, a highly powerful and vocal constituency. As a result, the land trust movement has not been totally exempt from right-wing fire. The Heritage Foundation, Fox News, and various property-rights groups all occasionally vilify land trusts and conservation easements, sometimes quite harshly.[8] But unlike movement conservatism's efforts to undermine climate science, the EPA, toxics regulation, and so many other branches of environmentalism, its attack on private land conservation has failed to gain traction. Land trust boards and staffs all around the country are filled with conservatives and Republicans working with passion to protect natural areas in the places they live. So why has the antienvironmental campaigning of the right, so successful in general, failed to separate conservatives from private land conservation?

There appear to be three sets of reasons, each of which contains critical lessons for the Green movement as a whole. First, the benefits of private land conservation are obvious, local, and attractive to a diverse constituency. People come to the cause with many different motivations and interests. Some may be concerned about protecting water quality, others with preserving habitat for hunting and fishing. Some land trust board members are keen ecologists focused on preservation of habitat, others are determined to preserve rural character or their community's distinctive sense of place. The land trust movement is a big tent. There is no orthodoxy to which adherents must subscribe. Cattlemen determined to preserve a critical mass of ranch lands are no less valued as land stewards than a group of local moms equally determined to prevent development of a beloved local forest. It doesn't matter how they come to love the land, but in private land conservation people come together in common cause to save it.

Land trusts may sometimes need to talk about the bad things that will happen if natural or open land is lost to development, but more often their rhetoric is positive and inspiring. The most effective ones focus their missions around a community's vision for its future and the positive values they are seeking to promote, whether it is the health and social benefits of community gardens in disadvantaged urban neighborhoods; the distinctive character and culture of farm and ranchlands; or the clean water, fresh air, and recreational opportunities provided by large expanses of forest. All of them in their own distinctive ways are manifestations of "in my backyard" motivation. It is no accident that the tag line of the national Land Trust Alliance is "Together, Conserving the Places You Love."

Not only are the benefits of protecting land from development diverse, but they are most often immediate, local, and easily understood. We have reviewed how the Great Estrangement resulted in part from the Green movement's shift in focus from its initial agenda of pollution, which personally and directly afflicted millions of Americans, to a second-order agenda dealing with largely invisible and (until recently) seemingly remote issues like toxics and global warming. Part of the reason why private land conservation has retained the support of the right is that it shares the immediacy of that initial 1970s Green agenda. The loss of farmland and ranchland to development; the relentless march of subdivision as suburbs sprawl farther and farther from city centers; the seemingly endless appetite for second homes in previously remote ecologically and scenically spectacular places; the loss, one by one, of open spaces in cities where buildable lots are increasingly rare—all of these trends are highly visible to hundreds of millions of Americans, rural, suburban, and urban.

The second set of factors that explains the bipartisan appeal of private land conservation arises from the architecture of the movement. Edmund Burke's concept of "little platoons," manifest in the variety of local civic organizations that so dazzled Alexis de Tocqueville in his survey of early American life, is given full expression in the twenty-first century by the land trust movement. This architecture—numerous local organizations close to their communities and thus reflecting their diversity and values—has made the movement one in which both liberals and conservatives feel at home. It also has allowed land trusts to preserve the grassroots nature of the early environmental movement. Most of the nation's 1,700 land trusts are truly bottom-up organizations that had their start with concerned citizens sitting around a kitchen table to organize their friends and neighbors to protect a beloved piece of land. Although some land trusts have grown to be enormous and highly professional, according to the Land Trust Alliance 2010 census 65 percent of land trusts still have fewer than ten staff members and 47 percent of them remain all volunteer. As a result, most land trusts are not large NGOs where professional staff tell their members what to think and do, but community organizations with strong local roots and boards that serve as accurate barometers of community sentiment. In most cases these land trusts work with, and not against, a community's sense of what it wishes to be. It is the vision and passion of their members that drives their transactions, not the prescriptions of remote professional Greens. For the larger organizations, their determination of which parcels are worthy of conservation may be informed by sophisticated science, but at the end of the day even those judgments are validated by the willingness of the relevant community to come together with money and time to support their work.

"Local" can be defined in different ways, but this grounding at a non-national level is an essential character of the land trust movement. Most of these organizations are focused on a neighborhood, town, or county. Sometimes they are organized around a river, valley, mountain range, or other landscape feature. Even the largest national organizations, such as The Nature Conservancy, operate largely through state and substate chapters. At whatever level "community" is defined, an essential objective of most land trusts is to be viewed as a trusted community-based organization, not an outsider telling communities what to do.

The use by the movement of the term "trust" also provides a critical lesson for other Green groups. After the Trust for Public Land helped to save a group of community gardens in New York City, the local users of these previously vacant plots—now vibrant community centers—needed to establish organizations to assume responsibility for their stewardship and operation. These communities, largely minority populations in disadvantaged parts of the city, chose the land trust as their vehicle. As Demetrice Mills, founding president of the Brooklyn Queens Land Trust, told me, the concept of trust was key: the community gardeners required an organization that would hold the lands in trust for them, and that they in turn could trust. These new land trusts have flourished, earning and keeping the trust of their members, and demonstrating that the model can succeed in the most challenging urban environments.

The widely distributed and largely local nature of the land trust movement has not impaired its effectiveness on the national stage. Instead, paradoxically, the *local* nature of the organizations in the movement is the "secret sauce" that has led to *national* legislative victories. In 1981 four land trusts, the Brandywine Conservancy, Iowa Heritage Foundation, Maine Coast Heritage Trust, and Napa County Land Trust, with funding and support from a couple dozen other land trusts and philanthropies, organized the Land Trust Exchange (now called the Land Trust Alliance) to share information and best practices among members of the fledgling movement and, critically, to create a framework for joint action on policy matters of mutual interest. Land trusts started coming together in 1985 for an annual rally, attended by 257 people the first year, and now regularly attracting almost 2,000. Today, the Land Trust Alliance network has grown to 1,200 member organizations that act together in a highly effective manner to advocate for the movement's common agenda in Washington, D.C.[9] Private land conservation's remarkable record of federal legislative success results from the Alliance's ability to mobilize a network of local grassroots organizations in each relevant congressional district and state, ready and willing to explain to their representatives and senators the *local* benefits of—and local bipartisan support for—the federal tax incentives and other policies and laws that enable and support private land conservation. On Alliance lobby day the movement can produce as many Republicans as Democrats, and strong showings of local support in both red and blue congressional districts. The mobilization of large bipartisan majorities to enable the legislative outcomes described above could not have been achieved by any of the individual land trusts acting alone. Nor could they have been achieved by a Washington, D.C.–based NGO, no matter how large or skilled, that talked policy without the support of a national network of politically engaged grassroots organizations. The lessons for the balance of the Green movement are obvious.

The final set of reasons for the continuing appeal of private land conservation to conservatives arises from its defining characteristic: it is private. Although private land conservation achieves a result similar to that achieved when the government protects land by regulation or acquisition, the limited nature of governmental involvement, limited fiscal impacts, and voluntary and market-based nature of the transactions make all the difference in terms of conservative comfort. In the paradigm transaction, a land trust—a private charity operating mostly with privately donated charitable dollars—acquires a conservation easement or land in a completely voluntary transaction from a willing seller or donor. If the land trust acquires an easement, the land stays in the private economy (often as sustainably harvested timberlands or a working ranch or farm).

From the perspective of a conservative motivated to limit the government's size and role in the economy, and anxious about ceding to the government—rather than the market—decisions about resource allocation and use, there is much to admire in private land conservation. The main actors and decision makers are nongovernmental—public charities directly accountable to their charitable supporters who vote with their dollars. The transactions in most cases do not add to the stock of public land or the growth of government.[10] And the cost to the public of the public benefit achieved is minimized because a limited and targeted tax incentive (similar to that which incentivizes all charitable giving) costs the public fisc far less than outright purchase by the government of the same land.[11]

Critically, private land conservation dodges the right's antipathy toward government coercion and regulation. There is no expropriation or exercise of eminent domain. The typical private land conservation transaction constitutes the *exercise* of private property rights: landowners decide when and how they wish to sell or donate their

land or development rights and, if a sale, at what price. Every transaction is a market transaction, with a willing buyer and willing seller
(or donor and charity) coming together for mutual benefit. Finally,
when a conservation easement is used, the land, although protected,
remains in private ownership and the owner continues to pay property taxes to the local government (although in many enlightened
towns the amount of property tax is reduced to reflect the property's diminished value to the landowner). The transaction has not
contributed to the stock of government-owned land, the growth of
the public sector, or an extension of federal government control into
local matters.

That conservatives continue to support private land conservation is
undeniable and the reasons are easy to understand. The more difficult question is whether the things that have allowed the land trust
movement to retain bipartisan support can be deployed or adapted
by the broader Green movement to achieve the same results. I think
they can. Land trusts, like their Green brethren, seek to prevent a
"parade of horribles" (habitat loss, sprawl, degradation of water quality), but speak largely in positive terms about the values of natural
places and community character. Green NGOs can and should do
the same. Private land conservation, like environmentalists generally, advocates solutions that serve many ends, but unlike many
Green NGOs, welcomes and embraces supporters motivated by a single cause (birds, farms, fishing, community gardens, water quality).
Land trusts may work on forestry projects that sequester greenhouse
gases or waterfront projects necessary to adapt to sea level rise, but
they do so in a way that does not require their supporters to align
themselves with a specific public policy response to climate change.
This in turn has enabled the land trust movement to build a "big

tent," welcoming conservative sportsmen, ranchers, westerners, and southerners, without the condescension and inauthenticity that so often have characterized the approach of left-leaning Green NGOs seeking expedient partnerships with those same groups. Green NGOs can learn to do the same. The land trust movement employs an architecture in which truly grassroots organizations predominate, and are networked not in the parent/subsidiary model of big national Green NGOs and their local affiliates (if they have them), but in a nonhierarchical web that both empowers the local organizations and channels local passions into effective political action at the national level. The broader movement can take steps in this direction. And finally, the private land trust movement employs a tool kit that, for practical and not ideological reasons, prefers private, non-coercive, market-based solutions where possible. The private land conservation movement highly values our public lands and supports government investment in land protection, but when a cheaper and equally effective tool, such as a conservation easement, is available, cost and efficiency rule the day, not ideological predisposition. The broader Green movement easily could move further toward a similar pragmatism.

Interestingly, the land trust movement's record of attracting substantial bipartisan support includes situations where private market-based tools are not being used, and state and local governments are raising public funds to protect conservation lands. Since 1988, state and local ballot measures to raise funding for land preservation through borrowing or other revenue-raising measures have succeeded in both red and blue areas of the country, raising more than $70 billion in public funding to protect land ($13.2 billion of this amount was approved in 2014 alone). Over this time period, according to The Trust for Public Land's "LandVote" database, 76 percent of local, county, and state ballot measures to raise public funds for land protection were approved by the voters.[12] Remarkably, these measures have passed in red states, including Arkansas, Arizona, Alabama, Colorado, Iowa, Mississippi, and Missouri, and in years, such as 2010, when the GOP was strongly ascendant (forty-one of forty-nine land conservation ballot measures, or 84 percent, passed in 2010 at a time when the same voters were returning control of the House to the GOP and Democrats suffered significant losses in the Senate and many state legislatures).

This record of voter behavior over a sufficiently long period demonstrates that it is not the nongovernmental nature of private land conservation that is the key factor in attracting bipartisan support. Instead, these ballot measures, like the land trust movement generally, succeeded due to the power of passionate attachment to place, a positive value–based rhetoric, the building of broad coalitions of diverse interests, and the effective mobilization of grassroots community action. These measures most often were initiated and pursued by coalitions of local organizations, including land trusts, working in informal networks with support from national organizations like The Trust for Public Land and its affiliate The Conservation Campaign. Again, there is much here for the Green movement as a whole to study and emulate.

Writing after the end of a long career as an environmental leader, Paul Hansen argued that "[t]he success of land conservation provides a striking contrast to the gridlock of the last twenty years on environmental issues and the recent decline in the environmental issue's popularity. . . . The zenith of their success shows the power of respectful engagement and compromise in conservation and provides a stark contrast to the nadir of in-your-face environmentalism."[13] While the ability of the land trust movement to preserve bipartisan support through the Great Estrangement gives us hope and a model for the rest of the Green movement to emulate, skeptics will ask if there really is common ground between right and left on environmental issues other than private land preservation. There is. Center Green, though not sitting entirely within the sweet spot of consensus between right and left, constitutes a modest redirection of the Green agenda, a new way of talking about that agenda, and specific policy positions on the major environmental issues that taken together have a reasonable chance of attracting support from both sides of the aisle and moving the Green agenda forward.

13

CENTER GREEN

"We can move forward, and clean up our climate, and develop green technologies, and . . . alternative energies . . . for hybrid, for hydrogen, for battery-powered cars, so that we can clean up our environment and at the same time get our economy going by creating millions of jobs." These words were spoken during the second debate between presidential candidates Barack Obama and John McCain. Do you know by which one? If you think it sounds a lot like the message we have been hearing from President Obama, you are correct, but you are wrong about who said it. It was the nominee of the Republican Party. And it was John McCain who promised to reduce emissions of greenhouse gases to 60 percent below 1990 levels if elected and supported a carbon cap-and-trade system to achieve it. So when I argue that there is a Center Green approach that can attract significant support from both parties at the highest levels, I should not be discounted as naïve, as so many on both right and left will argue. Bipartisan agreement on Green issues breaks out from time to time despite the best efforts of ideologues on both sides to prevent it. And the political success of the national land trust movement in building a robustly bipartisan base of support proves it can be sustained.

There are five hallmarks of the approach I call Center Green:

> It is built on values shared by right and left and uses language that is welcoming to conservative Americans.
> It focuses on the environmental goals shared by right and left, and is pragmatic about the policy tools used to achieve those goals.
> It sympathizes with concerns on the right about excessive and dysfunctional environmental regulation and prioritizes regulatory reform, simplification, and quality of enforcement.
> It employs both science and morality in making the case for conservation action, and redefines sustainability in a way easily understood by and acceptable to a broad swath of the American pubic.
> It seeks to rebuild environmentalism as a mass grassroots movement oriented toward political action.

The foundational insight of Center Green is that the values that animate the call to environmental action are shared by right and left. Both right and left in America are comfortable talking about values. Some of this talk reveals ideological differences about things like economic equality, but others—such as equality of opportunity—are deeply held in common. This means we should start with that part of the Green agenda that is most clearly linked to values embraced by the right, and reorient the rhetoric of the Green movement in the direction of values and arguments with which the right is familiar and comfortable.

Environmentalism is fundamentally about the continuity of civilization, an intergenerational project that revolves around respect for our ancestors and a sense of deep responsibility to our descendants. These are universal values. We may have present priorities, but prudence dictates that these be subordinated to the broader cause of the continuity of civilization, and the success of the great American experiment in particular. Although we are a society more obsessed with personal and economic liberty than any in history, all but the most libertarian extremes agree that liberty is coupled with responsibilities and rights are coupled with duties. We know that our appetite for material things must be restrained, both individually and socially. We may have moments of greater and lesser comfort with boundless greed, but acknowledgment of Burke's "moral chains upon [our] appetites" is deeply woven into American culture. Center Green is not shy about saying so. The problem is not that Americans are unwilling to make sacrifices—even the most casual familiarity with history demonstrates the opposite. The problem is that Americans only make sacrifices for things they understand and believe in. And so Greens must bring the case home, and feel comfortable—as conservatives always have—invoking without embarrassment love of home, love of place, and love of country, inspiring people to protect the things they love.

Language matters, especially in the public arena and the pursuit of change. The fascinating neopragmatist philosopher Richard Rorty, who saw culture as conversation and imagination as the "central human faculty," argued that the "talent for speaking differently, rather than for arguing well, is the chief instrument of cultural change."[1] Simply put, if the Green movement is to reach the American people, we must learn to speak differently and embrace a language rich with values shared between right and left. The core message of environmentalism needs to speak vividly to the values and emotions of the millions of Americans who are not secular rationalists. We would do well to study the language of the Evangelical Climate Initiative, which said "To ignore [climate change] is unthinkable. To grasp the problem with faith and courage, and with the wind of American ingenuity and goodness at our back, is morally right. . . ."[2] These are warm and engaging words. What Green wouldn't want to have given a speech calling on the audience to face the issue with courage and faith, and to have invoked "the wind of American ingenuity and goodness at our back." This will be the language of Center Green, language that is rich with values, language that unites, and language that inspires.

Much of conservatism's hostility to environmentalism arises not from disagreement with its goals but from its discomfort with the policy prescriptions advanced by Green NGOs to meet those goals. Conservatives dislike regulation when market solutions are available, and prefer an approach that balances environmental gain with economic cost. Center Green accepts and even embraces a robust debate over the right tools to do the job—that is, after all, at the heart of politics in a democracy.

There exists a significant gulf between the sides when it comes to the question of what tools to deploy to achieve our common goals. Liberals and conservatives have different views regarding the size and role of government, and the optimum balance in the economy between regulation and laissez-faire. Too often these differences have eclipsed the fact of a shared appreciation of the underlying problem, and neither side has been willing to set aside its policy preference and reach a compromise. Greens too often have allowed their stubborn pursuit of the optimum solution to result in no solution at all.

Center Green takes a pragmatic approach to the dichotomy between market and regulatory solutions. The balance between the two should depend in each instance on the efficacy and efficiency of the available tools, and not on ideological preference. We should not capitulate to the tendency of the right to fetishize any solution carrying the "market" label; there are plenty of cases, such as the banning and limitation of toxics, where old-fashioned regulation is still the only effective means of protecting public health and the environment. But Center Green recognizes that political feasibility may well be the main driver of the choice. In situations where a preferred regulatory solution would be dead on arrival as a political matter, we should take up the market solution and at least make a start on addressing the problem. Equally, when a sound market solution (like carbon cap-and-trade) is rendered impossible by the politics of the moment, then a regulatory solution (such as President Obama's Clean Power Plan, which limits greenhouse gas emissions from power plants) deserves our support.

———————

Center Green recognizes that some of the complaints from the right about environmental regulation are justified, and advocates regulatory reform as a goal where right and left can find common cause. As early as 1995, Bill Clinton's widely respected EPA administrator, Carol Browner, who came back to the White House in the early days of the Obama administration, recognized that much of the right wing criticism of regulatory excess was justified: "[T]he past 25 years have left us with a complex and unwieldy system of laws and regulations and increasing conflict over how we achieve environmental protection. The result of this history? An adversarial system of environmental policy. A system built on distrust. And too little environmental protection at too high a cost."[3] She was right. A Center Green approach aims to fix this: reform and simplify environmental regulation to make it better and cheaper.

As part of a mutual project to achieve long-overdue regulatory reform, both Greens and conservatives can come together in support of the proposition that in general government regulation should

be kept at the lowest possible level. The Green slogan "think globally, act locally" has embedded within it the conservative idea that
even problems of global scope do not necessarily require global
solutions. Regulation that takes account of local conditions and
that is enforced at the local level is more sustainable than federal
regulation that requires exceptions for local circumstances and is
interpreted and enforced by officials who are remote and unaccount-
able. For example, preservation of the lobster fishery in Maine was
enhanced in the mid-1990s by largely replacing traditional regulation with a "co-management" system where local councils of fishermen took responsibility for setting caps on the numbers of traps and
other matters. Lobstermen themselves became the chief enforcers of
the system, and according to most reports compliance rose and the
fishery returned to health.

Regulatory reform is not all that is required. In order for crucial
environmental laws and regulations to be sustained, they must be
administered skillfully and fairly. Greens must pay close attention
to the competence, training, and budgets afforded to those called on
to administer our environmental laws and regulations at the state
and federal level. New York State's Department of Environmental
Conservation, for example, has been chronically underfunded and
understaffed.[4] Well-meaning state employees find it impossible to
enforce regulations comprehensively, fairly, and promptly. This frustrates both sides: industry bemoans slow and quixotic environmental permitting that results in needless costs, and Green groups are
outraged that environmental laws are not being enforced. Ensuring adequate staffing and funding for the agencies that administer
our environmental laws and improving the quality, fairness, and
competence of that administration is another area where business
and Greens can find common cause. And when regulators or courts
make an obvious error, Greens must join the chorus of complaint.
For example, each time a farmer working the same dry upland his

family has farmed for generations is told by a bureaucrat that it is now, for technical reasons, a regulated wetland, the story goes viral among conservatives, undermining support for the whole concept of wetland regulation. When stupid results like this emerge from the regulatory process, Greens should join farm groups, property rights groups, and others in speaking out against the result. The sustainability of environmental regulation depends on it.

———————

The idea that the right rejects science and the left rejects morality is nonsense. The American story is one of a nation equally attached to high ideals and the application of the scientific method to advance every aspect of life. In the trauma caused by climate failure, some "postenvironmentalists" have come to question science as the traditional touchstone for diagnosis of environmental problems and development of solutions. They point out that some Greens have ignored the contingent nature of scientific knowledge, and appear to have hoped that the scientific basis for our policy agenda would somehow exempt the environmental agenda from the messy process of democratic decision making and compromise. While these are both mistakes, they don't mean that science should be discarded as the foundation for environmental policy.

The Center Green approach I am advocating preserves the place of science at the heart of environmentalism but requires us to remind policy makers and the public that scientific understanding should be seen as a *process*. A Carnegie Commission report gave a rare and unusually clear statement of the nature of scientific knowledge: "Scientists view their work as a body of working assumptions, of contingent and sometimes-competing claims. Even when core insights are validated over time, the details of these hypotheses are subject to revision and refinement as a result of open criticism within the scientific communities. Scientists regard this gradual evolution of their theories through empirical testing as the pathway to the *truth* [emphasis in the original]."[5]

Aldo Leopold was sensitive to this point in developing his views regarding ecology specifically, arguing that "[t]he ordinary citizen today assumes that science knows what makes the [biotic] community clock tick; the scientist is equally sure he does not. He knows that the biotic mechanism is so complex that its workings may never be fully understood."[6]

Environmentalists do not serve their own interests when they ignore the dynamic and tentative nature of scientific understanding. We always should acknowledge where the science has come from, and the possibility that it may end up somewhere else. If we don't, antienvironmental zealots with devious intent will do the job for us, and it will be hard to rebuild the movement's credibility. In the case of global warming, it is enough to say that the best science we have today suggests a certain result. There is no need to overstate the case or suggest a degree of certainty that is not there. And when the evidence starts to take us in a different direction, such as the realization in early 2013 that the standard climate models overstated the correlation between atmospheric carbon concentrations and temperature, Greens should be first to acknowledge the new information and adjust. The other side of the coin is equally important. The uncertainty and dynamism inherent in scientific understanding should never be used to provide an excuse for willful ignorance, and Center Green should never hesitate to call out deliberate blindness masquerading as legitimate debate.

Center Green also depends on an understanding of the boundary between science and policy. Sound science is a necessary condition for good policy, but not a sufficient one; policy making requires considerations of cost, public priorities, public opinion, and politics. The most interesting exploration of this dynamic between science and policy, in the context of the climate-change debate, is *Why We Disagree About Climate Change*, by British scientist Mike Hulme. He argues persuasively that most of the disagreement between right and left is not about what science says, but about what it means:

> We disagree about science because we have different under-standings of the relationship of scientific evidence to other things: to what we may regard as ultimate "truth," to the ways in which we relate uncertainty to risk, and to what we believe to be the legitimate role of knowledge in policy making. To help our discussions about climate change and to allow scientific knowledge to play its part in such discussions, we need to rec-ognize the limits to scientific knowledge. And we need to appre-ciate that such knowledge can be (perhaps inevitably will be) transformed in the process of leaving the laboratory and enter-ing the social world.[7]

Some Greens speak as if the climate-change debate should have been over once the influence of human activity on climate had been scientifically established. Instead, we must acknowledge that the science simply establishes a common understanding of the prob-lem, from which we then can have a vigorous debate over what the correct policy response to this common understanding should be. Scientists may have opinions on the correct policy, but science itself will not tell us what is the best thing to do. Without in any way giving a free pass to those who cynically distort climate science, the Green movement's tendency to confuse the proper realms of science and policy has contributed in part to the right's tactical decision to attack the science.

Center Green acknowledges that factors outside of the realm of science—moral arguments and aesthetics, for example—also are a valid basis for advocating certain conservation results; as Hulme says, "We must not hide behind science when difficult ethical choices are called for." Too often the Green movement, taught that everything must be based on compelling scientific arguments, is not entirely honest about why it seeks a result. For example, uncomfortable with arguing that a forest should be preserved because it is beloved by a community, or that a mountain should be protected because it is beautiful, a Green group may emphasize more esoteric, and even strained, ecological reasons. The Center Green approach calls for honesty about why a certain conservation result is desired. If it is ecological, then lay out the science. If it is not, then don't be shy about using the language of moral decision making, ethics, stewardship, beauty, or attachment to place. These are things to which both right- and left-leaning citizens can relate. And, over time, these types of statements will suggest to all sorts of conservatives that Green groups at least sometimes speak their language.

The use of the quasi-scientific concept of sustainability, long an important part of the Green toolkit, provides a good example of the synergy between science and morality. Sustainability, despite its overuse and abuse, remains a neat formulation. It does not deride or challenge the pleasures of present consumption, but it does raise the moral question of what duty we owe to the future.[8] The question can be answered in two different ways. One formulation, which ought to receive a rousing cheer from the right, simply asks whether our present consumption is selfish and irresponsible, depriving our progeny of similar pleasure, or is it prudent and disciplined—as all the gods of conservative ideology would demand—laying a foundation for the continuity of civilization and its advance.

There is also a more utilitarian formulation, where the economist calls for an equation solving for the optimal expenditure of capital: how much of our natural resources, wealth, and human capital should we use to increase our well-being today, and how much should we set aside and leave for future generations.[9] The right answer optimizes utility for all, current and future generations considered together. Of course this formula is easier to describe than to apply, since key elements of the equation are unknown and unknowable, including how scarce are our natural resources, how technology will develop in the future (which determines our need for those resources and the efficiency with which we consume them), and how much we should discount the interests of people born far into the future.

Under the Center Green approach I am advocating, it doesn't matter how you answer the question: the important thing is that both right and left demand that the question be asked. Whether we get there through a utilitarian calculus or through a moral imperative, the result is the same: we owe the future consideration and restraint, and must make our best efforts to figure out how much. We can disagree about how much restraint, but cannot disagree about the imperative of sustainability: it is never sufficient to point to a decline in our present consumption or wealth as a reason to avoid the prudent protection of the planet's ability to supply our future inputs and absorb our future outputs. This is what sustainability means, and it is devastating to market fundamentalism, which views lost jobs or higher costs for business as determinative reasons for declining to act in the interests of the planet's future.

Finally, Center Green declines to use sustainability in the sense of a balanced status quo that is perfectly calibrated to carry us forward to the indefinite future, and instead emphasizes sustainability as resilience, meaning the ability of healthy ecological systems to cope with change. Nature is dynamic, embedded with cycles on all time scales: cycles of population, abundance, climate, species extinction, and chemistry. Nature on Earth is subject to all manner of shocks and dislocations: cosmological events such as meteor strikes, solar flares and tides; geological events such as volcanic eruptions, earthquakes and tsunamis; climatic events, both random (such as forest fires) and cyclical (such as El Niño and La Niña, and, in longer time frames, the advance and retreat of the polar ice caps) as well as biological processes, as dominant species, such as man and dinosaur, rise and fall and create and destroy ecosystems. The thing that is powerful and enduring and that must be protected is the ability of nature to cope with these cycles and to recover from these shocks—

its resilience. Resilience of a natural system is what determines its ability to continue providing "regulating services" (climate, mitigation of flooding, control of disease, processing of waste, preservation of water quality) and also "supporting services" (such as soil formation, continuation of photosynthesis and nutrient cycling).

Center Green also declines to deploy "sustainability" as some sort of quasi-scientific imperative that trumps normal debates about policy. Both environmental historian William Cronon and food guru Michael Pollan have argued that sustainability is fundamentally undemocratic, at least when sustainability advocates use the term to suggest that decisions regarding how to live can be made by simply requiring experts to solve the sustainability equation. Cronon argues that sustainability "tempts us to believe that we no longer need to debate whether the market or government will solve our problems. We're just going to gather together, agree on what's sustainable, and then do it."[10] This undemocratic flavor of the concept of sustainability has contributed to the right's antipathy toward the Green movement. I suggest we deploy the concept of sustainability only as an analytical tool, and not as an imperative that trumps the debate over any particular environmental issue, and also that we should try to move the conversation toward the more durable concept of resilience.

———————

The ninth commandment asks Green NGOs to build a new grassroots movement focused on political engagement. There is growing evidence that the Green establishment accepts this mandate, such as the effort by 350.org and 1,500 other NGO partners culminating in the People's Climate March in September 2014, which its organizers generously estimated turned out over three hundred thousand people on the streets of Manhattan. But remember that approximately twenty *million* people participated in the first Earth Day in 1970, and that high level of popular support provided the foundation

for a decade of bipartisan legislative action. Today, the Green movement has yet to demonstrate either the capacity for sustained popular mobilization, or its translation into political results. The Center
Green approach to political action is focused on overcoming these
challenges.

The American political system is not good at tackling big issues
that pit a broad public interest against special interests. No cause is
broader or more universal than the environment. Arrayed against
environmentalists are the special interests adversely affected by conservation, such as polluters and real estate developers, who engage
in politics with all the vigor that humans bring to greedy ambition
and defense of their existing prerogatives. As a result, we face a deep
structural imbalance of passion between greed and altruism, where
the specifically interested are far more motivated than those advocating for the general public good. To succeed in this unequal contest, Greens need nearly flawless political execution.

The main Center Green strategy for improving environmentalism's political effectiveness is to balance the sophisticated lobbying
work of NGOs with equally professional and sustained political mobilization at the grassroots level. Green politics must go retail, with
the millions of members of Green organizations of all sorts making
political work as habitual as their recycling. The Green movement
must regain its standing as a mass movement having the numbers
and energy that will get it taken seriously by the political class. This
does not mean the type of "mobilization" favored by establishment
Green NGOs, in which members receive carefully crafted "messaging"
from head offices in Washington and New York instructing them to
dispatch form letters and form emails to politicians. Instead, Center
Green aims to model grassroots mobilization on the "little platoons"
of the local land trust movement, where directors, members, and
volunteers meet face-to-face, where communication is interactive,
not top-down, where a decision to take political action is based on a
genuine understanding of, and keen interest in, the issue, and where

that action consists not just of low-sacrifice moves like clicking the send button for an email, but also of higher-sacrifice acts like driving out on a rainy night to appear in person at a town board meeting.

The fact that this sort of engagement is grounded in the local does not mean that political action cannot be well coordinated and national in scale. The land trust movement demonstrates that local groups can be networked effectively. When that network is modeled not on the hierarchical hub-and-spoke but on the highly distributed model where local nodes are connected with each other as well as with the center, then the whole network can hum with thinking, learning, and messaging that flows up, down, and sideways among like-minded Greens around the country. The experience of the land conservation movement is clear and compelling: having a policy paper showing how open land helps the economy is good; having a poll showing how many folks in the district are in favor of open space is better; but having a dozen ranchers from the district, including a couple of major campaign contributors, sufficiently involved and motivated to travel to Washington and show up in the representative's office is best.

It is the most elementary truth about politics that increasing the number and diversity of voices behind a message increases its political strength. It is one thing for the lawyers and policy experts at NRDC to call for, say, additional wetland protections. It is quite another when that call is joined by 1,700 local land trusts, urban-based and largely minority environmental justice organizations, hunting and fishing groups, and the American Farmland Trust. Paul Hansen of the Izaak Walton League, who spent a career trying to get the hunting/fishing, land conservation, and environmental groups to work together, lays out multiple examples where this kind of cooperation produced dramatic results.[11] The power of broader partnerships was illustrated vividly by the success of so many of the open-space and land conservation bond acts, state constitutional amendments, and similar state referendum campaigns launched during the past twenty years, as a result of which voters approved more than $70 billion in public funding for open-space and land conservation. Typical of the coalitions assembled to support these efforts was the Iowa Water and Land Legacy coalition of sportsmen, businesses, agricultural interests, conservationists, and outdoor recreation advocates that achieved a resounding victory in Iowa in 2010. Critically, these coalitions typically included substantial representation from sportsmen groups, and attracted widespread bipartisan support. In late 2014 the private land conservation movement teamed up with NGOs including the Congressional Sportsmen's Foundation, Feeding America, United Way, Independent Sector, and others in support of a bill that contained enhanced conservation easement incentives and other provisions supported by the charitable sector more broadly. Their extraordinary joint effort resulted in a House vote, in the most difficult possible political circumstances, that fell only eight votes short of the two-thirds threshold required under the relevant procedural rules. It was a near-victory that the conservationists could not have achieved on their own.

There are encouraging examples outside of the land conservation arena. One is the defeat in November 2010 of a ballot measure in California (Proposition 23) designed to roll back state standards for carbon emissions reductions. Nearly six million voters were mobilized by a coalition that included more than 130 health, social justice, religious, and Green groups, mostly local.[12] And on the national stage, the Alliance for Climate Protection organized its "We" media campaign in cooperation with partners from outside the Green movement (including the Girl Scouts of America and United Steelworkers). The People's Climate March in 2014 was launched by a partnership including groups as diverse as Catholic colleges, health care and steelworkers' unions, the International Federation of Business and Professional Women, Amnesty International, the American Society of Landscape Architects, the National Lawyers Guild, and hundreds of NGOs from every corner of civil society. Although some of these efforts failed to achieve their goals, they demonstrated that unconventional partnerships can be forged in support of Green causes, that funders will fund these efforts, volunteers will volunteer, and there is nothing intrinsic to the Green movement that prevents it from employing these strategies.

Finally, in a democracy the ultimate political currency ought to be voters, but the reality of today's political scene is that the ultimate political currency is currency. And here the Green movement has been at a major disadvantage because of its architecture: it is led largely by Section 501(c)(3) charities that cannot make political contributions or otherwise support or oppose any candidate for office. As a result, the movement as a whole is disconnected from the strategizing and leadership of direct political action, which has been left mainly to the national and state Leagues of Conservation Voters. Since 1969 the national LCV (now supplemented by independent state leagues in over thirty states) has independently scored candidates on their environmental records, given endorsements, rewarded the greenest politicians with independent support, and penalized the least green by supporting their opponents. Although doing good and vital work, the national and state leagues have been unable to scale up their direct political action to the required level, resulting in efforts that one of my Green colleagues characterized as "spitting in the wind." In 2010, the national LCV said that it (and its affiliated political action committees, LCV Action Fund and LCV Victory Fund) spent only $5.5 million on independent expenditure campaigns. In contrast, during the same cycle, the Koch brothers' Super PAC Americans for Prosperity, the originator of the "No Climate Tax Pledge," claims to have spent $40 million.[13]

Unlike most environmental NGOs, businesses in the extractive industries, coal-burning utilities, real estate developers, and other opponents of the Green agenda are free to spend unlimited amounts on independent political action in support of or opposition to candidates for office. Until meaningful campaign finance reform arrives and the *Citizens United* decision is overturned, the Green movement must do more than howl at the millions directed against the environmental agenda by business interests and right wing PACs and Super PACs. We have plenty of proenvironment billionaires: we need to convince them to match the funding of our opponents until the country comes to its senses and brings the political money game to a close. Tom Steyer provides a useful example. His NextGen Climate Action Super PAC (Super PACs are limited to "independent action," such as running ads on television, and cannot give money directly to any campaign) intends to return climate change to the center of American political dialogue, with the goal of making it a major issue in the 2016 presidential race. In another encouraging development, in 2013 the America's Conservation PAC was formed, co-chaired by former interior secretary Ken Salazar (a Democrat) and hedge-fund manager and philanthropist Louis Bacon (a Republican), and initially headed by former land trust executive and Department of the Interior official Will Shafroth, to support on a bipartisan basis candidates "who are committed to invest in and expand access to our great outdoors and heritage, and conserve our working lands and wildlife."[14] This PAC, dedicated to supporting candidates from both parties, will be able to reward Republicans bucking their party's right wing and help conservation-minded Republicans fend off primary challenges by Tea Party candidates critical of their conservation records.

———

I am under no illusion about the ease of steering the environmental-politics supertanker from its current course through the rocky straits of hyperpartisanship to a place with room for maneuver sufficient for some Center Green positions to achieve bipartisan support. The most active voices on each side have a history of attacking centrist views even more vehemently than the views of their ideological opponents. The one thing most of the critics of this book will mis-understand is that Center Green is based on the idea that there are *some* issues on which a bipartisan consensus is possible, not the illu-sion that there can be agreement on *all* aspects of the environmental agenda. Moreover, the dialogue and compromise necessary to create action in the sweet spot of consensus does not foreclose vigorous debate on the areas of disagreement. The right might argue for cap-and-trade while the left argues for a carbon tax, but the fact that both are willing to consider the necessity of some action presents an opportunity that no responsible environmentalist should pass up. We have for too long let an argument about tools—regulation or market incentives—paralyze us, like sailors staring at a hole in the side of their ship arguing caulk vs. plug while the vessel slowly sinks into the sea.

There are many discouraging examples that foreshadow the sorts of attack Center Green is likely to attract. In February 2004, an *Out-side* magazine article attempted a balanced discussion of the pros and cons of permitting drilling in the Arctic National Wildlife Ref-uge. It offered the all-too-obvious conclusion that "both sides are too entrenched to see the other side clearly." The editor argued that "the final outcome of the dispute should not be achieved through poisonous invective, but through a healthy and open discussion of the facts on both sides."[15] Poisonous invective, however, is exactly what *Outside* magazine got, aimed at it from both sides. Extremists on both sides of that debate had a grudging respect for each other, and nothing but disdain for the moderate who sought to distract their respective partisans with a rational consideration of the facts. And the apostate, of course, sits in the lowest circle of hell. When the EPA under President Bush adopted mandatory reductions in nonroad diesel emissions, the move was immediately praised by the National Resources Defense Council, which commented that the initiative "will be the biggest public health step since lead was removed from gasoline more than two decades ago." The reaction

of other Greens? The *Washington Post* reported that other environmental NGOs were "apoplectic" at an NRDC statement—no matter
how fair and accurate—in support of the enemy, President Bush.
EPA administrator Whitman says that NRDC wrote and asked her
to stop quoting their statement of support.[16]

Another illustration of the special hostility directed by both sides
toward centrist rhetoric occurred in 2007, when Newt Gingrich was
penning his proenvironmental *Contract with the Earth*, Bjørn Lomborg
was retreating from his assault on environmentalism with his more
moderate book *Cool It*, and the climate movement was transition-
ing toward a more positive vision of resiliency and accelerating the
development of nonfossil energy sources. Everyone was expecting
action on cap-and-trade in the next administration. Twice during
2007 Andrew Revkin, a distinguished journalist, author, and blogger, reported in the *New York Times* that out of the "yelling match
between the political and environmental left and the right" there
seemed to be an emerging center willing to repudiate the most shrill
voices on both sides and "urge a move to the pragmatic center on
climate and energy."[17] Revkin quoted scientists who recognized the
reality of the global warming emergency, but urged a search for practical actions that could be taken immediately, and cautioned about
losing the attention and support of the public with a message of
unrelenting gloom unaccompanied by implementable solutions. The
reaction to Revkin's piece was swift and loud. *Grist* staff writer David
Roberts headlined "NYT's Andy Revkin pens another stinker on the
so-called 'center' of the climate debate," and called Revkin's piece
"awful" and "preposterous," arguing that "extremists" were those
who were appropriately "impassioned and urgent" and that the possibility of a center in the climate wars was an illusion.[18]

For many on both the right and the left, the idea of bipartisanship
is nothing but a naïve copout. The blogger Duncan Bowen Black,
better known by his pseudonym Atrios, even coined a disdainful
neologism based on longtime centrist *Washington Post* columnist

David Broder. He wrote: "We normally think of 'High Broderism' as the worship of bipartisanship for its own sake, combined with a fake 'pox on both their houses' attitude. But in reality this is just the cover Broder uses for his real agenda, the defense of what he perceives to be 'the establishment' at all costs."[19] Others criticize the center as being nothing more than a matter of tone, a reaction to shrill discourse that has no real point of view, described by Roberts as "[s]elf-appointed Reasonable People [who] define themselves in opposition to ranting and raving Dirty Hippie strawmen. 'We're not like them. We don't raise our voices.'"

The sort of centrism I am advocating is not primarily about tone, as illustrated by the specific Center Green substantive positions on climate change, fracking, and Keystone described in the following chapters. Center Green represents a distinctive point of view that seeks to find a part of the environmental agenda that can, on its merits, earn the support of a sufficient number of moderates and conservatives to permit urgently needed action. I am not the first person to reach this conclusion. *The Economist* editorial page, from the right, and Thomas Friedman, from the left, have endorsed the same basic idea. As Friedman put it: "[A] new green ideology, properly defined, has the power to mobilize liberals and conservatives, evangelicals and atheists, big business and environmentalists, around an agenda that can both pull us together and propel us forward."[20] This thesis began to be played out in the world of realpolitik before the Obama administration took office, but was quickly swamped by the peculiar politics of the moment. Viewed in historical perspective, both the right's general antipathy to the environment since the mid-1990s and the sinking of centrist Green solutions in the hyperpartisanship of the last decade are anomalies. They tell us the shape and extent of our short-term challenge, but little about the longer-term probability that a Center Green approach can move the agenda forward with bipartisan support.

14

CENTER GREEN ON
CLIMATE CHANGE

S o what does it look like when the Center Green approach is applied to a specific issue? How do the resulting policy positions and political tactics differ from those suggested by Green orthodoxy? Because climate change is at the same time the most difficult environmental issue, the movement's highest priority, and a major cause of the Great Estrangement, it provides a critical test of Center Green.

Center Green starts with the following understanding of the underlying science: global warming caused in part by human activity is now an observed phenomenon. It is sure to have significant impacts on both natural systems and human culture, but exactly how much warming will occur and what those impacts will be are difficult to predict.

Over geological time many natural factors affect the average temperature on our planet, including variations in Earth's orbit, changes in the sun's energy output, and volcanic eruptions. Decaying plant matter and the oceans release about thirty-five times more carbon into the atmosphere each year than man does. But the overwhelming consensus of science is that at least a significant part of the climate change we are now observing is caused by the marginal contribution to that carbon loading caused by human beings, primarily from fossil-fuel emissions and changes in land use. The marginal CO_2 contribution of man is partially (about 30 percent) absorbed by the ocean (causing ocean acidification), and the balance has accumulated in the atmosphere, increasing atmospheric CO_2 from a preindustrial level of about 280 ppm to about 400 ppm now. The exact balance of causation between natural factors and human activity is in legitimate dispute, but the causal link to human factors is clear enough that we ought to have been doing what we could to curtail our impact on the climate.[1] We haven't. We have failed to make the necessary reductions in net emissions of greenhouse gases, and are suffering and will continue to suffer the consequences.

While there is no uncertainty over whether climate change exists or whether it is significantly affected by humanity's greenhouse gas emissions, it does remain uncertain how increasing carbon levels in the atmosphere—taking into account the many complex offsets and feedback loops—will correlate with air temperatures, sea levels, precipitation, storm activities, and sea level rise in the future.[2] The uncertainty arises mainly from the difficulty in predicting the impact of feedbacks, that is, mechanisms other than the "greenhouse effect" that come into play once the planet starts to warm, and which can either amplify or moderate the warming effects of increased atmospheric carbon. These include the impact on Earth's albedo—the reflection of sunlight from white surfaces, such as ice—which would decline as the ice caps melt, causing the Earth to absorb more of the sun's energy, and thus further accelerate the warming. The level of atmospheric aerosols is another critical factor, because aerosols can reflect sunlight and produce a cooling offset, or in certain cases, such as black soot, absorb energy and lead to further warming. Another critical feedback is ocean absorption of CO_2, which declines as the seas warm, making it even more difficult to limit atmospheric carbon once warming starts. Scientists also are looking carefully at the extent to which planetary warming is absorbed by the deep ocean, thus potentially mitigating the warming effect on the atmosphere. A feedback that the Intergovernmental Panel on Climate Change (IPCC) calls "most uncertain" is the impact of increased cloud cover caused by higher water vapor in a warmer atmosphere, which could possibly reduce solar energy absorbed by the Earth (and offset warming), or might increase the greenhouse effect (and exacerbate warming). The operation and impact of these multiple feedback mechanisms singly and in concert will almost certainly have a significant impact on the expected warming resulting from the greenhouse effect itself, which is why the predicted temperature rises under various carbon-emission scenarios have changed over time and are still so difficult to predict with the certainty sought by policy makers.

As if this calculus were not sufficiently complex, scientists know that the operation of these offsets and feedbacks is not necessarily linear. Many scientists are concerned about tipping points, where changes may accelerate once an underlying driver crosses a certain point. Examples highly relevant to climate outcomes include the pace of melting of large ice sheets (which could accelerate rapidly once a certain threshold of warming is reached), and the pattern of macro-scale ocean currents, such as the Gulf Stream, which could shift suddenly once warming progresses beyond a certain point. Moreover, the cumulative effect of all these factors (greenhouse effect with its related offsets, feedbacks, and possible tipping points) only provides an overlay to natural climate variability, also imperfectly understood, which may either amplify or offset the temperature increases caused by man.

The key point is that all of these uncertainties are about *how much*, not about *whether or not*, and thus are uncertainties that provide no justification for inaction. The best-case end of the range of outcomes still would be disruptive and expensive, and the worst-case end of the range potentially cataclysmic. Although we simply do not yet know the probabilities that attach to each possible outcome, we still can develop a coherent policy response using the "precautionary principle."[3]

The precautionary principle originally arose not in response to uncertainty about the exact climate impacts that we face, but as a response to those who argued that science had not conclusively established that global warming was real. Accordingly, it has been much hated both by some Greens (who regard it as an unacceptable retreat from full confidence in the dire predictions of climate-change models) and the anticlimate right (which generally regards it as a weasel concept designed to distract from what they see as flaws in global-warming science).[4] Despite these objections from right and left, the precautionary principle is hugely attractive to the average nonideological man on the street, who finds "better safe than sorry" to be a commonsense reaction to the uncertainty about exactly what sort of climate change we face. The principle has been enshrined in European law, and is the position adopted by the moderate GOP group ConservAmerica (formerly Republicans for Environmental Protection), whose policy paper on global warming states, "It is the conservative course of action to err on the side of caution when the stakes are so great." Even George Shultz, who held cabinet-level positions in several Republican administrations, has argued that the idea of precaution and insurance against risk should have great appeal to conservatives, citing Ronald Reagan's reaction to science showing holes in the ozone layer: "Ronald Reagan didn't say, 'You people who are skeptical are wrong and I'm going to push your nose in the mud and I'm going to try to convince you.' He said, 'Look, let's take out an insurance policy. At least, maybe in the back of your mind, you might say, maybe you're wrong. And the insurance policy is not necessarily going to cost us forever.' So he brought them into the tent and got support. I think what should happen now is the same sort of thing."[5]

We need to be pragmatic. It drives Greens mad that so many conservatives refuse to acknowledge the science behind climate change and repeat a litany of assertions that are patently false. But given the epistemological problem we have explored—that a certain set of conservative beliefs are stubbornly resistant to evidence—we must move the battle to a different ground. The precautionary principle allows us to acknowledge some degree of uncertainty and skepticism (i.e., in relation to the timing, nature, and impacts of global warming), and move beyond it to a discussion of risk, appetite for risk, risk mitigation, and ordinary prudence. Even optimists convinced that their house will never burn down have fire insurance. Of course, even if we come together in analyzing climate change in terms of risk and insurance, we may still disagree over the critical questions of how much coverage to buy, and how much of a premium (either in diverted expenditure or lost economic activity) we should be willing to pay.

The main split in the Green movement today in relation to climate change is between the old guard, who continue to pursue national and international legal limitations on carbon emissions, and the so-called Post Greens who believe the only fix is technological and that our resources should be focused on accelerating a technological solution. The Post Green optimists often cite Moore's law (predicting the doubling, approximately every two years, of the number of transistors in a dense integrated circuit), wishfully hoping that the pace of change in the alternative energy space will approach or match the exponential improvements achieved with microprocessors.[6] It is true that some technologies we can see on the far horizon—pB11 nuclear fusion, for example—could massively disrupt the current energy equation, solving our carbon-emission problem overnight.[7] Other, more probable innovations would make continuous incremental improvements in the cost and efficiency of alternative energy. But the timing and extent of innovation through technology are fundamentally unpredictable. We might end up with a magic bullet; we might end up with too little too late.

Certain Post Greens advocate massive public investments as the only way to precipitate the necessary technological advance to replace fossil fuels. It is true that well-structured public investment in basic research and development is fully justified to maintain American competitiveness and security, and should be able to attract support from both right and left (especially when such spending is controlled by the Department of Defense because of its military implications). But the Post Green's reliance on massive public spending in pursuit of breakthrough technologies leaves much to be desired as a policy response to climate change, primarily because investment of the magnitude advocated by the Post Greens is highly unlikely given the nation's fiscal condition and outlook. In addition, the track record for federal subsidization of nonfossil fuels is not promising. Although governments all over the world have, shamefully, provided massive tax and other subsidies to the fossil-fuels industry for years (estimated by the International Energy Agency at $548 billion globally for 2013),[8] oil and gas, as mature industries, are able to absorb such subsidies. The Green energy sector is neither as large nor as mature. Moreover, the alternative energy and new-technology subsidies contained in the Energy Act of 2005, passed with bipartisan support, were poorly structured, administered badly (by an under-resourced bureaucracy within the financially unsophisticated Department of Energy), and resulted in embarrassments like the failure of the solar energy company Solyndra in 2011 soon after the issuance of $535 million in federal loan guarantees.

So if Post Green is not a sufficient answer to global warming, what is? Center Green hits the reset button on environmentalists' approach to climate by making four fundamental changes in the movement's strategy and tactics: being realistic that globalist solutions, such as the 2015 Paris agreement, depend entirely on U.S. domestic politics to permit their implementation in the real world; refocusing in the domestic sphere on steps, however small, that are actually achievable and will make a real world impact on greenhouse gas emissions and/or absorption; ditching the sort of exceptionalism that subordinates all other agendas to the planetary climate emergency; and embracing a public conversation about adaptation and resilience.

Despite the renewed optimism engendered by the greenhouse gas emission reduction targets agreed at the Paris conference in 2015, the Green movement should remain skeptical about the efficacy of sweeping multilateral agreements setting forth requirements for signing countries to reduce emissions. As attractive as such one-stop, package-deal solutions may be in principle, their reduction targets are not enforceable and their track record is not promising. Rio failed in 1992, Kyoto failed in 1997, and Copenhagen failed in 2009. Before Paris, even veteran climate campaigners had reached a high level of frustration with the international process. Eric Pooley, then a Bloomberg reporter, who was there, wrote that "Copenhagen achieved a new level of incoherence. It was as if the bumbling clerks at an Alitalia ticket counter had suddenly been tasked with saving the world."[9] Moreover, a number of the states that did ratify Kyoto and undertake treaty obligations to reduce greenhouse gas emissions, such as Canada, Japan, and Russia, later withdrew, having no prospect of meeting their Kyoto targets.

Notwithstanding the soaring rhetoric that emerged from the 2014 United Nations Climate Summit, which Secretary General Ban Ki-Moon promised would lead to "a meaningful universal climate agreement in Paris,"[10] the agreement between President Obama and Chinese president Xi Jinping soon thereafter, and the result of the Paris conference itself, there remains significant doubt whether the targets and timetables agreed by diplomats will translate into actual reductions in emissions. The Paris agreement leaves the world questioning whether any U.S. administration will be able to obtain the congressional appropriations necessary for the United States to meet its financial commitments under the agreement, on which compliance by the less-developed countries is conditioned. Most significantly, the legal challenges to the president's Clean Power Plan leave in limbo the question of whether the administration has the power to effect the agreed reductions under existing law, and the congressional vote to scuttle the Clean Power Plan, taken just prior to the Paris conference, reminds us that, without a president willing to veto such legislation, a hostile Congress can prevent the United States from undertaking the emission reductions agreed in Paris. Without at least some measure of domestic bipartisan support, there is little prospect that U.S. commitments made at the international level can be fully implemented. Moreover, the Paris agreement creates a short fuse: in 2020 the agreed "ratchet mechanism" requires the United States to serve up revised targets. If U.S. domestic politics prevents implementation of our initial target and/or the proposal of even more ambitious reductions, then there is a real chance that the entire Paris agreement process will collapse. In effect, the Paris framework creates an urgent imperative and time frame for breaking our longstanding political deadlock on the environment.

Adherence by national governments to internationally agreed reduction targets may be highly uncertain, but this should provide no excuse for other actors. Individual and often uncoordinated voluntary actions by states, cities, and the private sector can make an immediate and meaningful difference. Even Secretary General Ban Ki-Moon admitted that the "most potentially transformational"—i.e., real—actions involve the private sector. This includes, for example, the public-private partnership announced at the Paris conference, in which twenty countries agreed to double their basic renewable energy research budgets and collaborate with twenty-eight global investors led by Bill Gates, who agreed to invest billions in the commercialization of the resulting clean energy solutions.

Center Green seeks to steer the Green movement away from its past pursuit of the universal and the illusory to a new focus on the specific and the real.

———————

Cap-and-trade is an elegant solution to carbon emissions reduction. It worked for acid rain and would have worked for carbon. Waxman-Markey should have passed. As a market-based solution it should have attracted conservative support. It is monumental hypocrisy for the right, so convinced that free-market capitalism provides all the answers, to refuse to take any action to allow that market to function as it should, by putting a price on the free-ride externality of carbon emissions. But "should have" and "could have" are not paths forward. A national solution implemented through federal legislative action may be possible someday, but it is not possible now or in the foreseeable future.

It is nonetheless tempting for the Green movement to pick itself up and try to rally behind another whole-economy market-based solution that limits carbon. One candidate is "cap-and-dividend" (sometimes called "cap-and-share"), an idea with many parents, which most recently was promoted by senators Bernie Sanders and Barbara Boxer in the form of the Climate Protection Act of 2013.[11] The idea is simple. The government would impose an escalating fee on carbon and methane emissions at their source, all or most of which (three-fifths in the Sanders-Boxer bill) would be returned directly to citizens, making up (or more than making up, in the case of modest energy users) for the increased costs of carbon-based energy. The balance would be used for research and development in alternative energy technologies. The idea is clever, and if it could be passed, I would support it. But it can't. Everyone with an interest in fossil energy would oppose it, including key coal state Democratic senators, and much of the GOP would condemn it as a redistributive tax.

One Green leader has recognized the fundamental lesson of the movement's failure in relation to climate change: "By insisting on a comprehensive plan rather than a first-steps strategy, climate change proponents have come away with next to nothing."[12] Greens, with their orderly minds and careful sense of priority, have long preferred solutions that are universal, top-down, and comprehensive—what Mike Hulme calls "elegant" solutions, like ratchet-down cap-and-trade. All such solutions have revolved around overly ambitious targets that call for sweeping percentage reductions over long periods.

In contrast to this preference for comprehensive, "elegant" solutions, Center Green advocates what some what some call "clumsy" solutions, meaning a diversity of approaches taken at more than one level of government, depending on what can gain public and political support at the time.[13] So, for the United States, Europe, Japan, Australia, and other affluent societies, this means taking whatever unilateral steps are politically feasible to create a cost for, and thus limit, carbon emissions. The Green movement should stop the internecine squabbling over whether regulation, taxation, or cap-and-trade schemes are more efficient or effective; the only question should be which is politically feasible in the relevant country. Japan, the U.K., Switzerland, and many of the Scandinavian countries were able to implement a carbon tax, and the EU, New Zealand, South Korea, and some others were able to start with cap-and-trade. It may be that regulatory limits applicable to high impact sectors such as electric generation are the only way forward in the United States at the federal level, and that our efforts should shift to political action at the regional, state, and local level (where California and the REGI states have opted for state or regional cap-and-trade systems).[14] Since it is already too late to keep the climate we once knew, the most important thing is not to let the perfect be the enemy of the good. The existence for the first time of some market signal that carbon emission is not free will be a breakthrough, even if that signal, incentive, or regulation will not itself effect the full amount of the necessary reduction. Any such tax, cap, or regulation would create the possibility of higher costs (or tighter restrictions) in the future, will shape investment activity and expectations (even if only at the margins), and will dramatically shift the debate from whether we need to do anything at all to whether what we are doing is adequate. It would provide a framework for an evolving recalculation of the desired tradeoff between the costs of climate change (which will escalate and become increasingly clear) and the price we are willing to pay to prevent or mitigate it (which should increase correspondingly).

Center Green seeks to determine what first small step is possible and then take it, notwithstanding that traditional Greens will moan about its farcical inadequacy, tokenism, and the moral hazard of deluding ourselves into thinking we have taken meaningful action when nothing short of preventing the tipping point of a 3.6 degree Fahrenheit increase in global temperature is acceptable. They will be wrong. The real feel-good delusion was twenty years of reliance on treaties with targets that governments could not or would not achieve.

We have encouraging models of state and regional initiatives to deal with greenhouse gas emissions, including REGI in the Northeast, and California's AB 32 (California Global Warming Solutions Act of 2006), and the Western Climate Initiative in the West. After Proposition 23 (which aimed to suspend AB 32 until unemployment abated) was defeated soundly in 2010, California's cap-and-trade scheme was finally launched in 2012. The scheme, which also includes declining mandatory caps, is designed to reduce California's greenhouse gas emissions to 1990 levels by the year of 2020. The Obama administration's Clean Power Plan, although national in scope, also wisely adopted a regionalist approach by giving each state a different greenhouse gas emission-reduction target based on that state's particular energy mix, and allowed each state flexibility to choose the means to meet its goal.

A U.S. senator who is part of the Senate "climate caucus," and who agrees that the movement needs to embrace and nurture the "small game" of state, local, and industry-by-industry action, offered an interesting analogy in a conversation with me in March 2014. Only a few years ago, at the national level, he observed, gay marriage was dead in the water, with no apparent path to progress. National polls were discouraging, showing little understanding of what the gay-marriage fight was about, and little support for the idea. But the movement soldiered on, relentless in its efforts to change hearts and minds, and succeeded in rebranding the issue as one of freedom and equality. Each incremental victory at the state level changed expectations, and within a short time the movement experienced the dramatic tipping point of the 2012 elections, and ultimately the U.S. Supreme Court's endorsement of the right of marriage equality in 2015. This, the senator argued, should be a model for climate change.

The next plank of Green climate orthodoxy that Center Green would discard is the idea of "climate exceptionalism." Mike Hulme describes climate exceptionalism this way: "We have made climate change the overriding project of this generation. We have been persuaded by our own rhetoric that it is on this project—and this project alone—that future generations will judge us. Veteran environmental campaigner George Monbiot has issued the rallying cry: 'Curtailing climate change must . . . become the project we put before all others. If we fail in this task, we fail in everything else.'"[15]

Environmental issues are important. But so were the battles against fascism and communism in the twentieth century. So was the threat of nuclear Armageddon. The fight to end racial segregation was fought within the same framework of law and politics in which all other issues are debated and resolved. It is tempting to argue that climate change constitutes a planetary emergency that somehow should be exempt from the normal political dialogue, risk analysis, and democratic yielding to the will of the majority. The perception that Greens seek this sort of exceptionalism is highly damaging. It has created rifts within the Green movement, where not all environmentalists agree, for example, that the low-carbon footprint of nuclear power or wind power should trump all other environmental considerations, and some Greens, such as novelist Jonathan Franzen, argue that obsession with our climate future has distracted from conservation action that is possible in the present.[16] Climate exceptionalism alienates potential allies, who simply cannot see that health care, education, or poverty alleviation must fall to the back of the queue, on the basis that they will be irrelevant in a world coping with the chaos and destruction of sea level rise and warming. And exceptionalism alienates conservatives most of all. It implies to them rejection of any sort of cost-benefit analysis, and a threat to throw both liberty and economic growth under the bus.

As one conservative group put it, "There can be no trumping of what the Framers called natural rights in the name of other things, even nature. Other rights claims, whether they be to the rights of species or to clean air, do not have the same fundamental status as 'Life, Liberty and the pursuit of happiness' and the other rights specified in the Bill of Rights. . . ."[17] This is not just right-wing rhetoric; this is a coherent concern that needs to be taken seriously.

This idea that the great existential threat of climate change trumps all other traditional Green concerns must be turned on its head. Instead, climate change as an issue must look to, celebrate, and benefit from progress in other parts of the Green agenda. Post Greens may dismiss traditional environmental issues like smog as subsidiary concerns, but smog is a far more powerful motivator to environmental activism than any number of Al Gore films or IPCC studies. Beijing's chronic smog promises to create a generation of Chinese environmental activists and provides the greatest hope for that nation to wean itself from dirty coal, with consequential reductions in greenhouse gases that are more meaningful than any others on the horizon of the possible.

Talk of adaptation to climate change is still discouraged among some orthodox Greens. They find the idea that we might adjust to a warmer planet to be a dangerous illusion, and one that risks distracting lawmakers and ordinary citizens from the urgent need to prevent or mitigate global warming. Center Green looks at adaptation more pragmatically. After superstorm Sandy and a series of other weather events in 2012–2013, citizens all along the East Coast began to turn serious attention to making their communities more resilient in the face of climate change. The debate over climate change as an "issue" abated and ordinary people, conservatives and liberals alike, asked what they needed to do to adapt to the new reality. The psychological shift was profound. Both big cities and small towns up and down the coast and its estuaries mobilized to understand their vulnerability and debate how their communities should respond. Conservatives who never would have attended a meeting on global warming came to workshops to discuss their town's response to sea level rise.

Another example of the power of public discussion of adaptation is Audubon's 2014 finding that climate change will cause the majority of North American bird species to lose more than 50 percent of their current range of habitat by 2080.[18] This provided American bird lovers with a tangible illustration of how climate change may affect their backyards and, importantly, provided hope that birds could be saved from extinction both by taking action now to prevent further warming and by investing in the protection of natural lands necessary for those species to migrate successfully to more hospitable climates. By incorporating adaptation into a grim climate-change warning, the message was transformed into one that was both hopeful and action-oriented.

Will this sort of focus and work on adaptation prevent future global warming? No. But it sows the seeds for future environmental action by raising the collective consciousness regarding the importance of environmental conditions generally and climate change specifically. It converts the issue from a global abstraction to a local reality. It engenders a sense of individual responsibility for and participation in decisions regarding the future, and shows how long-held convictions regarding the subject and the partisan divisions they support can melt away in the face of a common threat. Climate change is global, and for years our failed efforts to prevent it were taken primarily at the global level. But adaptation to climate change is essentially local, and thus provides important opportunities for the sorts of grassroots action and local collaboration that will lay the foundation for the Green movement in the twenty-first century.

With Green orthodoxy tweaked in these ways, a comprehensive Center Green approach to climate change would comprise the following:

> We should be clear and unyielding in declaring that science overwhelmingly supports the proposition that anthropomorphic climate change is a reality, while acknowledging a significant degree of uncertainty regarding both its extent and effects.
> We should ditch apocalyptic rhetoric, while not ignoring worst-case scenarios. The job of Greens is to convince the public that we *can* prevent catastrophic levels of global warming without reverting to a premodern lifestyle.
> We should acknowledge that technological innovation may well provide powerful tools for both mitigation and adaptation, and support policies designed to promote such innovation, while at the same time not putting all of our eggs in the technology breakthrough basket.
> The public sector should provide generous support for basic research and development in relation to nonfossil energy sources, but allow venture capitalists and markets to fund the commercialization of the most prospective technologies.[19]
> Just as we insist on clear-eyed acceptance of the reality of human influence on climate change, we ourselves must not indulge in the wishful thinking that nonfossil energy can quickly replace fossil fuels. The International Energy Agency estimates that in 2035 just 31 percent of the world's electricity generation will come from renewables.[20] So our pursuit of a fossil-fuel-free future in the long term must not blind us to the necessity of living with fossil fuels in the short term. In that short term, Center Green priorities are: (1) Support whatever will reduce the share of coal as an electric generating fuel as soon as possible, in both

the developed and developing world (this includes support for regulatory standards for carbon emissions when more efficient mechanisms, such as a carbon tax or cap-and-trade approach, are politically infeasible); (2) Accept the reality that natural gas (which has 51–57 percent of the CO_2 emissions per unit of energy output compared to coal) is the cleanest possible transition fuel to a fossil-fuel-free future and strive to make natural gas production as clean as possible by strictly regulating the management of methane leakage and conduct of hydraulic fracturing; (3) Prioritize actions that will mitigate the impact of fossil-fuel combustion during the transition, such as continuing enhancement of vehicle efficiency standards, and requiring state-of-the-art technology to capture and store carbon emissions from electric power stations; and (4) Prioritize the fight against deforestation, which is estimated to cause about 20–25 percent of the world's annual CO_2 emissions (and which, ironically, may be exacerbated by rising demand for land caused by government incentives for biofuels such as cellulosic ethanol).

> America should continue to participate in the U.N. process, encourage others to meet their Paris agreement targets, and do its best to meet its own target, but without overselling the extent to which Paris constitutes a "solution" to global warming. If America is to lead, it must first restore its domestic politics to a place where it is able to meet its commitments and be a reliable partner. Moreover, applying the "first do no harm" principle, no president should allow any international agreement that requires Senate ratification to poison the prospects for making bipartisan progress on the incremental domestic steps that actually reduce emissions and mitigate climate change.

> Finally, we should welcome increasing public interest in adaptation, which gives people a greater understanding of the consequences of global warming and offers incentives to both mitigate the warming trends and adapt to the consequences.

But what about politics? Even if Green NGOs realigned to this Center Green approach to climate change, would the GOP—the same GOP whose ascendant wing recently banned, in North Carolina, any state official from considering sea level rise caused by global warming in planning for the state's future coastal development—make a U-turn and change its position? Actually, it might. The deep split in the party in relation to climate change was revealed in a November 2013 Pew poll, which found that just 25 percent of Tea Party Republicans say there is solid evidence for global warming, while 61 percent of non–Tea Party Republicans believed there was.[21] That is a remarkable difference for confreres within the same party, and provides strong evidence that when Tea Party influence abates, the GOP as a whole will swing dramatically back toward support for pragmatic action in relation to climate. Given the goals and nature of politics, in the long term it is inevitable that political calculation and political self-interest will reassert themselves over ideological fervor as drivers of policy. Ridding the conservative movement of its irrational denial of the problem, and getting it refocused on solutions and adaptations that reflect conservative values, should be a critical priority for the Republican Party. According to other recent Pew polling, almost 80 percent of Latino and other immigrants say there is solid evidence for global warming and about 65 percent say it is clearly caused by human activity.[22] The same poll showed that 67 percent of voting-age Americans under twenty-nine say that climate change is a "very/somewhat serious problem." Can the GOP hope to gain any traction with tomorrow's majorities if it steadfastly ignores a problem that tomorrow's majorities believe to be both obvious and urgent?

The adult supervision within the GOP knows the answer. In a recent op-ed in the *New York Times*, the Republican EPA administrators who served presidents Nixon, Reagan, Bush I, and Bush II admitted with regret that the best market solution—a carbon tax—

was not now politically feasible, but argued that Republicans should nonetheless support President Obama's climate action plan: "We can have both a strong economy and a livable climate. All parties know that we need both. The rest of the discussion is either detail, which we can resolve, or purposeful delay, which we should not tolerate."[23]

15

CENTER GREEN ON THE HEADLINE ISSUES

Hydro-fracturing and Keystone

With climate change largely absent from the headlines for a half-dozen years, "environmentalism" might seem, to the very young and those with short memories, to be a movement about a method of hydrocarbon extraction called hydraulic fracturing ("fracking" for short) and Keystone XL, which would have been the final phase of an obscure oil pipeline system in Canada and the American midwest. It seems a fair test of Center Green to ask if its approach to these two issues would bridge the gap between right and left, allow a mutually acceptable resolution, and permit the Green movement to focus on more important things.

Both fracking and Keystone are manifestations of a long struggle over hydrocarbons. The good news is that when the (hopefully long) history of *Homo sapiens* is written, the period of our dependence on long-dead organic matter pried at great cost from the earth should prove to have been both vital and brief. Vital, because it provided the energy that powered the industrial and technological revolutions and the emergence of billions of people from poverty. Brief, because as brilliantly as our technology has allowed us to reach and economically exploit ever deeper and scarcer resources, those resources are, at the end of the day, finite. So we will transition to other energy sources—the only question is when.

In the meantime, we stand at a pivotal moment of opportunity in relation to energy policy that requires us to build on the points of consensus between right and left. Both share a healthy under-standing of the extent to which our dependence on foreign oil has required us to support unsavory regimes, tarnish our ideals, and sacrifice American lives and American treasure. Both understand that continued American competitiveness and prosperity depend on American leadership in emerging technologies, and that alternative energy is a field likely to produce technological advances that will stand at the core of the twenty-first century economy.

This is already an area where common ground has produced bipartisan efforts. James Woolsey, often aligned with neoconserva-tives, director of the CIA under President Clinton, and later a foreign policy advisor to Senator John McCain, drove a hybrid that sported a bumper sticker reading "Osama Bin Laden Hates This Car."[1] For a decade, a significant part of the right-wing foreign policy and defense establishment has characterized the need to transition to a post-fossil-fuel future as a national security imperative. This has led to some encouraging cross-political and cross-ideological coali-tions. One, called "Set America Free," includes the Hudson Institute, a right-wing think tank, and the religious conservative Gary Bauer, as well as the Apollo Alliance (an ambitious clean-energy initiative launched after 9/11) and the NRDC.

In the meantime, however, Greens and conservatives remain locked in a ritualistic struggle in which Greens seek to starve the world of carbon energy on the basis that this will raise prices and accelerate the transition to renewables, and conservatives, in furi-ous reaction, fall in behind Sarah Palin's inane chant of "drill, baby, drill." Rather than working through a long agenda of complex energy policy choices, the two sides periodically pick a single fight to symbolize their differences, rally the troops, and serve as a litmus test of ideological purity. The proposal to drill in the Arctic National Wildlife Refuge served this purpose for a number of years. ANWR was elevated to the headlines when one side or the other thought it would serve some purpose, whereupon the right would simply repeat their mantra of jobs and growth, and Greens would again find themselves on the defense, struggling to answer the charge that caribou were more important than people. Wait a year and repeat. And then, with the world energy markets changing more than at any time in the last two decades, with profound economic, political, and national security challenges and opportunities, the public debate revolved around a once-obscure hydrocarbon recovery technique known as fracking and a single 875-mile addition, Keystone XL, to the 190,000-mile North American crude and petroleum liquids pipeline network. What does Center Green have to say about these two talismanic issues?

The distinction between Center Green and traditional environmentalism is illuminated perfectly by a single issue. For many Green NGOs fracking has been a gift: a retail issue that has attracted deep grassroots concern and activism, rekindling some of the popular revulsion and passion that animated the movement in the 1970s. But in the spirit of the 2010s decade, it was not a careful book like Rachel Carson's *Silent Spring* that sparked the public outcry, but a documentary film, Josh Fox's *Gasland* (and its sequel, *Gasland Part II*), a click away on everyone's favorite device, featuring dramatic footage of exploding kitchen faucets. Old-school Greens, egged on by a ground swell of popular support, started campaigns to ban fracking.

The wave of popular concern about this technique of hydrocarbon extraction came at a moment when many Green NGOs were worried that the natural gas revolution, notwithstanding its potential to render dirty coal uneconomic, would simply postpone the longed-for sunset of hydrocarbons and dawn of the age of renewables. Barely had the natural gas revolution taken flight when the Sierra Club supplemented its commendable "Beyond Coal" campaign with an ill-conceived "Beyond Natural Gas" campaign. This campaign conflates legitimate concerns about fracking with a policy preference that we proceed directly to an all-renewable economy, despite the complete impossibility of realizing that dream and the inconvenient truth of much higher greenhouse gas emissions if natural gas were to be taken out of the energy mix during the transition to the age of renewables.[2]

On the other side of the Green house, the Environmental Defense Fund developed a sensible program to strengthen regulation of fracking, improve enforcement, and empower local communities to have a voice in the rules set for fracking in their own communities. The no-fracking Greens were furious. Change.org started a petition drive to dissuade the Bloomberg Philanthropies from supporting EDF, and other groups charged EDF with the ultimate sin of "filling a role that's closer to what industry's interests are,"[3] echoing the old Green belief that "industry interests" and environmental goals can never be aligned.

So, substantively, what would be the Center Green position on fracking? First, its analysis would be grounded in reality and not aspiration. The reality is that technology has disrupted the energy equation just as it has virtually all other aspects of life. Fracking and related technologies have driven the price of natural gas (Henry Hub, MMBtu) to a trading range, after 2009, typically between $2 and $4 (from $5 to $10 before 2009, with occasional spikes over that range) and dramatically reduced our dependence on imported energy. Fracking is not going away. Moreover, Center Green cannot ignore the fact that the natural gas revolution has the potential to finally break the country's reliance on its dirtiest energy source, coal.

When conservatives accuse the Green movement of waging a war on coal, Center Green proudly pleads "guilty."[4] Although coal still

is America's number one source of fuel for electric generation, supplying approximately 38–39 percent of our power, it is indisputably
the fuel source with the greatest impact on the environment, due
to open-pit mining and mountain top removal, the high level of
greenhouse gases and other pollutants emitted when it is burned,
and the large volume of toxic coal ash left behind. According to the
U.S. Energy Information Agency, combustion of natural gas emits
only 51 to 57 percent of CO_2 per unit of energy output compared to
coal (depending on the type of coal).[5] Confirming the EIA analysis,
a Harvard study concluded that generating one kilowatt-hour of
electricity from coal releases twice as much CO_2 to the atmosphere
as generating the same amount from natural gas.[6] ExxonMobil predicted in December 2011 that natural gas will replace coal as the primary fuel for electricity generation in the United States by 2025.[7] If
it turns out to be true, history could very well record that fracking
made the single greatest human contribution to the mitigation of
global warming.

So for Center Green the challenge is how to regulate fracking and
other emergent technologies to protect public health and the environment. The gas industry has long argued that fracking itself, carried out far below the depth of aquifers, does not carry with it the
risk of groundwater contamination. An independent expert study
by seven environmental scientists funded by the National Science
Foundation confirmed that gas and chemicals from fracking "very
rarely" seep upward to contaminate groundwater.[8] Instead, the study
finds that observed contamination results almost exclusively from
the failure in the steel and cement casings of wells, the risk of which
can be greatly reduced by regulations requiring best practices (such
as testing) to ensure well integrity, together with effective enforcement of those regulations. And, importantly, the study found that
the greater environmental threat arises from the large amounts of
contaminated wastewater that result from the fracking process.
Wastewater can be disposed of safely through limited treatment

and reuse for subsequent fracking, or by advanced water treatment to produce water usable for irrigation and other purposes. Instead, much of the wastewater is now used or stored untreated, delivered to treatment centers not equipped to deal with the relevant chemicals, or injected deep underground, often in places and in a manner that causes small but sometimes significant earthquakes.

So what does the best independent science suggest as a policy matter? Congress erred in 2005 when it amended the Clean Water Act to remove hydraulic fracturing fluids from the scope of "underground injections" regulated under that law without substituting any other regulatory framework. Michael Bloomberg, in defending his foundation's grants to EDF, put it well: "[I]t's clear we need stricter regulation. That means oversight of everything from well sealing to fracking fluid so that we can ensure the safety of the air, land, and water wherever fracking takes place."[9] Center Green agrees. And fracking should not be allowed everywhere, including in or near national and state parks and forests, or in municipal watersheds. Chemical composition of fracking fluids should be reported. Process water should be treated at plants equipped to remove all the hazardous chemicals or safely reinjected. Possible seismic impacts should be studied before permits are granted, and reinjection should not be permitted where the seismic risks are material. Testing of well integrity and strict control of methane leaks at the wellhead should be required. And regulations themselves are not sufficient. State legislators must adequately fund enforcement of fracking regulations (preferably at the expense of upstream developers).

Responsible drillers no longer dispute the need for enhanced regulation. At the annual oil and gas confab CERAWeek in Houston in 2014, the former chairman of Shell was reported as saying that regulatory standards combined with regulatory control and enforcement were key, and that industry and regulators must do more to solve problems associated with land and water use.[10] A Center Green approach would try to harness some of the energy now directed at the fruitless quest to ban fracking altogether, and focus it on these higher priority objectives.

———————

As I write, I am watching a long train of ominous-looking black tank cars snaking south along the sinuous west bank of the Hudson River. Inside them is a highly volatile crude oil from the Bakken shale formation under North Dakota and Montana, headed to refineries. I have seen derailments before along this section of track, and think of the pictures of the small Canadian town of Lac-Mégantic, where over forty people died in the thousand-yard blast radius caused by a derailment of the same ill-designed tank cars carrying the same highly volatile Bakken crude. My neighbors and I could be next. And the ecological consequences for the Hudson River could be devastating.

Crude oil is transported by rail only when pipelines are unavailable. Pipelines are safer and cheaper than rail or trucks. No one contests this. Most pipeline leaks are small, quickly contained in a small area, and readily cleanable. Pipelines do spring larger, catastrophic leaks, but these are quite rare (occurring at about the same rate as commercial jet crashes result in fatalities). But just as flying is far safer than driving, pipelines are far safer for the environment, and for people in the environment, than any of the alternative means of transporting petroleum.

So future historians will no doubt strain to explain why, given all the ecological challenges facing the planet, the environmental cause célèbre in America in the early twenty-first century was a proposal by a Canadian pipeline company to make an incremental addition to the country's enormous existing pipeline network. The answer is that the Green movement, hugely frustrated by its inability to accomplish anything meaningful in the fight against climate change, was drawn to this single simple thing that was easy for the public to understand, appeared to be winnable (all that was needed was a friendly president to deny a necessary permit), could become a focus and rallying cry for the movement as a whole, and could be leveraged as a pivotal moment, a "line in the sand," where the movement could finally claim to have turned back the relentless forward march of the carbon economy.

The choice by the Green movement to put all its chips on fighting Keystone XL was flawed from the outset. Because the choice of Keystone was more tactical than substantive, its opponents had difficulty agreeing on and articulating the case against the pipeline. The facts were and are that the Canadians, for political and economic reasons of their own, had already chosen to develop the relatively dirty tar-sand product to be carried south by Keystone, and no single transportation option was going to change that. It was an awkward fact that with the tar sands already in production, the pipeline was a far safer and environmentally preferable way to get this crude to market than trains and tankers. Three of the four phases of the Keystone pipeline were already built. Early articulated objections by environmentalists revolved around the safety of the pipeline and its route, objections that were largely resolved when the pipe was rerouted to avoid the ecologically sensitive Sand Hills region of Nebraska and much of the Ogallala aquifer that underlies the Great Plains. Keystone opposition then became a position in search of a rationale.

With little else to go on, the case against Keystone simply morphed to become a proxy for concern about climate change, despite two inconvenient truths. The first is that stopping the pipeline would be highly unlikely to prevent the greenhouse gas emissions associated with the Canadian tar sands, because—as the U.S. State Department and many others concluded—the tar-sand oil would find its way to markets even without Keystone XL. And the second is that even if the defeat of Keystone caused the Canadians to abandon the development of the crude that would have been transported by it, the EPA-estimated 18.7 million metric tons per year of incremental carbon emissions (compared with conventional crude oil) associated with producing and burning the tar-sand crude transported by Keystone is only what the *New York Times* called "an infinitesimal slice" of the global total[11] (and only about

17–20 percent higher than the greenhouse gas emissions that would result from "well-to-wheels" use of an equivalent amount of conventional crude). But to many in the movement, even those who admit that the pipeline itself would hardly rank on any list of substantive Green priorities, this is beside the point. As Tom Steyer, a major funder of the anti-Keystone effort, said, "The Keystone XL pipeline is a line in the sand that signifies whether our country has the courage, the commitment and the capacity to be a global leader in addressing the challenge of climate change before it's too late."[12] Or, as Gail Collins wrote in a *New York Times* op ed, "If the pipeline isn't built, the oil will still get to the refineries by train, but at least we wouldn't appear to be encouraging the energy industry to drill the worst stuff possible."[13] Quite aside from whether dragging out permitting for six years constitutes "encouraging," it is a stark admission that, at the end of the day, the fight was all about appearances. So the principal Green political fight of the decade was over a symbol—a symbol of whether the country was or was not ready to take climate change more seriously. Not surprisingly, one of the first things the new GOP-controlled Congress did in 2015 was to pass another bill approving Keystone, but it then failed to muster the votes necessary to override President Obama's veto. In November 2015 many Greens celebrated their long-sought victory, when the Obama administration denied the Keystone permit, largely, as the president admitted, to avoid undercutting America's "global leadership" on climate change, particularly in view of the coming climate change conference in Paris. Whether this denial of the Keystone permit constitutes a pivotal moment in energy policy remains to be seen. Nor is the Keystone matter itself finally settled. TransCanada's CEO said the company remains "absolutely committed" to building Keystone XL, and is exploring the option of filing a new application. With all GOP presidential candidates remaining in favor of Keystone, a resubmitted application would most likely be approved if any of them makes it to the White House. And in the meantime, oil imports from Canada continue to increase and close to one million barrels of oil each day roll across the country on oil trains, each one a human and ecological disaster waiting to happen.

What would a Center Green approach to Keystone have been? Center Green is no fan of tar sands, California bitumen, coal, or other energy sources whose carbon emission profiles (as a result of extraction, refining, and/or combustion) are high relative to the alternatives (like natural gas). So Center Green opposes the development of Canadian tar sands. Center Green would campaign for continuous improvement in the safety of all liquid and gas pipelines, and would have supported, out of an abundance of caution, rerouting the line to avoid vulnerable conservation lands such as the Sand Hills. But Center Green stands against squandering precious political capital on largely symbolic battles, and insists that the fights we pick are prioritized carefully. No one has claimed seriously that preventing a single pipeline sat anywhere near the top of opportunities to make a real dent in global greenhouse gas emissions. Center Green rejects the idea that we should deny the petroleum industry needed bits of infrastructure along the supply chain in a futile attempt to force fossil fuels from the economy before an economic alternative exists. And Center Green clearly rejects the denial of needed pipeline network when the consequence is rail and truck transportation, with its significantly increased risk to human and environmental safety, and higher carbon footprint. The NRDC policy statement on Keystone says, "Tar sands oil has no place in the clean energy economy." NRDC is correct. But we don't have a clean energy economy. We have a transitional economy, and Center Green seeks to avoid the hypocrisy of attacking everything about hydrocarbons at the same time that we still wish to consume more of them per capita than most other countries on the planet.

The sad irony of the Keystone debacle is that the enthronement of Keystone opposition as the litmus test of Green orthodoxy actually has retarded progress to the clean energy future that Keystone opponents, and all Greens, desire. In recent polls, anywhere from 57 to 68 percent of Americans said they supported permitting of Keystone XL.

The House passed at least eight separate bills authorizing construction of the pipeline. Fifty-three senators, including nine Democrats, signed a letter to the president urging approval. And how much did the rest of the Senate Democrats care? When it looked like a vote for Keystone could help reelect Louisiana Democrat Mary Landrieu in her runoff, fourteen Democratic senators threw the Greens under the bus and sided with the GOP in support of approval, falling only one vote short of the sixty required. Many sources indicated that the president himself viewed Keystone as a distraction. So what did Keystone opposition yield Greens? Notwithstanding the symbolic (and possibly temporary) victory, the fact remains that we created significant political complications for a friendly president, gave the GOP a useful wedge issue in the 2014 midterms, produced a potent issue that energized the worst of the anti-Green right, and squandered political capital that should have been deployed for far more substantive and important causes.

16

GETTING TO GREEN

What You Can Do

A ll of the strategies advanced by this book for transcending
the Great Estrangement and moving toward Center Green
share a common predicate for execution: political leadership. The Great Estrangement occurred because of top-down signals
from movement ideologues that environmental concern was not
consistent with being a true conservative. And so ideological and
political leaders on the right are the ones who must change that signal and again make it safe for the party faithful to care for nature
while retaining their conservative identities.

The 2016 Republican primaries and presidential election present an
unparalleled opportunity for Republican politicians brave and wise
enough to take up this challenge. In 2012, a desperate desire to unseat
President Obama at all costs overshadowed more strategic thinking
about how to position the GOP for national success in the long term.
During the current cycle, more Republicans are focused on the urgent
need to craft a message that will appeal to the approximately 35 percent of voters who now characterize their ideology as "moderate," and
the roughly 40 percent who self-identify as unaffiliated or independent.

Environmental issues present the perfect platform for pivoting toward these moderates and independents. The anti-Green passions of the right have somewhat cooled since 2012. The irresistible power of demographics is showing its hand as older white males shrink as a percentage of the electorate; younger and more diverse GOP voters, and potential GOP voters, hold more mainstream views on Green issues. In 2015, Pope Francis caught the attention of many Americans, including many conservatives, with his powerful proenvironmental message. And in 2016, Americans of all political persuasions share concerns about exploding oil trains, food safety, children's health, water quality, disappearing lakes, depleted aquifers, air pollution, severe drought, increasingly extreme weather, sea level rise, sprawl, and many other environmental issues. The GOP's national candidates cannot afford once again to be forced into a cranky corner by the party's crankiest primary voters.

There is an alternative. My advice to ambitious Republicans: Sound the call to stewardship of the natural world in the rich language of American values and moral responsibility with which so many GOP primary voters are comfortable. Bone up by reading a few environmental speeches by Theodore Roosevelt, Barry Goldwater, and Richard Nixon. Recognize the intimate connection with nature forged by the country's tens of millions of hunters, anglers, and outdoor enthusiasts. There is no need to be seen to capitulate to all of the left's prescriptions with respect to climate change; indeed, your strategists will probably tell you to not to use those words. That's fine. Talk about the unfinished business of clean water and clear air, the gross irresponsibility and market-warping effects of pollution, the risks of tampering with nature on a global scale, and the need to hand our children a world where nature remains resilient and adaptable, a world where people can flourish. Stress that Americans must lead this effort. Remind everyone that human health and the protection of the natural world is not a Republican or Democratic issue. Remind them of the great tradition of GOP conservation leadership and the inspiring outbreak of bipartisanship that midwifed the birth of modern environmentalism in the 1970s.

In a country desperate for bridges across the great political divide, be the unifying leaders the people want, not by mouthing platitudes that the voters have learned to distrust, but by proposing a concrete Center Green agenda that both sides, and most Americans, can support.

What would a GOP presidential primary contender have to gain by following my advice? He or she instantly would be distinguished from the rest of the primary crowd. Once the anti-Green taboo is broken by a leading conservative taking up the Green mantle, the odds are that the other candidates, saddled with the party's stale policies that reek of climate denial and capitulation to big coal interests, will look foolish by comparison. The far-right ideologues may howl, but 60 percent of GOP voters say they are neither members nor supporters of the Tea Party, and most of them are broadly supportive of environmental goals, even if they have doubts about over-regulation and government bureaucracy. There is every reason to expect that the six million activist hunters and anglers, and the five million local land trust members, all of whom care passionately about conservation and many of whom are GOP primary voters, will be attracted to your corner. And when the general election comes along, that large group of Americans who call themselves "moderates" will be grateful that your name is on the ballot.

———————————

The usual environmental polemic ends with a call to individual action, often to "think globally, act locally." This slogan suggests that you acknowledge that environmental problems are global in scope, but then implies that the primary solutions are personal in scale: recyle, compost, change to low wattage lights, and drive a hybrid. This is not how this book will end.

Instead of "think globally, act locally," the mantra of Greens should be "think ethically, act politically." "Think ethically" is meant to suggest that the path to motivation for Green action does not lie in individuals looking outward to problems that are large and seemingly intractable, but in looking inward to their own ethical compasses. The Green movement should not be selling a one-size-fits-all cognitive or moral framework (the "competing religion" of hard-right lore); it should be confident that dedication to ethical action will lead most people to a place where conservation and stewardship of the natural world seem right. There is little prospect in the short run that a conservative in Kansas will adopt the lifestyle choices of the liberal coasts—the Saturday morning trip to the farmers' market in the Prius, for example—especially if told to do so by liberal Greens. But a call to be a thoughtful person who takes ethics seriously and whose actions reflect one's underlying values is an admonition to which both those in Kansas and in suburban Connecticut should be equally receptive. Most importantly, ethical thinking grounded in personal values can be powerful enough to change over time political positions that were born merely of mimicry and conformity. If a positional belief like climate-change denial is a shirt worn to express solidarity with one's community, a lifetime of Al Gore PowerPoints will not change that. But an appeal to the denier's deeply held values, such as personal responsibility, prudence, generosity, and caring for others, especially if leavened with some personal connection with nature, just might.

"Act politically" in my formulation reflects the fact that environmental issues are political issues, meaning that changes in public policy, and not merely changes in personal behavior, are required for them to be solved. Of course, recycling and composting are good things to do, but they are not sufficient. Once your personal ethical compass tells you what is right and what wrong, then "act politically" is intended to signal that passivity is unacceptable, and that you must step up to your responsibilities as citizen. The civil rights movement did not suggest that it was enough to tackle your own personal racial prejudice, hoping that over time the cumulative effect of individual actions would change the world. The civil rights movement understood that change could be accomplished only by the mobilization of a mass movement of citizens aimed at holding those in power accountable for their actions. "Act politically" means networking with your fellow Greens and holding accountable politicians who ignore our common interest in the health and resilience of the world, or who find it financially or politically expedient to represent the interests of those who profit from pollution or unsustainable exploitation of our natural resources.

The Green as stern nanny or hectoring preacher is a model that has not worked. Although Center Green does not tell people what to think or how to live, it does ask everyone to try to connect with that deeply human part of themselves that cares about the natural world, other creatures, and the future. Most importantly, Center Green seeks to inspire all Americans with a positive vision of our future: a vision that includes a resilient planet where humans can flourish; revolutionary improvements to human health and longevity; a vision that each future generation of American children will share the medical, mental, and imaginative benefits of exposure to nature; and a vision of healthy and vibrant American cities, reinvented to deeply integrate the experience of green spaces into urban life.

––––––––––

Woven through this book is a long letter of advice for the staffs and boards of Green organizations and for ordinary people who consider themselves environmentalists. If you are one of these, then you should by now understand what I think you should do to move the Green movement forward: make a concerted effort to reconnect conservatives and moderates to their long tradition of conservation and offer them an authentic welcome back into the movement; facilitate this by abandoning the antigrowth and antibusiness thinking that has infected the movement and embracing a philosophy that puts people first; try to recapture the connectedness, spirit, and political effectiveness of environmentalism as a genuine mass movement; use the national land trust movement as a model to start to heal the Great Estrangement; and prioritize an agenda that can be advanced on a nonpartisan basis. This is a lot of work. It would be easier if we could wave a wand and eliminate the malevolent influence of conservative demagogues and polluter money that holds so many conservative voters and politicians in its spell. But blaming the Koch brothers and Fox News, as much as that blame may be merited, is not a plan to move forward. Greens who believe that environmental issues are serious and urgent must be the ones to take the first step across the partisan divide. Those advances will be ridiculed and rebuffed, at least initially, but the time has never been better to give it a try.

In the event you do not consider yourself an environmentalist, then I will follow my own advice and not tell you what to think or do. But if you have read this far I think it is reasonable to infer that you have some interest in nature and conservation. I offer one modest suggestion for your consideration: join some kind—any kind—of local group that is concerned with the outdoors, nature, or the environment. I don't ask you to accept any particular belief or to align with any particular policy. I do ask that if you like to plant flowers in your front yard, then hook up with a local gardening group. Is there a local nature trail that you enjoy walking? There is probably a local land trust that takes care of the forest or maintains the trail—join it. Are you an angler? Don't fish alone. An urban local food fanatic? Connect with your Slow Food chapter, farmers' market, or community garden. Hoped to be an ornithologist when you were younger? Find your local Audubon group. You get the point. All I ask is that the group be sufficiently local that it has live events or meetings, occasions where you can connect in person with like-minded folks. Signing up to join a group online is not good enough; this is not about sending money and receiving emails. It is about connecting in person and becoming part of an interactive network of folks who

are like-minded in at least one respect. Why do I make these suggestions? Once you are embedded in one of Burke's "little platoons," you
will be part of a group of people engaged in some way with nature.
And once you connect with the natural world you will begin to care
for it. Once you begin to care for your local place, you will most likely
act together with others to protect it. And once you are acting in
defense of your local place, you will have become a valuable part of
the broader Green community caring for the world.

If you consider yourself to be politically conservative, I ask you
to look beyond talk radio and the conservative politicians of the
moment, and reflect on the history of conservatism in America.
Think about the difference between positions on issues of the day,
and the deeper principles that are supposed to inform the evolution
of those positions over time. These principles include the mandate
to look beyond greed and materialism to the long project of civilization building in which we respect the achievements of our ancestors
and care deeply about our progeny. They include the fundamental
conviction that citizens must balance the allure of personal freedom
with the harder truth of personal responsibility. It is that moral call
to respect and responsibility that led the Republicans of a century
ago to lead the conservation movement and lay its contemporary
foundations. It is that sort of long-term thinking, together with the
conviction that prosperity, growth, and American strength depended
utterly on a healthy environment, that led Barry Goldwater, Richard
Nixon, and the conservatives of the 1970s to create the EPA and the
entire framework of environmental law, the same framework that
the talking heads on today's Fox News ridicule and would demolish. The conservatism that comes at you from the talking heads at
Fox News is something new, barely twenty years old, and is largely
disconnected from the great tradition of American conservative
thought. All I ask is that you realize that there is another way to be a
conservative and a patriot.

Finally, if you are a baby boomer, I ask you to shoulder a special responsibility to reconnect with the idealism of your youth, and use your wealth and wisdom to end the Great Estrangement and help the country realize the vision of Earth Day. The baby-boom generation that came out twenty million strong on Earth Day in 1970 may still belong to the Sierra Club, but they have been focusing on other things during the past forty years. They have done their work, raised their families, and largely retired. But they have not retired their dreams or their values. Many are now grandparents, and focused even more intently on the question of what world they will leave to their progeny. I am convinced that millions of them will reconnect with the idealism that made them think in 1970 that they could change that world. And this time, they will bring to the cause not only their idealism and voices, but their life experience and wealth. Carly Simon exhorted us to "let the dreamers wake the nation." Now we have the time and money, so let's do it.

———————————

F. Scott Fitzgerald wrote of the day in 1927 when Charles Lindbergh completed the world's first transatlantic flight and landed safely at Le Bourget Field in Paris: "For a moment people set down their glasses in country clubs and speakeasies and thought of their old best dreams." America the beautiful and bountiful, a land that will nurture and inspire our grandchildren as it is did our grandparents, is one of our oldest and best dreams. The political divide that separated half the country from a long tradition of caring for the Earth is a shallow and ephemeral thing. It arose only in the last twenty years and soon will be gone. Depoliticizing our love of nature and place will press the reset button on the environmental movement and unleash a force powerful enough to overcome today's venal partisanship and reconnect us with one of America's oldest and best dreams.

Acknowledgments

I owe a huge debt to my friends and colleagues in the numerous environmental organizations with which I have worked. I am inspired every day by their selfless dedication.

This book would not have been possible without the experience, skills, and support provided by my long career at Sullivan & Cromwell LLP. My partners, colleagues, and clients have taught me a great deal, and the diversity of their perspectives on environmental issues has been key to unlocking some of the insights in this book. Needless to say, all of the views expressed in this book are mine personally, and in no way represent the views of the firm or of any of its clients.

I continue to be dazzled by the quality and culture of W. W. Norton. This book benefited enormously from the rigorous ministrations of editor Star Lawrence, to whom I am truly grateful. Assistant editor Ryan Harrington smoothed the way to publication with confident professionalism. Copy editor Nancy Green saved me on more than one occasion from embarrassing error, while at the same time indulging certain idiosyncrasies.

I want to thank Simon Roosevelt, Ned Sullivan, and Rand Wentworth, each of whom read the manuscript as a work in progress and shared invaluable comments. Each of them is a Green leader of extraordinary skill and accomplishment, and epitomizes the values advocated in this book.

Notes

PROLOGUE

1 Industry estimated the cost of reducing sulfur and nitrogen dioxide pollution to be $1,500 per ton, the EPA estimated $600–800 per ton, and its environmental proponents estimated $300 per ton. Over the decade following the enactment of the law, the actual costs were less than $200 per ton. The estimated benefits are from a report by George W. Bush's Office of Management and Budget. Paul Walden Hansen, *Green in Gridlock, Common Goals, Common Ground, and Compromise* (College Station: Texas A&M Press, 2013), 32–33.

2 Ted Nordhaus and Michael Shellenberger, *Break Through: Why We Can't Leave Saving the Planet to Environmentalism* (Boston: Mariner Books, 2009), 33. Nordhaus and Shellenberger cite the Environics Research Group, "Socio-Cultural Trends: 3SC," 2004, www.americanenvironics .com.

3 Pew Research Center for the People and the Press, "Partisan Polarization Surges in Bush, Obama Years," http://www.people-press.org/2012/06/04/partisan-polarization-surges-in-bush-obama-years/(June 4, 2012).

4 David Brooks argues that this myopia is shared by both right and left, calling it "the No. 1 political fantasy in America today, which has inebriated both parties. It is the fantasy that the other party will not

exist. It is the fantasy that you are about to win a 1932-style victory that will render your opponents powerless." David Brooks, "Ryan's Biggest Mistake," *New York Times*, August 23, 2012, http://www.nytimes .com/2012/08/24/opinion/brooks-ryans-biggest-mistake.html?_r=0.

5 Michael Shellenberger and Ted Nordhaus, "The Death of Environmentalism: Global Warming Politics in a Post-Environmental World" (paper delivered at the Environmental Grantmakers Conference, October 2004), www.thebreakthrough.org/images/Death_of_Environmentalism .pdf; and Adam Werbach, "The Death of Environmentalism and the Birth of the Commons Movement," speech reprinted at www.grist.org/article/ werbach-reprint (December 2004).

6 Shellenberger and Nordhaus, "Death of Environmentalism," 7.

7 Ibid., 10.

8 Jonathan Haidt, *The Righteous Mind: Why Good People Are Divided by Politics and Religion* (New York: Pantheon, 2012).

9 My work as a lawyer has never included acting as a lobbyist or policy advocate for resource or energy companies in relation to environmental or political matters. My role as an outside finance lawyer to these clients has been to help raise funding for large energy, resource, and infrastructure investments.

10 "Record High 42% of Americans Identify as Independent" (Gallup poll, January 8, 2014), http://www.gallup.com/poll/166763/Record -High-Americans-Identify-Independents.aspx.

CHAPTER 1: THE GREEN AGENDA IN A HYPERPARTISAN AMERICA

1 Based on the growth in "Function 300," one of the approximate score of budget categories that measure spending by function rather than by the agency spending the money.

2 Pew Research Center telephone poll conducted October 4–7, 2012, as reported in Keith Johnson, "On Climate Change, Some Arguments Shift," *Wall Street Journal*, January 26–27, 2013, A4. See also Seth Motel, "Polls show most Americans believe in climate change, but give it low priority," FactTank (September 23, 2014), Pew Research Center, http:// www.pewresearch.org/fact-tank/2014/09/23/most-americans-believe -in-climate-change-but-give-it-low-priority/.

3 As discussed later, demographics may accomplish what Green advocacy could not. The same poll shows that 67 percent of Americans between

the ages of eighteen and twenty-nine believe that global warming is a "very/somewhat serious problem."

4   Petra Bartosiewicz and Marissa Miley, *The Too Polite Revolution: Why the Recent Campaign to Pass Comprehensive Climate Legislation in the United States Failed* (report prepared for the Symposium of the Politics of America's Fight Against Global Warming), 74, http://www.journalism .columbia.edu/system/documents/684/original/CLIMATE_CHANGE _FULL_WITH_COVER.pdf.

5   H.R. 2042, the "Ratepayer Protection Act," seeks to delay implementation of the rules until such time as all judicial review has been completed. And Oklahoma Attorney General Scott Pruitt has commenced an action seeking a preliminary injunction to stay the EPA's Clean Power Plan rules pending final determination of the inevitable legal challenge. The Supreme Court's June 2015 decision remanding the EPA's 2012 power plant mercury emission rules has emboldened those determined to stop the new EPA carbon limits from ever taking effect.

6   Paul Walden Hansen, *Green in Gridlock: Common Goals, Common Ground, and Compromise* (College Station: Texas A&M Press, 2013), 151.

7   http://sustainableagriculture.net/blog/function-300-letter/.

8   http://www.cbo.gov/publication/42728.

9   http://www.boone-crockett.org/pdf/FY12Function300Analysis.pdf.

10 See, e.g., Nicholas Institute of Environmental Policy Solutions, Peter Hart Research and Public Opinion Strategies, August 25–28, 2005, quoted in Ted Nordhaus and Michael Shellenberger, *Break Through: Why We Can't Leave Saving the Planet to Environmentalists* (Boston: Mariner Books, 2009), 32.

11 See, e.g., Pew Research Center for the People and the Press, "Little Consensus on Global Warming, Partisanship Drives Opinion," June 14–19, 2006, http://www.people-press.org/2006/07/12/little-consensus-on-global -warming/.

12 http://www.gallup.com/poll/153875/worry-water-air-pollution-historical -lows.aspx.

13 Hansen, *Green in Gridlock*, 16.

14 Australia's carbon tax was abolished in July 2014, with the government promising to replace it with a "direct action" plan to pay big polluters to cut carbon emissions. Australia maintained its commitment, achieved on a bipartisan basis, to cut emissions by 5 percent from 2000 levels by 2020.

15 GLOBE Climate Legislation Study, 4th ed., February 27, 2014; see http:// www.globelegislators.org/publications/legislation/climate.

16 "Climate-change laws, Beginning at home," *The Economist*, January 19, 2013.

17 Pew Research Center for the People and the Press, "Partisan Polarization Surges in Bush, Obama Years," http://www.people-press.org/2012/06/04/partisan-polarization-surges-in-bush-obama-years/(June 4, 2012). See also Pew Research Center, "Political Polarization in the American Public, How Increasing Ideological Uniformity and Partisan Antipathy Affect Politics, Compromise and Everyday Life," June 12, 2014.

18 Nolan McCarthy, Keith Poole, and Howard Rosenthal, *Polarized America: The Dance of Ideology and Unequal Riches* (Cambridge: MIT Press, 2008).

19 Pew, "Partisan Polarization Surges."

20 Based on "landslide" (>20 percent more Republican than country as a whole) and "strong" (10–20 percent more Republican) districts. See Nate Silver, "As Swing Districts Dwindle, Can a Divided House Stand?" *New York Times*, December 27, 2012. In 2014 the Rothenberg Political Report estimated that 223 House seats were "safe" for the GOP.

CHAPTER 2: IT WASN'T ALWAYS THIS WAY:
A BRIEF HISTORY OF CONSERVATION AND THE RIGHT

1 Roger Scruton, *How to Think Seriously About the Planet: The Case for an Environmental Conservatism* (Oxford: Oxford University Press, 2012), 5.

2 George Perkins Marsh, *Man and Nature: or, Physical Geography as Modified by Human Nature* (New York: Charles Scribner, 1864), 36.

3 Today's conservatives would do well to note that TR's dedication to capitalism was balanced by a fierce distrust of monopoly and other forms of concentrated economic power, and an insistence on true equality of opportunity—the need to give a "square deal" to the "little guy." Today's Republicans should study TR not only for his understanding that conservatism required a commitment to conservation, but also for his political acumen.

4 Quoted in Benjamin Kline, *First Along the River: A Brief History of the U.S. Environmental Movement* (Lanham, MD: Rowman & Littlefield, 2011), 63.

5 Although many environmentalists acknowledge and celebrate these origins of the Green movement in America, some contemporary conservatives try to put a distance between themselves and these early conservative conservationists. Showing signs of the antiestablishmentarianism that later flowered in the Tea Party, Gordon Durnil, in a mid-1990s work promoting conservative environmentalism, casually

dismisses the conservative conservation tradition as having "originated more or less as a hobby for the wealthy and elite in our society. For folks with names such as Roosevelt." Gordon Durnil, *The Making of a Conservative Environmentalist* (Bloomington: Indiana University Press, 1995), 181.

6   See discussion in Hal K. Rothman, *The Greening of a Nation? Environmentalism in the United States Since 1945* (Fort Worth: Harcourt Brace College, 1998), 16–18.

7   Donald C. Swain, quoted in Kline, *First Along the River*, 69.

8   The most notable exception was the fight to prevent the construction of the Echo Park Dam in Dinosaur National Monument, which provided a preview of the political battles to follow.

9   The speech is worth watching: https://youtu.be/5LpspwToZwA.

10   In his syndicated column, which appeared in newspapers on January 26 and 27, 1970, some titled "Mr. Nixon and Pollution" and some "Pollution Control and Bureaucracy," Buckley wrote: "I take it as axiomatic that no one has the right to pollute the air I breathe, or the water I drink, and that the latitudinarian habits of a society whose frontier was always bigger than any of us have finally caught up with us, generating a common revulsion."

11   Lindbergh was keenly interested in biodiversity and used his celebrity to support the World Wildlife Fund, the International Union for the Conservation of Nature, The Nature Conservancy, and the Oceanic Foundation.

12   John R. E. Bliese, *The Greening of Conservative America* (Boulder, CO: Westview Press, 2001), 11.

13   "Greening Bush," *The Economist*, March 5, 2005, 34 (as to Sierra Club) and Bliese, *Greening of Conservative America*, 275 (as to REP).

14   In July 1969, Angelinos awoke to their radios and televisions announcing, "The children of Los Angeles are not allowed to run, skip, or jump inside or outside on smog alert days by order of the Los Angeles Board of Education and the County Medical Association." Quoted in Kline, *First Along the River*, 88.

15   In 1964 the federal government registered its highest popularity in the polls. Franklin Foer, "New Frontiers of Failure," *The New Republic*, December 9, 2013, 3.

16   Kline, *First Along the River*, 90.

17   John C. Whitaker, "Earth Day Recollections: What It Was Like When the Movement Took Off," *EPA Journal* 14, no. 8 (July–August 1988).

18   Rothman, *Greening of a Nation*, 106–7.

19 Ibid., 122.

20 Quoted in Rothman, *Greening of a Nation*, 123.

21 Quoted in Bliese, *Greening of Conservative America*, 11.

22 Russell Train, *A Memoir* (Privately published, 2000), 180.

23 Train reports that the timing was carefully chosen by Nixon to make it his first official act of the decade. Train, *Memoir*, 188.

24 Richard M. Nixon, "Statement About the National Environmental Policy Act of 1969" (January 1,1970), available at the American Presidency Project website, http://www.presidency.ucsb.edu/ws/?pid=2557.

25 For example, President Nixon, although generally supportive of the aims of the 1972 Clean Water Act amendments, vetoed the bill because he objected to its cost, estimated at $24 billion. His veto was promptly overridden by the Senate by a vote of 52–12 (with 17 votes to override coming from Republicans) and by the House by a vote of 247–23 (with 96 of the override votes coming from Republicans). Nixon then asserted executive authority to impound the appropriated funds, but was overruled by the Supreme Court.

26 HR 17255, the weaker version of the act, first passed by the House.

27 Rothman, *Greening of a Nation*, 125.

28 Russell Kirk, "Common Reader for Everyday Ecologists," *New Orleans Times-Picayune*, September 20, 1971.

29 Justin Gillis, "The Montreal Protocol, a Little Treaty that Could," *New York Times*, December 9, 2013.

CHAPTER 3: WHAT WENT WRONG: THE GREAT ESTRANGEMENT

1 Hal K. Rothman, *The Greening of a Nation? Environmentalism in the United States Since 1945* (Fort Worth: Harcourt Brace College, 1998), 112–13.

2 Ibid., xii.

3 Theda Skocpol, *Naming the Problem: What It Will Take to Counter Extremism and Engage Americans in the Fight against Global Warming* (report prepared for the Symposium on the Politics of America's Fight Against Global Warming, February 14, 2013), http://www.scholarsstrategynetwork.org/sites/default/files/skocpol_captrade_report_january_2013_0.pdf.

4 Aaron McCright, Chenyang Xiao, and Riley E. Dunlap, "Political polarization on support for government spending on environmental protection in the USA, 1974–2012," *Social Science Research* 48 (2014), 251–60.

5 The gap is measured in "points," meaning the difference in the vot-

ing records between the parties, where 0 represents opposition to all legislation identified by the LCV as a priority, and 100 means a perfect Green voting record. Skocpol, *Naming the Problem*, 60–61.

6 Benjamin Kline, *First Along the River: A Brief History of the U.S. Environmental Movement* (Lanham, MD: Rowman & Littlefield, 2011), 115.

7 Philip Shabecoff, *A Fierce Green Fire: The American Environmental Movement*, rev. ed. (Washington, D.C.: Island Press, 2003), 204.

8 Ibid., 200.

9 Edith Efron titled her book *The Apocalyptics: Cancer and the Big Lie.* The cancer controversy is discussed in Shabecoff, *Fierce Green Fire*, 217–18.

10 Rothman, *Greening of a Nation*, 180.

11 Kline, *First Along the River*, 122.

12 Rothman, *Greening of a Nation*, 181.

13 Shabecoff, *Fierce Green Fire*, 243.

14 Like his Democratic successor, President Clinton was largely confined to actions he could take without Congress, including protecting significant lands with national-monument designations and strengthening clean air standards through administrative action.

15 Kline, *First Along the River*, 142. Ms. Chenoweth-Hage, who told the *New York Times* that federal agents in black helicopters were landing on Idaho farms to enforce the Endangered Species Act, also famously called environmentalism "a cloudy mixture of New Age mysticism, Native American folklore, and primitive earth worship." Rocky Barker, "Chenoweth's Logic Aimed at Environment Is Flawed," *Idaho Falls Post Register*, February 18, 1996, quoted in Bruce Yandle, *The Market Meets the Environment* (Lanham, MD: Rowman & Littlefield, 1999).

16 See Pew, "Partisan Polarization Surges." See also Dan Farber, "Environmental Values and Political Polarization," Legal Planet, November 6, 2012, www.legal-planet.org/2012/11/06/environmental -values-and-political-polarization/.

17 Jim Peterson, "Death of a Sawmill," *Wall Street Journal*, December 29, 2005, A11.

18 Christine Todd Whitman, *It's My Party Too* (New York: Penguin, 2005), chap. 5.

19 *New York Times*, March 16, 1999, quoted in Kline, *First Along the River*, 161.

20 See, e.g., Daniel Henninger, "Enviromania," *Wall Street Journal*, August 7, 2008, A11.

21 These and many other similar comments are collected on the Environment page of www.rightwingwatch.org.

22 Thurman Arnold, *The Folklore of Capitalism* (New Haven: Yale University Press, 1937), 359.

23 Frederick Buell, *From Apocalypse to Way of Life: Environmental Crisis in the American Century* (New York: Routledge, 2014), 19.

24 McCright, Xiao, and Dunlap, *Political Polarization*, 252.

25 Ibid., 258.

26 Sierra Club press release, February 7, 2001.

27 Gordon Durnil, *The Making of a Conservative Environmentalist* (Bloomington: Indiana University Press, 1995), 144.

28 Joe McGinniss, *The Rogue: Searching for the Real Sarah Palin* (New York: Crown, 2011), 91.

29 Whitman, *It's My Party Too*, chap. 5.

30 Whitman quotes the National Wildlife Federation as making this statement only three months after Bush took office. Whitman, *It's My Party Too*, chap. 5.

31 Ibid.

32 Ibid.

33 Newt Gingrich and Terry L. Maple, *A Contract with the Earth* (New York: Plume, 2008), 187.

34 Quoted in Kline, *First Along the River*, 121.

35 http://groups.yahoo.com/neo/seac-discussion/conversations/topics/1019.

36 Statement by Audubon's then-president, David Yarnold, quoted in Felicity Barringer, "Q&A: Back to the Future With Environmental Bipartisanship," *New York Times*, October 22, 2012.

37 Paul Walden Hansen, *Green in Gridlock: Common Goals, Common Ground, and Compromise* (College Station: Texas A&M Press, 2013), 144.

38 S. Robert Lichter, "Liberal Greens, Mainstream Camouflage," *Wall Street Journal*, April 21, 1995, A10.

39 "Ship of Fools," *The Economist*, November 13, 2008, 44.

40 Jonathan Chait, "The Revolution Eats Its Own: How Republican moderates go silently to their doom," *The New Republic*, October 25, 2012, 33–34. See also Allen McDuffee, "Rick Santorum: 'Smart people' will never side with conservatives," *Washington Post*, September 15, 2012.

41 Michael Shellenberger and Ted Nordhaus, "The Death of Environmentalism: Global Warming Politics in a Post-Environmental World" (paper delivered at the Environmental Grantmakers Conference, October 2004), www.thebreakthrough.org/images/Death_of_Environmentalism .pdf, 33.

CHAPTER 4: THE ULTIMATE WEDGE ISSUE: CLIMATE CHANGE

1 Fred Krupp and Mariam Horn, *Earth: The Sequel, The Race to Reinvent Energy and Stop Global Warming* (New York: W. W. Norton, 2008), 9.

2 *Wall Street Journal*, July 24, 2002, A14.

3 Holman W. Jenkins, Jr., "Personal Score-Settling Is the New Climate Agenda," *Wall Street Journal*, March 1–2, 2014, A13.

4 David Thomas, "Anti-Christ of the Green Religion," (London) *Daily Telegraph*, January 20, 2002.

5 "The litany and the heretic," *The Economist*, January 31, 2002.

6 "Thought control: The scourge of the greens is accused of dishonesty," *The Economist*, January 11, 2003.

7 Mr. Lomborg now serves as director of the Copenhagen Consensus Center. The Copenhagen Consensus is a movement, promoted by *The Economist* and others, that uses cost-benefit analysis to assert that addressing problems other than climate change, such as air pollution, health, and literacy, are better investments for humanity.

8 See, for example, Peter J. Jacques, Riley E. Dunlap, and Mark Freeman, "The Organization of Denial: Conservative Think Tanks and Environmental Skepticism," *Environmental Politics* 17, no. 3 (2008), and the interview of the sociologist Robert Brulle, "Robert Brulle: Inside the Climate Change 'Countermovement,'" PBS *Frontline*, September 30, 2012.

9 Jacques, Dunlap, and Freeman, "The Organization of Denial," 360–61.

10 Ibid., 349.

11 These include Frederick W. Meyer, "Stories of Climate Change: Competing Narratives, the Media, and U.S. Public Opinion 2001–2010" (February 2012), available at www.shorensteincenter.org; and Robert J. Brulle, Jason Carmichael, and J. Craig Jenkins, "Shifting Public Opinion on Climate Change: An Empirical Assessment of Factors Influencing Concern over Climate Change in the U.S., 2002–2010," *Climatic Change* 114, no. 2 (February 2, 2012): 169–88. These findings are reviewed in Theda Skocpol, *Naming the Problem: What It Will Take to Counter Extremism and Engage Americans in the Fight against Global Warming* (report prepared for the Symposium on the Politics of America's Fight Against Global Warming, February 14, 2013), available at http://www.scholarsstrategynetwork.org/sites/default/files/skocpol_captrade_report_january_2013_0.pdf, 74–83, particularly as they explain the rapid deterioration in public concern about global warming following its 2007 peak.

12 The correlation is plotted by Skocpol in *Naming the Problem*, 78.

13   Josh Rosenau, "Will Climate Change Denial Inherit the Wind," www.ncse
.com/news/2013/04/will-climate-change-denial-inherit-wind-0014786.

14   Quoted in Paul Krugman, "The Ignorance Caucus," *New York Times*,
February 11, 2013.

15   According to Gallup, in March 2007, 41 percent of respondents, the
highest ever, reported that global warming worried them a great
deal. This was also the conclusion of Brulle, Carmichael, and Jenkins,
"Shifting Public Opinion on Climate Change."

16   Skocpol, *Naming the Problem*, 10.

17   Ibid., 90.

18   Quoted in *Environment & Energy Daily*, www.eenews.net/EEDaily/print/
2013/03/11/1.

19   *We Believe in America, 2012 Republican Platform*, 16, 19.

20   Coral Davenport, "Senate Democrats' All-Nighter Flags Climate
Change," *New York Times*, March 12, 2014.

21   Jenkins, "Personal Score-Settling Is the New Climate Agenda."

CHAPTER 5: MARKET FUNDAMENTALISM:
THE ANTIENVIRONMENTAL ORTHODOXY OF THE RIGHT

1   Philip Shabecoff, *A Fierce Green Fire: The American Environmental Movement*, rev. ed. (Washington, D.C.: Island Press, 2003), 282.

2   Thomas R. Wellock, *Preserving the Nation: The Conservation and Environmental Movements 1870–2000* (Wheeling, IL: Harlan Davidson, Inc.,
2007), 208.

3   Benjamin Kline, *First Along the River: A Brief History of the U.S. Environmental Movement* (Lanham, MD: Rowman & Littlefield, 2011), 172.

4   Shabecoff, *Fierce Green Fire*, 132.

5   For an early analysis, see, e.g., Organisation for Economic Co-opera-
tion and Development, *Environmental Performance in OECD Countries:
Progress in the 1990's* (Paris: OECD, 1996) and OECD, *Integrating Environment and Economy* (Paris: OECD, 1996). An interesting example of
the economy vs. environment fallacy is the opposition by the National
Association of Manufacturers to sulfur dioxide emissions reduction in
the 1980s, claiming that acid rain controls, if adopted, would "achieve
only the dubious distinction of moving the United States toward the
status of a second class industrial power by the end of the century"
(quoted in John R. E. Bliese, *The Greening of Conservative America* [Boul-

der, CO: Westview Press, 2001], 21). Instead, the cap-and-trade scheme both achieved a historic reduction in acid rain and allowed a surge of industrial innovation and growth.

6 James Surowiecki, "Waste Away," *New Yorker*, May 6, 2002.

7 The 2004 GOP Platform reflected this view, advocating that environmental stewardship efforts should be focused at the state and local level: "As the laboratories of innovation, they should be given flexibility and authority to address many environmental concerns." The platform document is available at http://www.presidency.ucsb.edu/papers_pdf/25850.pdf (unpaginated).

8 For example, Gordon Durnil, the self-professed "conservative environmentalist," writing in 1995, seemed to fear the process, cost, and bureaucracy of government regulation more than the limiting effect on corporate and individual action. As a result, he advocated straightforward rules requiring zero discharge of toxic substances instead of a traditional scheme of permitting and regulation. He explained that "attempts to *regulate* such substances have not resulted in a terribly efficient or successful set of programs. . . . Regulatory standards tend to be excuses which enable governments to set exceptions for the discharge of various poisons into the waters of North America through the collection of fees and issuance of permits" [emphasis in the original]. Gordon Durnil, *The Making of a Conservative Environmentalist* (Bloomington: Indiana University Press, 1995), 26.

9 Marc Landy and Charles Rubin, *Civic Environmentalism: A New Approach to Policy* (Washington, D.C.: George C. Marshall Institute, 2001), 8.

10 Durnil, *Making of a Conservative Environmentalist*, 183.

11 Matthew Carolan, "Double Agent for the Greens?" review on the website of the Acton Institute for the Study of Religion and Liberty, http://www.acton.org/pub/religion-liberty/volume-6-number-4/double-agent-greens.

12 Tom Hamburger, "Sen. Inhofe, denier of human role in climate change, likely to lead environment committee," *Washington Post*, November 5, 2014.

13 Jonathan Allen and Erica Martinson, "EPA wears the bull's-eye," *Politico*, June 20, 2012.

14 See, e.g., Kimberley Strassel, "The Real Obama Climate Deal," *Wall Street Journal*, January 25, 2013, A11.

15 Dan Farber, "Environmental Values and Political Polarization," *Legal Planet*, November 6, 2012, www.legal-planet.org/2012/11/06/environmental-values-and-political-polarization/.

16 Tom Hamburger, Kathleen Hennessey, and Neela Banerjee, "Koch brothers now at the heart of GOP power," *Los Angeles Times*, February 6, 2011.

17 Wellock, *Preserving the Nation*, 239.

CHAPTER 6: UNEASY ABOUT GROWTH: THE ANTICAPITALIST TENDENCY IN ENVIRONMENTALISM

1 James Gustave Speth, *The Bridge at the End of the World: Capitalism, the Environment, and Crossing from Crisis to Sustainability* (New Haven: Yale University Press, 2008), 117.

2 Clive Hamilton, *Growth Fetish* (Crows Nest, Australia: Allen & Unwin, 2003), xvi. Hamilton makes the arguments, familiar to many of us, that we fetishize growth, but that it does not bring us happiness, or even necessarily mitigate social problems such as unemployment, poverty, overwork, or lack of employment security. Hamilton observes that in a society where our main role is to be a consumer, we "seek fulfillment but settle for abundance." He proposes a "new politics of happiness" that encourages people to "pursue a rich life instead of a life of riches."

3 The estimates differ because of different assumptions about the percentage of the population that will join the labor force, trends in self-employment, and other factors.

4 For example, when the "Group of 10" NGOs (now called The Green Group) published its first major position paper in 1986, it characterized overpopulation as one of the "root causes" of environmental problems. See Robert Cahn, ed., *An Environmental Agenda for the Future* (Washington, D.C.: Island Press, 1985), 4.

5 Marian R. Chertow, "The IPAT Equation and its Variants," *Journal of Industrial Ecology* 4 (2000), 13.

6 The bet is the subject of a recent book by Yale history professor Paul Sabin, *The Bet: Paul Ehrlich, Julian Simon, and Our Gamble over Earth's Future* (New Haven: Yale University Press, 2013).

7 Cass R. Sunstein, "The Battle of Two Hedgehogs," *New York Review of Books*, December 5, 2013, 21.

8 Ted Nordhaus and Michael Shellenberger, *Break Through: Why We Can't Leave Saving the Planet to Environmentalists* (Boston: Mariner Books, 2009), 17.

9 Interestingly, this idea was stated with some eloquence in the 2000 GOP Platform, which read: "Economic prosperity and environmental protection must advance together. Prosperity gives our society the wherewithal to advance environmental protection, and a thriving natural environment enhances the quality of life that makes prosperity worthwhile." By 2004, this concept of economy and environment advancing together had been abandoned in favor of prioritization of the economy: "Republicans know that economic prosperity is essential to environmental progress." The 2000 platform document is available at http://www.presidency.ucsb.edu/ws/index.php?pid=25849 (unpaginated), and the 2004 platform document at http://www.presidency.ucsb.edu/papers_pdf/25850.pdf (unpaginated).

10 This argument has been made by many authors, based largely on Abraham Maslow's "hierarchy of needs," a pyramid with the basic material needs (food, shelter, and security) at the base, followed by the needs for status, belonging, and self-esteem, above which sit higher needs such as self-realization, purpose, and fulfillment. See A. H. Maslow, *The Farther Reaches of Human Nature* (New York: Viking, 1971). This analytical paradigm is sometimes confused with an iterative sequence, in which humans need to satisfy the needs at a lower level in order to progress to the next level, leading some to argue that affluence is required in order for people to become interested in nature and committed to a broad environmental agenda. This argument ignores the fact that poor people living rural, agricultural, and traditional lives often are more connected to nature than the urban affluent. Without in any way underestimating the soul-searing burdens of extreme poverty, it is equally offensive to endorse the blanket proposition that the poor are incapable of achieving self-realization or personal fulfillment. The point is simply that in general, with respect to an entire population, a rise in overall affluence is correlated with increasing support for the Green agenda.

11 Speth, *Bridge at the End of the World*, 116.

12 Garrett Hardin, "The Tragedy of the Commons," *Science* 162, no. 3859 (December 13, 1968): 1243.

13 Speth, *Bridge at the End of the World*, 8. Some conservatives don't like to speak about "market failures," but ascribe the tragedy of the commons and externalities to "market absence. " See, e.g., Roger Scruton, *How to Think Seriously About the Planet: The Case for an Environmental Conservatism* (Oxford: Oxford University Press, 2012), 141.

14 Russell Kirk, *The Conservative Mind: From Burke to Eliot,* 7th rev. ed. (Washington, D.C.: Regnery, 2001), 140.

15 Naomi Klein, "Capitalism vs. the Climate," *The Nation,* November 29, 2011. See also Klein, *This Changes Everything: Capitalism vs. the Climate* (New York: Simon & Schuster, 2014).

16 Dinesh D'Souza, "The Gathering Storm, Mass Affluence and Its Discontents," *Philanthropy,* November/December 2000.

17 Frederic D. Krupp, "New Environmentalism Factors in Economic Needs," *Wall Street Journal,* November 20, 1986.

18 USCAP included more than twenty CEOs of major American corporations and the leaders of EDF, NRDC, the Pew Center on Global Climate Change, the World Resources Institute, The Nature Conservancy, and the National Wildlife Federation (which dropped out in 2009).

19 Doug Parr, "C4's What the Green Movement Got Wrong: Environmentalists Respond," The Guardian Environment Blog, November 4, 2010, www.theguardian.com/environment/blog/2010/nov/04/c4-what-green-movement-wrong.

20 John Cavanagh and Jerry Mander, eds., *Alternatives to Economic Globalization: A Better World Is Possible* (San Francisco: Berrett-Koehler, 2002), 122–24.

21 Wes Jackson, quoted in Heather Rogers, *Green Gone Wrong: How Our Economy Is Undermining the Environmental Revolution* (New York: Scribner, 2010), 191.

22 Danielle Sacks, "Working With the Enemy," http://www.fastcompany.com/60374/working-enemy (September 2007).

23 Andrew Goldstein, "Too Green for Their Own Good," *Time,* August 26, 2002.

24 Coral Davenport, "Keystone Pipeline May Be Big, but This Is Bigger," *New York Times,* April 22, 2014, F2.

25 Robin Mann, quoted at www.content.sierraclub.org/naturalgas/content/beyond-natural-gas, accessed January 26, 2013.

26 "Sierra Club Natural Gas," *Wall Street Journal,* May 30, 2012, A12.

27 Speth, *Bridge at the End of the World.*

CHAPTER 7: THE GREEN MOVEMENT AT FIFTY

1 Quoted in Petra Bartosiewicz and Marissa Miley, *The Too Polite Revolution: Why the Recent Campaign to Pass Comprehensive Climate Legislation*

in the United States Failed (report prepared for the Symposium of the Politics of America's Fight Against Global Warming), 27.

2 Intergovernmental Panel on Climate Change, *Climate Change 2014: Mitigation of Climate Change* (New York: Cambridge University Press, 2014), also available at http://www.ipcc.ch/report/ar5/wg3/. The findings of the third phase of the report were leaked to the *New York Times* and others. See Justin Gillis, "U.N. Says Lag in Confronting Climate Woes Will Be Costly, Waiting to Cut Carbon Emissions Could Outstrip Technology's Ability to Preserve Planet, Report Warns," *New York Times*, January 17, 2014, A8.

3 In a 2011 speech at the Yale School of Forestry and Environmental Studies, Shellenberger and Nordhaus estimated that in 2009–2010 alone, Green NGOs spent over $1 billion promoting action in response to climate change. Speech by Michael Shellenberger and Ted Nordhaus, "The Long Death of Environmentalism" (February 25, 2011), http://the breakthrough.org/archive/the_long_death_of_environmenta.

4 See, for example, the back-and-forth between Professor Skocpol and Thinkprogress.org climate blogger Joe Romm (a former DOE official) (Joe Romm, thinkprogress.org posts on January 18, 2013, and March 21, 2013, and Professor Skocpol's replies in the comments).

5 Reliable numbers are hard to find. Bartosiewicz and Miley cite the Center for Responsive Politics, which estimates that in 2007–2009 opponents spent $492 million in lobbying against carbon legislation, versus around $35 million spent by Green groups in support of it. Bartosiewicz and Miley, *Too Polite Revolution*, 5. Much more was spent by the Green side between 2008 and 2010—at least $368 million, and probably more than $560 million according to one controversial estimate. Matthew C. Nisbet, *Climate Shift, Clear Vision for the Next Decade of Public Debate* (2011), http://climateshiftproject.org/ report/climate-shift-clear-vision-for-the-next-decade-of-public -debate/. Whatever the exact number, corporations and Green NGOs do not play on a level field, because most Green NGOs are public charities whose lobbying activities are limited by the tax laws.

6 Theda Skocpol, *Naming the Problem: What It Will Take to Counter Extremism and Engage Americans in the Fight against Global Warming* (report prepared for the Symposium on the Politics of America's Fight Against Global Warming, February 14, 2013), 74, http://www.scholarsstrategy network.org/sites/default/files/skocpol_captrade_report_january _2013_0.pdf, 96, 107.

7 Quoted in Auden Schendler, *Getting Green Done: Hard Truths from the Front Lines of the Sustainability Revolution* (New York: Public Affairs, 2009), 5.

8 Benjamin Kline, *First Along the River: A Brief History of the U.S. Environmental Movement* (Lanham, MD: Rowman & Littlefield, 2011), 191.

9 Thomas R. Wellock, *Preserving the Nation: The Conservation and Environmental Movements* (Wheeling, IL: Harlan Davidson, Inc., 2007), 10–11. He also observes: "By the end of the twentieth century, the environmental movement had lost its bipartisan appeal . . . leaving the movement unsure of its future course," p. 4.

10 Jeffrey M. Jones, "In U.S., Alternative Energy Bill Does Best Among Eight Proposals, Two-thirds favor expanded drilling and exploration for oil and gas" (Gallup poll, February 2, 2011), http://www.gallup.com/poll/145880/alternative-energy-bill-best-among-eight-proposals.aspx.

11 A. Leiserowitz, E. Maibach, C. Roser-Renouf, and J. D. Hmielowski, *Climate Change in the American Mind: Public support for climate & energy policies in March 2012* (Yale University and George Mason University, Yale Project on Climate Change Communication, 2012), http://environment.yale.edu/climate/files/Policy-Support-March-2012.pdf.

12 Lymari Morales, "Green Behaviors Common in U.S., but Not Increasing, Nearly all recycle, making it the most common environmentally friendly action" (Gallup poll, April 9, 2010), http://www.gallup.com/poll/127292/green-behaviors-common-not-increasing.aspx.

13 Pew Research Center, "Economy, Jobs Trump All Other Policy Priorities in 2009, Environment, Immigration, Health Care Slip Down the List" (January 22, 2009), http://www.people-press.org/2009/01/22/economy-jobs-trump-all-other-policy-priorities-in-2009/.

14 Jeffrey M. Jones, "Americans Increasingly Prioritize Economy Over Environment, Largest margin in favor of economy in nearly 30-year history of the trend" (Gallup poll, March 17, 2011), http://www.gallup.com/poll/146681/Americans-Increasingly-Prioritize-Economy-Environment.aspx.

15 Frank Newport, "Economy, Government Top Election Issues for Both Parties, Differ most widely on climate change, deficit" (Gallup poll, October 9, 2014), http://www.gallup.com/poll/178133/economy-government-top-election-issues-parties.aspx.

16 Philip Shabecoff, *A Fierce Green Fire: The American Environmental Movement*, rev. ed. (Washington, D.C.: Island Press, 2003), 139.

17 Raymund Flandez, "Nature Conservancy Faces Flap Over Fundraising Deal to Promote Swimsuit Issue," *The Chronicle of Philanthropy*, March 6, 2012. http://philanthropy.com/article/Swimsuit-Deal-Causes-Flap -at/156923/. The average age was reported to have increased to sixty-five. See Paul Voosen, "Conservation: Myth-busting scientist pushes greens past reliance on 'horror stories,'" April 3, 2012, http://www .eenews.net/stories/1059962401.

18 Paul Walden Hansen, *Green in Gridlock: Common Goals, Common Ground, and Compromise* (College Station: Texas A&M Press, 2013), 79.

19 Lisa Curtis, "Don't call me an environmentalist," http://grist.org/ green-jobs/dont-call-me-an-environmentalist/.

20 The "Green jobs" enthusiasts are also highly motivated by the goals of poverty alleviation and social justice, and seek to align the environmental movement with those goals. See, for example, the work of Anthony Kapel "Van" Jones, who, among other things, founded Green for All and served as an advisor early in the administration of President Obama.

21 Bartosiewicz and Miley, *Too Polite Revolution*, 70.

22 Shabecoff, *Fierce Green Fire*, 255.

23 Joel Kotkin, *The Next Hundred Million: America in 2050* (New York: Penguin, 2010).

24 These groups included a group of two thousand business owners from South Florida who were organized as a lobbying force by American Business for Clean Energy, The Hip Hop Caucus, the National Latino Coalition on Climate Change, and the Commission to Engage African Americans on Energy, Climate Change and the Environment, among others.

25 Quoted in Bartosiewicz and Miley, *Too Polite Revoution*, 63–64.

26 Adam Rome, *The Genius of Earth Day: How a 1970 Teach-In Unexpectedly Made the First Green Generation* (New York: Hill and Wang, 2013), 210–11.

27 Nicholas Lemann, "When the Earth Moved, What happened to the environmental movement?" *New Yorker* (April 15, 2013).

28 The term "conservation" also has some difficult baggage. As the word was used in America in the twentieth century, it carried a strong connotation of the husbanding of natural resources such as timber and minerals, as opposed to a broader sense of protecting nature for a variety of reasons other than ensuring that resources continue to be available to support economic activity. In 1969, the United Nations

and the International Union for Conservation of Nature defined "conservation" as "the rational use of the environment to achieve the highest quality of living for mankind." USAID, Glossary for Natural Resource Management, http://rmportal.net/help/additonal -help-docs/archive/natural-resource-management-glossary-and -keywords/nrm-glossary. This definition is not bad, as it recognizes that a healthy environment supports not only wealth, but health, beauty, knowledge, and spirituality.

29 Dr. Mike Hulme, then director of the Tyndall Center for Climate Change Research, quoted in Andrew Revkin, "A New Middle Stance Emerges in Debate over Climate," *New York Times*, January 1, 2007.

30 Shellenberger and Nordhaus, *Death of Environmentalism*, 13. They observed, with only a touch of exaggeration, "The assumption here is that the American electorate consists of 100 million policy wonks eager to digest the bleak news we have to deliver" (p. 28).

31 Daniel Kahneman, *Thinking: Fast and Slow* (New York: Farrar, Straus and Giroux, 2011).

32 Kahan's theories as they apply to climate change are discussed in Judith Shulevitz, "Why do people deny science?," *The New Republic*, October 21, 2013, 16.

33 See Dan M. Kahan, "Making climate-science communication evidence-based: all the way down," in M. Boykoff and D. Crow, eds., *Culture, Politics and Climate Change: How Information Shapes Our Common Future* (New York: Routledge, 2014), 203. See also Dan M. Kahan and Donald Braman, "Cultural Cognition and Public Policy," *Yale Law & Policy Review* 24, no. 149 (2006).

34 Shulevitz, "Why do people deny science?," 18.

35 Bartosiewicz and Miley, *Too Polite Revolution*, 49, citing a Rasmussen Reports May 2009 poll.

36 Eric Pooley, *The Climate War: True Believers, Power Brokers, and the Fight to Save the Earth* (New York: Hyperion, 2010), 205, 387.

37 Bartosiewicz and Miley, *Too Polite Revolution*, 59.

38 Hansen, *Green in Gridlock*, 80. The Green Group membership fluctuates and is not publicly reported. As of 2013 Hansen reported that it includes (in alphabetical order) American Rivers, Apollo Alliance, Center of International Environmental Law, Clean Water Action, Defenders of Wildlife, Earthjustice, Environment America, Environmental Defense Fund, Friends of the Earth, Greenpeace, Izaak Walton League, Land Trust Alliance, League of Conservation Voters, National Audu-

bon Society, National Parks Conservation Association, National Religious Partnership for the Environment, National Tribal Environmental Council, National Wildlife Foundation, Native American Rights Fund, Population Action International, National Resources Defense Council, Oceana, Pew Environmental Group, Physicians for Social Responsibility, Population Connection, Rails to Trails Conservancy, Sierra Club, The Trust for Public Land, Union of Concerned Scientists, World Resources Institute, and World Wildlife Fund.

39 Emily Miller, "Democratic front group hyped as hunters by media in gun control fight," *Washington Times*, April 5, 2013.

40 Shabecoff, *Fierce Green Fire*, 226

41 Established in 1981, the informal group was first called the "Group of Ten," consisting of the core of the environmental establishment (excluding those organizations, such as Greenpeace, focused on direct action and thus lacking a strong Washington, D.C., presence and lobbying capacity). See note 38.

42 Members include groups such as the Boone and Crockett Club, Ducks Unlimited, Izaak Walton League, Pheasants Forever, The Wildlife Society, Theodore Roosevelt Conservation Partnership, and U.S. Sportsmen's Alliance.

43 Quoted in Hansen, *Green in Gridlock*, 87.

44 Hansen, *Green in Gridlock*, 83, 88.

45 Rome, *Genius of Earth Day*, 58–59.

46 Wellock, *Preserving the Nation*, 147.

47 Hal K. Rothman, *The Greening of a Nation? Environmentalism in the United States Since 1945* (Fort Worth: Harcourt Brace College, 1998), 41–42.

48 Quoted in Kline, *First Along the River*, 133.

49 Rome, *Genius of Earth Day*, 280.

50 Nicholas D. Kristof, "I Have a Nightmare," *New York Times*, March 12, 2005.

51 The dark, light, and bright distinction was coined by Alex Steffen. See Steffen, ed., *Worldchanging: A User's Guide for the 21st Century* (New York: Abrams, 2011).

52 Viridian Green (chosen because viridian green was considered an entirely artificial, i.e., designed and not natural, shade of green) was conceived by Bruce Sterling. Philosophically and practically, it was essentially coextensive with mainstream Bright Green, with perhaps a greater emphasis on design. See Bruce Sterling, "Viridian: The Manifesto of January 3, 2000," http://www.viridiandesign.org/manifesto .html.

53 For years Greens have been looking to define the transition from third-
to fourth-wave environmentalism, and arguing about whether it has
occurred. By consensus, the "first wave" was the conservation movement that originated in the nineteenth century and climaxed with
Teddy Roosevelt; the "second wave" is the popular movement marked
by the first Earth Day in 1970 and ensuing decade of environmental
progress. The "third wave" is usually taken to mean the maturing of the
Green movement into inside-the-Beltway professional organizations
dominated by lawyers, lobbyists, and scientists, sometime partnering
with corporations. The USCAP coalition in which big Green and big
business worked together to advance a climate-change cap-and-trade
compromise was probably the climactic moment of the third wave,
which is often distinguished by its emphasis on Green technologies
and the transition to a "Green economy." The fourth wave is used to
mean the movement that will replace the third, but there consensus
stops, with each of the shades of Green claiming to be the successor to
Green history. Bill McKibben and the new activists like 350.org are the
most widely acknowledged claimants to the fourth-wave title, which
for them means the transition to a Green movement dominated by
local organizations and activists, a movement that is participatory,
populist, and unencumbered by ties to the corporate sector, but which
also retains a strong whiff of antigrowth conviction and other limitations that so crippled their predecessors.

54 Bright Greens sometimes are also called "neo-environmentalists" and
the Bright Green label often is used to include Nordhaus and Shellenberger and their so-called breakthrough school.

55 Fred Krupp and Mariam Horn, *Earth: The Sequel, The Race to Reinvent
Energy and Stop Global Warming* (New York: W. W. Norton, 2008), 9.

56 Ted Nordhaus and Michael Shellenberger are typical critics, referring
to these lifestyle choices as "ecologically irrelevant" and arguing,
"What downscalers offered was not a better way to reduce emissions,
but rather, a way to reduce guilt." See, e.g., Nordhaus and Shellenberger, "The Green Bubble," *The New Republic*, May 20, 2009.

57 Schendler, *Getting Green Done*. Other Dark Greens have labeled this
group Lazy Greens, characterizing them as folks who are unwilling to
make the sort of deep sacrifice that Dark Greens insist on, and who
are seen as wanting to shop their way to sustainability. The journalist Heather Rogers devoted an entire book, *Green Gone Wrong*, to criticizing these well-intentioned habitués of Whole Foods: "Couched in

optimism that springs from avoiding conflict, the current approach asks if taking care of ecosystems must entail a Spartan doing without when saving the planet can be fun and relatively easy." Rogers, *Green Gone Wrong: How Our Economy Is Undermining the Environmental Revolution* (New York: Scribner, 2010), 4.

CHAPTER 8: GETTING TO GREEN, STEP ONE: RECONNECTING CONSERVATIVES WITH CONSERVATION

1 Russell Kirk, *The Conservative Mind: From Burke to Eliot*, 7th rev. ed. (Washington, D.C.: Regnery, 2001), 8.
2 For this reason I rejected Russell Kirk, whose work is much better known by contemporary American conservatives. Kirk's brand of Burkean conservatism ignores—indeed, is overtly hostile to—the libertarian strain that has been so influential in American politics.
3 Edmund Burke, *Maxims and Opinions, Moral, Political and Economical, with Characters* vol. 1 (London: C. Whittingham, 1804), 53.
4 Clinton Rossiter, *Conservatism in America: The Thankless Persuasion* (New York: Vintage Books, 2nd ed., rev., 1962), 31.
5 Edmund Burke, *Reflections on the Revolution in France* (Oxford: Oxford University Press, 1993), 95.
6 Both conservatism and conservation are derived from the Latin word *conservare*, which means to keep, preserve, cherish, and treasure that which is worthy.
7 *The Report of the President's Commission on Americans Outdoors* (Washington, D.C.: Island Press, 1987), 14.
8 Russell Kirk, *Redeeming the Time* (Wilmington, DE: ISI Books, 1996), 33.
9 William Harbour, *The Foundations of Conservative Thought* (Notre Dame: University of Notre Dame Press, 1982), 102–3.
10 Edmund Burke, "A Letter to a Member of the National Assembly, in Answer to Some Objections to His Book on French Affairs, 1791," *The Works of the Right Honourable Edmund Burke*, vol. 4 (London: John C. Nimmo, 1887), 51.
11 Benjamin Kline, *First Along the River: A Brief History of the U.S. Environmental Movement* (Lanham, MD: Rowman & Littlefield, 2011), 53.
12 Edwin Way Teale, "February 2," *Circle of the Seasons: The Journal of a Naturalist's Year* (New York: Dodd, Mead, 1953).
13 Kirk, *The Conservative Mind*, 44.

14   Rossiter, *Conservatism in America*, 41.

15   Barry Goldwater, *The Conscience of a Majority* (New York: Prentice Hall, 1971).

16   Edmund Burke, *A Vindication of Natural Society: or, a View of the Miseries and Evils arising to Mankind from every Species of Artificial Society. In a Letter to Lord **** by a Late Noble Writer*, 2nd ed. (London: R.J. Dodsley, 1757).

17   For example, in the course of opposing the acid rain cap-and-trade scheme adopted in 1990, industry estimated the cost of reducing sulfur and nitrogen dioxide pollution to be $1,500 per ton. Over the decade following the enactment of the law, the actual costs proved to be less than $200 a ton. Paul Walden Hansen, *Green in Gridlock: Common Goals, Common Ground, and Compromise* (College Station: Texas A&M Press, 2013), 32–33.

18   This list was compiled by Yale economist William D. Nordhaus in 2013 based on an analysis by Greg Mankiw. See Nordhaus, *Climate Casino: Risk, Uncertainty, and Economics for a Warming World* (New Haven: Yale University Press, 2013), 314. See also www.carbontax.org/who-supports/conservatives/.

19   Ben Geman, "GOP Leaders Slam Door on Carbon Taxes," *The Hill*, July 16, 2012, http://thehill.com/policy/energy-environment/238111-boehner-mcconnell-slam-door-on-carbon-taxes.

20   Quoted in Alan Crawford, *Thunder on the Right: The "New Right" and the Politics of Resentment* (New York: Pantheon, 1980), 222.

21   David Brooks, "The Day After Tomorrow," *New York Times*, September 13, 2010.

22   William F. Buckley, Jr., "Mr. Nixon and Pollution" (sometimes titled "Pollution Control and Bureaucracy"), a syndicated column that appeared in various newspapers on January 26–29, 1970.

23   I do not underestimate the magnitude of the valuation problem. This is particularly vexing in relation to natural areas, where the act of destroying the aesthetic beauty of a place simultaneously undercuts the motive to save it.

24   The 1990 amendments to the Clean Air Act that set sulfur-dioxide emissions caps and then distributed tradable permits also worked. Acid rain–causing emissions were reduced more than 30 percent from 1990 levels (per EPA estimates), and cost industry overall only about 25 percent of the amount originally estimated by the EPA.

25   See, e.g., Kirk, *The Conservative Mind*, 8.

26   Hansen, *Green in Gridlock*, 12.

27 I do not condone flag burning. As a legal matter, I believe it should be protected expression. My mother, a World War II veteran not encumbered by my knowledge of constitutional law, found it rude and disrespectful and thought it should not be tolerated. That is a view I understand and respect.

28 Philip Shabecoff, *A Fierce Green Fire: The American Environmental Movement*, rev. ed. (Washington, D.C.: Island Press, 2003), 63.

29 Message to Congress transmitting the Council on Environmental Quality's Annual Report, February 19, 1986.

30 Marc Landy and Charles Rubin, *Civic Environmentalism: A New Approach to Policy* (Washington, D.C.: George C. Marshall Institute, 2001), 5.

31 Newt Gingrich and Terry L. Maple, *A Contract with the Earth* (New York: Plume, 2008), 15.

32 The poll was conducted for The Nature Conservancy by the bipartisan research team of Fairbank, Maslin, Maullin, Metz & Associates (D) and Public Opinion Strategies (R), June 16–19, 2012, http://www .nature.org/newsfeatures/pressreleases/poll-conservation-is-patriotic -and-has-bipartisan-support.xml.

CHAPTER 9: IS CONSERVATIVE ENVIRONMENTALISM REALLY POSSIBLE?

1 Durnil wrote: "Instead of joining in the environmental discussions, instead of making their case, instead of discussing potential solutions, industry officials built barriers to dialogue. They seemed to try very hard to live up to the reputation given to them by their nemesis, the organized environmental groups. That reaction was disturbing to me, because I had spent a lifetime in support of industry. My most basic philosophical beliefs include the thought that we cannot succeed as a free nation without a free market economic system. I expected more from the captains of industry." Gordon Durnil, *The Making of a Conservative Environmentalist* (Bloomington: Indiana University Press, 1995), 108. Durnil kept his faith in "captains of industry" and decided the immoral response of industry was due to the influence of their lobbyists.

2 Matthew Carolan, "Double Agent for the Greens?" review on the website of the Acton Institute for the Study of Religion and Liberty, http:// www.acton.org/pub/religion-liberty/volume-6-number-4/double

-agent-greens. Carolan also reviewed the book unfavorably in *National Review*, February 12, 1996, 58.

3 www.perc.org.

4 John R. E. Bliese, *The Greening of Conservative America* (Boulder, CO: Westview Press, 2001).

5 Rod Dreher, *Crunchy Cons: How Birkenstocked Burkeans, gun-loving organic gardeners, evangelical free-range farmers, hip homeschooling mamas, right-wing nature lovers, and their diverse tribe of countercultural conservatives plan to save America (or at least the Republican Party)* (New York: Crown Forum, 2006).

6 Newt Gingrich and Terry L. Maple, *A Contract with the Earth* (New York: Plume, 2008), 185.

7 Julie Hirschfeld David, "Gingrich Accepting Gore Invite Lands on Love Seat with Pelosi," Bloomberg, December 1, 2011, http://www .bloomberg.com/news/articles/2011-12-02/gingrich-accepting-gore -invite-lands-on-love-seat-with-pelosi.html.

8 Newt Gingrich, *Drill Here, Drill Now, Pay Less: A Handbook for Slashing Gas Prices and Solving Our Energy Crisis* (Washington, D.C.: Regnery, 2008). The book and its title obviously are designed to appeal to the "drill, baby, drill" faction of his party. There are few better examples of polit-ical expediency than the contrast with his statement only one year before that "[b]y weaning industrial societies from their dependence on fossil fuels, the world would be a far better place," Gingrich and Maple, *Contract with the Earth*, 48.

9 "No Endorsement for the White House," *The Green Elephant* 8, no. 2 (Fall 2004): 1.

10 Interview by author with Rob Sisson, president of ConservAmerica, January 7, 2014.

11 Coral Davenport, "Conservative Group Plans to Push Republicans Toward Action on Climate, Cleaner Energy," *National Journal*, August 19, 2012.

12 The companies leaving the coalition included BP America, ConocoPhil-lips, and Caterpillar.

13 Felicity Barringer, "Q&A: Back to the Future with Environmental Bipartisanship," *New York Times*, October 22, 2012.

14 Jon M. Huntsman, Jr., "The G.O.P. Can't Ignore Climate Change," *New York Times*, May 7, 2014, A25.

15 Frank Newport, "Four Years in, GOP Support for Tea Party Down to 41%, Support for the movement nationwide drops to 22%" (Gallup

poll, May 8, 2014), http://www.gallup.com/poll/168917/four-years-gop
-support-tea-party-down.aspx.

16 Jonathan Chait, "The Revolution Eats Its Own: How Republican moderates go silently to their doom," *The New Republic*, October 25, 2012, 32.

17 Jacob S. Hacker and Paul Pierson, *Off Center: The Republican Revolution
& The Erosion of American Democracy* (New Haven: Yale University Press,
2005), 225.

18 Pew Research Center, "GOP Deeply Divided Over Climate Change,"
November 1, 2013, http://www.people-press.org/2013/11/01/gop-deeply
-divided-over-climate-change/. This intraparty split on Green issues is
consistent with the divide between populist Tea Party Republicans and
"establishment" Republicans on other issues. For example, 2014 Pew
Research showed that 68 percent of establishment Republicans support
free-trade agreements, compared to only 39 percent of the populists; 64
percent of the establishment believe that immigrants strengthen the
United States, compared to only 17 percent of the populists. William A.
Galston, "Restive Republicans Target the Ex-Im Bank," *Wall Street Journal*, July 2, 2014, A13.

19 According to the 2010 census, the average population of a congressional district is around 710,000. Of these, votes cast average about
280,000 per district. Assuming on average roughly 25 percent of those,
or 70,000, are registered Republicans, the 25,000–30,000 Republicans
who prioritize conservation issues is a significant number.

20 Author interview with Rob Sisson.

21 Coral Davenport, "Why Republicans Keep Telling Everyone They're
Not Scientists," *New York Times*, October 31, 2014, A18.

22 Study by Responsive Management, cited by Paul Walden Hansen,
Green in Gridlock: Common Goals, Common Ground, and Compromise (College Station: Texas A&M Press, 2013), 88.

23 Speech at Center for Strategic and International Studies, April 23,
2007.

24 Not all of the moderate Republicans defeated in primary battles with
Tea Party candidates have gone quietly into the sunset. One, Bob
Inglis, a former GOP representative from South Carolina, formed the
Energy and Enterprise Initiative at George Mason University and is
actively promoting a carbon tax offset by equal tax cuts, so that it cannot fairly be accused of increasing the total tax burden or the size of
the federal government. Inglis argues that a carbon tax is necessary
to remedy an obvious market failure, and claims that he has found a

receptive audience in "young Republicans, federalist societies, energy clubs at business schools, [and] young evangelicals." Brad Plumer, "Could Republicans Ever Support a Carbon Tax? Bob Inglis Thinks So," *Washington Post*, March 14, 2013.

25 See, e.g., Stephen C. Rockefeller and John C. Elder, eds., *Spirit and Nature: Why the Environment Is a Religious Issue—An Interfaith Dialogue* (Boston: Beacon Press, 1992). One of the most successful books of this type is E. O. Wilson's *The Creation* (New York: W. W. Norton, 2006).

26 "Greening Bush," *The Economist*, March 5, 2005.

27 Ibid.

28 The Evangelical Climate Initiative, "Climate Change: An Evangelical Call to Action" (2006), http://www.npr.org/documents/2006/feb/evangelical/calltoaction.pdf.

29 Polling shows that only a minority of white evangelical Protestants agreed that climate change was real, and evangelical groups are divided on the EPA's proposed rule on carbon pollution. Theodore Schleifer, "Religious Conservatives Embrace Pollution Fight," *New York Times*, July 31, 2014, A17.

30 *Caritas in Veritate*, June 29, 2009.

31 Schleifer, "Religious Conservatives Embrace Pollution Fight."

32 Jeet Heer, "The Last Time Conservatives Dismissed a Major Encyclical, It Ended Terribly for Them," *The New Republic*, June 17, 2015.

33 Erica Werner and Matthew Daly, "GOP Dismisses Pope Francis' Climate Thoughts," http://www.usnews.com/news/politics/articles/2015/06/19/pope-francis-climate-message-yields-little-gop-response.

34 Joel Gillespie, "The Red, the Blue and the Green," *Onearth*, Spring 2005, 48.

35 John G. Taft, "The Cry of the True Republican," *New York Times*, October 23, 2013, A29.

36 See, e.g., in addition to Jonathan Haidt, *The Righteous Mind: Why Good People Are Divided by Politics and Religion* (New York: Pantheon, 2012) and Daniel Kahneman, *Thinking: Fast and Slow* (New York: Farrar, Straus and Giroux, 2011), discussed above; Margaret Heffernan, *Willful Blindness: Why We Ignore the Obvious at our Peril* (New York: Bloomsbury, 2012); and Cass R. Sunstein, *Going to Extremes: How Like Minds Unite and Divide* (New York: Oxford University Press, 2009).

37 Inglis also received the 2015 Profile in Courage award from the JFK Library. See Eric Holthaus, "This Man Is America's Best Hope for Near-Term Climate Action, He's a Republican," *Slate*, May 13, 2015.

38 Aaron McCright, Chenyang Xiao, and Riley E. Dunlap, "Political polar-

ization on support for government spending on environmental protection in the USA, 1974–2012," *Social Science Research* 48 (2014): 258.

39 Walter Lippmann, *A Preface to Politics* (N.p.: CreateSpace, 2012), 86.

40 Thomas R. Wellock, *Preserving the Nation: The Conservation and Environmental Movements* (Wheeling, IL: Harlan Davidson, Inc., 2007), 245.

41 Pew Research Center, "GOP's Favorability Rating Takes a Negative Turn," July 23, 2015, http://www.people-press.org/2015/07/23/gops-favorability-rating-takes-a-negative-turn/.

42 "Greening Bush," *The Economist*, March 5, 2005, 34.

43 Karl Rove, "Rove: The GOP's Path Back to Power," *Newsweek*, November 14, 2008.

44 In Colorado, for example, nineteen of the twenty-six candidates endorsed by Colorado Conservation Voters were elected in 2008. In Wisconsin, though, Governor Scott Walker was reelected in 2014 despite the fact that the national League of Conservation Voters, together with the Wisconsin League of Conservation Voters, named him to the national "Dirty Dozen in the States" citing his "abysmal [environmental] record" and launching a $1 million television advertising campaign against the GOP presidential aspirant. Press release, "Governor Walker Named to 'Dirty Dozen,' Wisconsin League of Conservation Voters Launches $1 Million Campaign," October 8, 2014, www.wispolitics.com/1006/WLCV10082014.pdf.

45 Jeffrey Hart, *The Making of the American Conservative Mind: National Review and Its Times* (Wilmington, DE: Intercollegiate Studies Institute, 2005), 362.

CHAPTER 10: GETTING TO GREEN, STEP TWO:
A PHILOSOPHY THAT PUTS PEOPLE FIRST

1 See, for example, Michael Zimmerman, J. Baird Callicott, George Sessions, Karen Warren, and John Clark, eds., *Environmental Philosophy: From Animal Rights to Radical Ecology*, 3rd ed. (Upper Saddle River, NJ: Prentice Hall, 2001).

2 The so-called Gaia hypothesis is a close cousin of "deep ecology" and also has served as a lightning rod for ridicule by many of the Green movement's enemies. First articulated by British scientist James Lovelock in 1969, it started out as a scientifically respectable observation that biotic and nonbiotic (rocks, oceans, climate) elements of

the planet affect each other, create feedback effects, and thus coevolve in a kind of mutual dance. This was then extended to the more controversial idea that it is life itself that acts to maintain the stability of the nonbiotic environment, suggesting that the planet is somehow self-regulating and even self-healing. The less subtle and most popular form of the hypothesis takes the metaphor literally, and posits that the Earth is (or at least ought to be regarded as) a singular integrated living being, like the Greek goddess Gaia, for whom the idea was named. The temptation to turn the environment into a female injured by patriarchal culture made the Gaia hypothesis a favorite for the ecofeminist movement, and a cheap target for anti-Greens of all sorts.

3   Michael E. Zimmerman, General Introduction, Zimmerman et al., *Environmental Philosophy*, 3.

4   Professor Zimmerman includes in his anthology "anthropocentric reformism," by which he means all mainstream thinking that grudgingly admits that humans will be apt to consider their own collective interests as the primary measure of environmental decision making. This line of thought, the professor writes in his introduction, was omitted from the first edition of the anthology but was included in subsequent editions not because of its intellectual merit but because "young people feel despair . . . in the face of the grim future envisioned by some radical ecologists but also in face of the unlikely prospects of the revolutionary changes purportedly needed to avert such a future." With the feelings of young people as a rather unlikely driver of the philosopher's search for truth, these essays were included in the anthology, albeit as representatives of a somewhat suspect approach on the margins of academic respectability.

5   Christopher D. Stone, "Should Trees Have Standing? Toward Legal Rights for Natural Objects," *California Law Review* 45 (1972), 450.

6   Aldo Leopold, *A Sand Country Almanac, and Sketches Here and There* (New York: Oxford University Press, 1949), 224–225.

7   The temptation to embrace simple moralities is manifest across various areas of our national life, and is a hazardous development in a world that is ever more complex and requires ever more subtle solutions. The former Episcopal chaplain at MIT, the Rev. Amy Ebeling McCreath, put it as follows: "There is a great danger in the loss of complexity in our national conversation about morality. The sound-biting of morality impoverishes us intellectually and leaves little room for . . . our complex, rich, and often ambiguous reality. . . . [I]t preempts genu-

ine dialogue, discourages self-reflection, and encourages the demonization of others." *Princeton Alumni Weekly*, March 9, 2005, 22.

8 One environmental leader called this tendency a "misanthropic nostalgia for a 'natural' past that didn't include human beings." It has been a major contributor to Green political failures. In 2008, the U.S. birthrate spiked to its highest level in nearly a half century, and awoke the inner Malthus in a number of Greens, who started speaking openly about children as part of the problem. In a rare mistake (an error in communication, not science), Nature Conservancy chief scientist Peter Kareiva wrote that not having children was the most effective way of reducing "carbon scenarios" and becoming an "eco-hero." Kareiva, "Children and Their Carbon Legacy: A Way to Be an Eco-Hero?" *Cool Green Science*, blog.nature.org, March 11, 2009, http://blog.nature.org/conservancy/2009/03/11/children-and-carbon-legacy-population-eco-hero-carbon-emissions/.

9 See the examples cited in Joel Kotkin, *The Next Hundred Million: America in 2050* (New York: Penguin, 2010), 213 and n. 15.

10 D. T. Max, "Green Is Good, The Nature Conservancy wants to persuade big business to save the environment," *New Yorker* (May 12, 2014), 59.

11 Quoted in Verlyn Klinkenborg, "Land Man," *New York Times Book Review*, November 5, 2006, 30.

12 James Gustave Speth, *The Bridge at the End of the World: Capitalism, the Environment, and Crossing from Crisis to Sustainability* (New Haven: Yale University Press, 2008), 199–204.

13 C. A. Dubray, "Nature," *The Catholic Encyclopedia*, vol. 10 (online edition, 1999).

14 See Genesis 1:28: "And God blessed them, and God said unto them, Be fruitful, and multiply, and replenish the earth, and subdue it: and have dominion over the fish of the sea, and over the fowl of the air, and over every living thing that moveth upon the earth."

15 *Laudato Si'*, 49, 104.

16 Thirteenth-century scholars developed the concepts of *natura naturata* and *natura naturans*, literally meaning "natured nature" and "naturing nature."

17 The distinction between God and his work has been an irksome one for theologians. If God and his work are actually different things (*natura naturans* is different from *natura naturata*), this raises, as *The Catholic Encyclopedia* puts it, "the question of the existence and nature of God and of his distinction from the world." A rather big question.

18 Alberti applied the idea to architecture and saw *natura naturans* as consisting in the "laws" that governed that art, such as harmony. When we look at a building, we do see columns and pediments, but more fundamentally what we see, what gives us pleasure, and what turns mere building into architecture are the laws, rules, archetypes, and principles that are not themselves visible, but are manifest in the visible.

19 Going full circle back to the question of creation, the distinction between created nature (*natura naturata*) and creating nature (*natura naturans*) has been resurrected recently by a quantum physicist, Wolfgang Smith, who sees the collapse of the wave function, whereby potential becomes manifestation, as the action of *natura naturans* creating *natura naturata*. We now know that what we perceive as matter is really the organization of energy, and yet most educated Americans have no grasp of quantum reality. I agree with the late Heinz Pagels, who warned us in the early 1980s that the intellectual mastery of the "cosmic code" was a fundamental challenge for civilization.

20 Carl O. Sauer, *Agricultural Origins and Dispersals* (New York: American Geographic Society, 1952), https://archive.org/details/agriculturalorig 033518mbp.

21 For this calculation WCS researchers considered human population density greater than one person per square kilometer, areas within 15 km of a road or river with human traffic, land occupied by agricultural or urban uses, and lands producing enough light to be regularly visible to a satellite at night. See Eric W. Sanderson et al., "The Human Footprint and the Last of the Wild," *BioScience* 52, no. 10, 891 (October 2002): 894.

22 Bill McKibben, *The End of Nature*, 2nd ed. (New York: Anchor Books, 1999).

23 Daniel B. Botkin, *Discordant Harmonies: A New Ecology for the Twenty-First Century* (New York: Oxford University Press, 1990), 68–71.

24 An inspiring example is the "daylighting" of the Saw Mill River through densely urban Yonkers, New York, spearheaded by Ned Sullivan, the visionary president of Scenic Hudson, a New York State environmental organization.

25 2004 speech by Adam Werbach, www.grist.org/article/werbach-reprint.

26 Christopher Solomon, "Rethinking the Wild, The Wilderness Act Is Facing a Midlife Crisis," *New York Times*, July 6, 2014, SR1.

27 Michael Soulé, quoted in D. T. Max, "Green Is Good, The Nature Conservancy wants to persuade big business to save the environment," *New Yorker* (May 12, 2014), 60.

28 Leopold, *Sand Country Almanac*, 199.

29 Sanderson et al., "Human Footprint," 902.

30 Michael Pollan, *Second Nature, A Gardener's Education* (New York: Dell, 1991).

31 The WCS scientists who developed the human-footprint analysis made the same point in the dry language of science by observing simply that humans, who have a demonstrated capacity to modify the environment, can choose to apply that capacity to "modify the environment to enhance natural values, not degrade them." Sanderson et al., "Human Footprint," 902.

32 David Rothenberg, "Wild Thinking: Philosophy, Ecology and Technology," in Michael Tobias, J. Patrick Fitzgerald, and David Rothenberg, eds., *A Parliament of Minds* (Albany: State University of New York Press, 2000), 172.

33 Leopold, *Sand Country Almanac*, 68.

34 "Working miracles: Can technology save the planet?" *The Economist*, July 6, 2002, 13.

35 The more radical elements of the Green movement have expressly rejected the gardener model. Earth First!, for example, has stated that "We reject even the notion of benevolent stewardship as that implies dominance." Thomas R. Wellock, *Preserving the Nation: The Conservation and Environmental Movements* (Wheeling, IL: Harlan Davidson, Inc., 2007), 228. They forget that it is our big brains and technology that create the fact of dominance, not any philosophical approach to our interaction with other species. Short of self-extermination or relocation to another planet, choosing to exercise our dominance in a benevolent way is the most we can do.

36 Some economists call the latter approach "instrumental value theory" (i.e., the nonhuman world is valuable only as an instrument to contribute to the well-being of humans) and the former approach the "intrinsic value" theory (i.e., the natural world has value whether or not humans attach value to it or decide that it contributes to their welfare). One economist making this distinction is Clive Hamilton. He identifies three flavors of "instrumental value" theory, correlating roughly with a strict utilitarian view where nature is valued at what it can fetch as a commodity in the market, a modified view that recognizes the limits to growth and calculates value on a long-term basis, and a third view that also admits to its calculation the softer values of preserved nature. See Hamilton, *Growth Fetish* (Crows Nest, Australia: Allen & Unwin, 2003), 191–93. When I speak of a utilitarian calcula-

tion as part of the answer to "why save nature," it is in the spirit of the softest of Hamilton's flavors of "instrumental value," and, most importantly, sits side by side with an equally valid moral calculus.

37 Conservation biologist John Terborgh is typical when he writes that "[u]ltimately, nature and biodiversity must be conserved for their own sakes, not because they have present utilitarian value. . . ." Terborgh, *Requiem for Nature* (Washington, D.C.: Island Press, 2004), 38.

38 Max, "Green Is Good," 59.

39 *Audubon Strategic Plan 2012–2015, A Roadmap for Hemispheric Conservation*, http://www.audubon.org/sites/default/files/documents/audubon _strategic_plan_-_web_2012.pdf.

40 Nelson, Gaylord, *Beyond Earth Day: Fulfilling the Promise* (Madison: University of Wisconsin Press, 2002).

41 The Millennium Ecosystem Assessment commissioned by the United Nations looked at these "ecosystem services" in four categories: provisioning services (food, water, timber, fiber); regulating services (affecting climate, flood, disease, waste, and water quality); cultural services (recreation, aesthetic and spiritual benefits); and supporting services (soil formation, photosynthesis, and nutrient cycling). *Millennium Ecosystem Assessment Synthesis Report*, republication final draft, March 23, 2005, www.millenniumassessment.org.

42 Robert Costanza et al., "The value of the world's ecosystem services and natural capital," *Nature* 387 (May 15, 1997): 253–60.

43 *Millennium Ecosystem Assessment*, 16.

44 Michael Shellenberger and Ted Nordhaus, "The Death of Environmentalism: Global Warming Politics in a Post-Environmental World" (paper delivered at the Environmental Grantmakers Conference, October 2004), www .thebreakthrough.org/images/Death_of_Environmentalism.pdf, 33.

45 Jonathan Haidt, *The Happiness Hypothesis* (New York: Basic Books, 2006), 242.

46 *Laudato Si'*, 116.

47 Ecumenical Patriarch Bartholomew, "Sins Against Nature and God: We Are All Accountable for Ignoring the Global Consequences of Environmental Exploitation," *Huffington Post*, July 17, 2010.

48 Gregory E. Kaebnick, *Humans in Nature: The World As We Find It and the World as We Create It* (Oxford: Oxford University Press, 2014), xiii.

49 See, e.g., C. Peterson and M. E. P. Seligman, *Character Strengths and Virtues: A Handbook and Classification* (Washington, D.C.: American Psychological Association and Oxford University Press, 2004). In a comprehensive sur-

vey, Peterson and Seligman identified twenty-four character strengths leading to six higher-level virtues: wisdom, courage, humanity, justice, temperance, and transcendence. Some assert that the universality of these virtues has its roots in evolutionary advantage, some that they are necessary to a sustained collective culture that also is consistent with respect for the personal autonomy of others. One way or another, they appear to be hardwired both into human nature and our collective sense of what is required to live together and sustain civilization.

50 See Thomas E. Hill, Jr., "Ideals of Human Excellence and Preserving Natural Environments," *Autonomy and Self-Respect* (Cambridge: Cambridge University Press, 1991), 104–17.

51 See, e.g., William J. Bennett, *The Book of Virtues* (New York: Simon & Schuster, 1993). Bennett was George Bush's secretary of education. The book, with chapters on self-discipline, compassion, responsibility, courage, honesty, and the like, drew praise from Rush Limbaugh, Margaret Thatcher, and many others on the right.

52 Peter Forbes, *The Great Remembering: Further thoughts on land, soul, and society* (San Francisco: The Trust for Public Land, 2001), 61–62.

53 Ted Nordhaus and Michael Shellenberger, *Break Through: Why We Can't Leave Saving the Planet to Environmentalists* (Boston: Mariner Books, 2009), 94.

54 Ibid., 102.

55 "Natural Beauty—Message from the President of the United States," *Congressional Record*, 89th Congress, 1st session, vol. 111, pt. 2 (February 8, 1965), 2085–89.

56 *Laudato Si'*, 157.

57 See S. R. Kellert and E. O. Wilson (eds.), *The Biophilia Hypothesis* (Washington, D.C.: Island Press, 1995).

58 "Environmental psychology" and its close cousin "conservation psychology" are growing fields that explore this and other ideas about the psychological dimension of the human relationship with nature.

CHAPTER 11: GETTING TO GREEN, STEP THREE: REFORMING THE GREEN MOVEMENT

1 See, e.g., Mark VanVugt, "Averting the Tragedy of the Commons: Using Social Psychological Science to Protect the Environment," *Current Directions in Psychological Science* 18, no. 3 (June 1, 2009).

2   Nicholas D. Kristof, "I Have a Nightmare," *New York Times*, March 12, 2005.

3   Paul Ehrlich, *The Population Bomb* (New York: Ballantine Books, 1968), prologue. Apocalyptic rhetoric set the tone on the first Earth Day in 1970, when U.C.-Davis "systems ecologist" Kenneth Watt is widely reported to have declared in his speech at Swarthmore, "We have about five more years at the outside to do something," and on the same day Harvard biochemist George Wald predicted that "civilization will end within 15 or 30 more years unless immediate action is taken. . . ."

4   Paul Voosen, "Conservation: Myth-busting scientist pushes greens past reliance on 'horror stories,'" April 3, 2012, http://www.eenews. net/stories/1059962401.

5   Justin Gillis, "Freezing Out the Bigger Picture," *New York Times*, February 11, 2014, D3.

6   International Energy Agency, *Global carbon-dioxide emissions increase by 1.0 Gt in 2011 to record high*, May 24, 2012, http://www.iea.org/news roomandevents/news/2012/may/name,27216,en.html.

7   Nordhaus says, "Humans are in effect spinning the roulette wheel when we inject CO_2 and other gases into the atmosphere. The balls may land in the favorable black pockets or in the unfavorable red pockets, or possibly in the dangerous zero or double-zero pockets. . . . A sensible policy would pay an insurance premium to avoid playing the roulette wheel of the Climate Casino." William D. Nordhaus, *The Climate Casino: Risk, Uncertainty, and Economics for a Warming World* (New Haven: Yale University Press, 2013), 300.

8   *Time*, August 26, 2004, A60.

9   Michael Shellenberger and Ted Nordhaus wrote that "the environment community ha[s] still not come up with an inspiring vision . . . that a majority of Americans could get excited about." Shellenberger and Nordhaus, "The Death of Environmentalism: Global Warming Politics in a Post-Environmental World" (paper delivered at the Environmental Grantmakers Conference, October 2004), www.thebreakthrough.org/ images/Death_of_Environmentalism.pdf, 16.

10 "Clinton, Bush Share Laughs and Memories at Launch of Scholars Program," *Wall Street Journal*, September 9, 2014, A8.

11 Paul Hansen, whose career included service as executive director of the Izaak Walton League and head of The Green Group, recently wrote an extended cri de coeur in which he bemoans the entrenched hostility of the movement to compromise, the constant internecine bick-

ering and lack of commitment to results: "[N]ational environmental leaders came under intense criticism for any thought of compromise and were accused of being out of touch with their grass-roots. If they had any inclination to make the best deal that public opinion and political will made possible, they were accused of being too close to power, too accommodating, and even too professional. Environmental leaders who adopted the proven strategy for success by negotiating responsibly or considering compromise to obtain the best deal possible at the time faced ridicule or worse. Some even lost their jobs due to efforts to work across political parties or constituencies. We tend to celebrate the most passionate and charismatic defenders of the faith, not the most strategic and effective dealmakers who are responsible for most of the progress." Hansen, *Green in Gridlock: Common Goals, Common Ground, and Compromise* (College Station: Texas A&M Press, 2013), 21.

12 Thomas R. Wellock, *Preserving the Nation: The Conservation and Environmental Movements* (Wheeling, IL: Harlan Davidson, Inc., 2007), 151.

13 Hansen, *Green in Gridlock*, 125.

14 See, e.g., James Gustave Speth, *The Bridge at the End of the World: Capitalism, the Environment, and Crossing from Crisis to Sustainability* (New Haven: Yale University Press, 2008), xiii.

15 Quoted in James Surowiecki, "Waste Away," *New Yorker*, May 6, 2002.

16 Wellock, *Preserving the Nation*, 191.

17 See, for example, Mark Sagoff, *Price, Principle and the Environment* (Cambridge: Cambridge University Press, 2004).

18 The free-market environmentalist answer to this objection is extremely odd. Terry Anderson answers Sagoff as follows: "Turning moral values into political issues . . . becomes another form of rent-seeking, wherein people with one set of moral values get what they want at the expense of others." Terry L. Anderson and Donald R. Leal, *Free Market Environmentalism*, rev. ed. (New York: Palgrave Macmillan, 2001), 24. This idea confuses "rent seeking" by for-profit entities and individuals, which is a form of economic free riding, with the noneconomic idea of citizens simply seeking to satisfy their preferences, and be true to their values, within the context of the political process.

19 Jared Diamond, *Collapse: How Societies Choose to Fail or Succeed* (New York: Viking, 2005), 17.

20 *Time*, August 26, 2002, A59.

21　Paul Hawken, Amory Lovins, and L. Hunter Lovins, *Natural Capitalism: Creating the Next Industrial Revolution* (Boston: Little, Brown and Company, 1999).

22　Reported in Andrew Revkin, "Report Tallies Hidden Costs of Human Assault on Nature, *New York Times,* April 5, 2005.

23　www.riskybusiness.org.

24　Matthew Feinberg and Robb Willer, "The Moral Roots of Environmental Attitudes," *Psychological Science* 24, no. 1 (January 2013): 56–62.

25　Robb Willer, "Is the Environment a Moral Cause?" *New York Times,* February 27, 2015.

26　Speth, *Bridge at the End of the World,* 227.

27　Ibid., 195.

28　Shellenberger and Nordhaus disagree, arguing that sharp focus on environmental issues forces the Green movement to deal only with "symptoms" and that "the tendency to put the environment into an airtight container away from the concerns of others" leads to defensiveness and isolation. *Death of Environmentalism,* 29.

29　Marshall Ganz, a lecturer at the Kennedy School of Government, Harvard, quoted in Petra Bartosiewicz and Marissa Miley, *The Too Polite Revolution: Why the Recent Campaign to Pass Comprehensive Climate Legislation in the United States Failed* (report prepared for the Symposium of the Politics of America's Fight Against Global Warming), 67.

30　Vishaan Chakrabarti, "America's Urban Future," *New York Times,* April 16, 2004.

31　Ibid. See also Vishaan Chakrabarti, *A Country of Cities: A Manifesto for an Urban America* (New York: Metropolis Books, 2013).

32　William Cronon, "Saving the Land We Love: Land Conservation and American Values," keynote address at the Land Trust Alliance Rally, Madison, Wisconsin, October 17, 2005, www.williamcronon.net/writing/LTA_Plenary.htm.

33　Jon Christensen, Robert McDonald, and Carrie Denning, "Ecological Urbanism for the 21st Century," *Chronicle of Higher Education,* January 22, 2012, http://chronicle.com/article/Ecological-Urbanism-for-the/130384/.

34　Joel Kotkin, *The Next Hundred Million: America in 2050* (New York: Penguin, 2010).

35　Peter Kareiva, "Urban Conservation," *Nature Conservancy Magazine* (2012).

CHAPTER 12: A MODEL FOR CENTER GREEN:
THE LAND TRUST MOVEMENT IN AMERICA

1 Social scientists have compared economic trends, severe weather events, science news, and other factors as drivers of changing public opinion about climate change. The most significant driver: partisan statements as amplified by the media. See the discussion at Theda Skocpol, *Naming the Problem: What It Will Take to Counter Extremism and Engage Americans in the Fight against Global Warming* (report prepared for the Symposium on the Politics of America's Fight Against Global Warming, February 14, 2013), http://www.scholarsstrategynetwork.org/sites/default/files/skocpol_captrade_report_january_2013_0.pdf.

2 The Apollo Project was launched in 2003 and called for a $300 billion, ten-year effort to accelerate the transition to clean energy.

3 Ted Nordhaus and Michael Shellenberger, *Break Through: Why We Can't Leave Saving the Planet to Environmentalists* (Boston: Mariner Books, 2009), 7.

4 Letter from Thomas Jefferson to William Caruthers, March 15, 1815, http://founders.archives.gov/documents/Jefferson/03-08-02-0272.

5 Richard Brewer, *Conservancy: The Land Trust Movement in America* (Hanover, NH: University Press of New England, 2003), 39.

6 This pamphlet is available online at http://www.gpo.gov/fdsys/pkg/CZIC-ht166-w59-1968/pdf/CZIC-ht166-w59-1968.pdf.

7 http://www.landtrustalliance.org/about/land-trust-census/.

8 See, e.g., http://www.foxbusiness.com/government/2013/01/21/land-trust-scams-on-rise/, and Property Rights Foundation of America, http://prfamerica.org.

9 The author is a member of the board of directors of the Land Trust Alliance. For a concise account of the early history of the Land Trust Alliance, see Brewer, *Conservancy*, 176–84.

10 In some cases a land trust acquiring land in fee will donate or sell that land to the government to be added to a park or other public lands, but even in that case the fiscal impact is usually less than direct action by the government, and the transaction is noncoercive to the landowner.

11 For example, if the fair market value of a fee interest in forestland is $100,000, then the cost to the government of acquiring the land would be $100,000. In contrast, the value of the easement limiting timber operations and preventing development will be only a portion of that, say $60,000, since the family still owns the land and can still get some

value by doing limited sustainable timber harvesting. When the family deducts the $60,000 donation, at a 35 percent tax bracket, the cost to the government is only $21,000.

12 http://www.landvote.org.

13 Paul Walden Hansen, *Green in Gridlock: Common Goals, Common Ground, and Compromise* (College Station: Texas A&M Press, 2013), 117, 120.

CHAPTER 13: CENTER GREEN

1 Richard Rorty, *Contingency, Irony and Solidarity* (Cambridge: Cambridge University Press, 1989), 7.

2 The Evangelical Climate Initiative, "Climate Change: An Evangelical Call to Action" (2006).

3 Carol Browner, "The Earth Is in Your Hands," *EPA Journal*, Winter 1995, 4.

4 Environmental Advocates of New York, "Turning a Blind Eye to Illegal Pollution" (September 2013), www.eany.org/our-work/reports/.

5 *Concluding Report of the Carnegie Commission on Science, Technology, and Government* (April 1993), in Gordon Durnil, *The Making of a Conservative Environmentalist* (Bloomington: Indiana University Press, 1995), 93.

6 Aldo Leopold, *A Sand Country Almanac, and Sketches Here and There* (New York: Oxford University Press, 1949), 205.

7 Mike Hulme, *Why We Disagree About Climate Change: Understanding Controversy, Inaction and Opportunity* (Cambridge: Cambridge University Press, 2009), 106.

8 The most often cited definition of sustainability came from the United Nations Brundtland Commission in 1987: "[D]evelopment that meets the needs of the present without compromising the ability of future generations to meet their own needs." Another version of the concept, promoted by the Footprint Network, asks whether human activity is "right-sized" for the planet; to the extent we are taking resources or producing waste in excess of the planet's ability to replace those resources and absorb that waste, then our "footprint" is not sustainable. See www.footprintnetwork.org.

9 Described by Professor Kenneth Arrow in the Taplin Environmental Lecture, Princeton University, March 5, 2002.

10 "Out of the Wild, Two acclaimed authors discuss how the language we use shapes the planet we live on. A conversation between William Cronon and Michael Pollan," *Orion*, November/December 2013.

11 See Paul Walden Hansen, *Green in Gridlock: Common Goals, Common Ground, and Compromise* (College Station: Texas A&M Press, 2013), 97.

12 Petra Bartosiewicz and Marissa Miley, *The Too Polite Revolution: Why the Recent Campaign to Pass Comprehensive Climate Legislation in the United States Failed* (report prepared for the Symposium of the Politics of America's Fight Against Global Warming), 80.

13 Tom Hamburger, Kathleen Hennessey, and Neela Banerjee, "Koch brothers now at heart of GOP power," *Los Angeles Times*, February 6, 2011.

14 *E&E Reporter*, December 12, 2013. The author is a contributor to this PAC.

15 David Masiel, "Crude Reality," *Outside* (Feburary 2004), http://www.outsideonline.com/1822186/crude-reality. See also note from the editor, "*Outside* and the ANWR Debate."

16 Christine Todd Whitman, *It's My Party Too* (New York: Penguin, 2005), chap. 5.

17 Andrew C. Revkin, "A New Middle Stance Emerges in Debate over Climate," *New York Times*, January 1, 2007, and "Challenges to Both Left and Right on Global Warming," *New York Times*, November 13, 2007.

18 David Roberts, "NYT's Andy Revkin pens another stinker on the so-called 'center' of the climate debate," www.grist.org/article/centrist-dog-food/ (November 14, 2007).

19 Atrios, "More Broder," comment in Eschaton blog, April 28, 2007, http://www.eschatonblog.com/2007/04/more-broder.html.

20 Thomas L. Friedman, "The Power of Green," *International Herald Tribune*, April 14–15, 2007.

CHAPTER 14: CENTER GREEN ON CLIMATE CHANGE

1 In September 2013 the United Nations' Intergovernmental Panel on Climate Change set the probability that humans are main cause of climate change at 95 percent.

2 For an excellent survey of the many different approaches to modeling the correlation between atmospheric carbon and global temperature (referred to by scientists as "climate sensitivity"), see "Climate Science: A Sensitive Matter," *The Economist*, March 30, 2013.

3 One definition of the precautionary principle, referred to as the "Wingspread Statement," was developed at a 1998 conference con-

vened by the Science and Environmental Health Network, and read in part: "When an activity raises threats of harm to the environment or human health, precautionary measures should be taken even if some of the cause and effect relationships are not fully established scientifically." See http://www.sehn.org/wing.html. Another formulation of the precautionary principle appears in the 1992 Rio Declaration: "[W]here there are threats of serious or irreversible damage, lack of full scientific certainty shall not be used as a reason for postponing cost-effective measures to prevent environmental degradation."

4 See, e.g., Robert W. Hahn and Cass R. Sunstein, *The Precautionary Principle as a Basis for Decision Making* (Washington, D.C.: AEI-Brookings Joint Center for Regulatory Studies, April 2005). The right also articulates a more principled objection to the precautionary principle, arguing that it can be applied in a manner that preempts a fulsome cost-benefit analysis that compares the risk to the cost of the risk mitigant.

5 "Common Ground on Energy, George Shultz and Thomas Steyer say bipartisanship is possible," *Wall Street Journal*, March 26, 2013, R5.

6 See, e.g., Oliver Morton writing in *Nature* (September 7, 2006): "If Silicon Valley can apply Moore's law to the capture of sunshine, it could change the world again." Quoted in Fred Krupp and Mariam Horn, *Earth: The Sequel, The Race to Reinvent Energy and Stop Global Warming* (New York: W. W. Norton, 2008), 14.

7 This is a technology without the radioactive by-products of nuclear fusion, achieved through the fusing of protons (not neutrons) with nonradioactive boron-11. See Krupp and Horn, *Earth: The Sequel*, 234.

8 International Energy Agency, "Energy Subsidies," http://www.worldenergy outlook.org/resources/energysubsidies/. See also "Energy Subsidies— Fueling Controversy," *The Economist*, January 11, 2014.

9 Eric Pooley, *The Climate War: True Believers, Power Brokers, and the Fight to Save the Earth* (New York: Hyperion, 2010), 424.

10 Ban Ki-moon, "Making Headway Against Climate Change," *Wall Street Journal*, September 26, 2014, A11.

11 California entrepreneur and author Peter Barnes did much to popularize the notion. Bill McKibben also has supported cap-and-dividend.

12 Paul Walden Hansen, *Green in Gridlock: Common Goals, Common Ground, and Compromise* (College Station: Texas A&M Press, 2013), 35.

13 G. Prins and S. Rayner, *The wrong trousers: radically re-thinking climate*

policy (Oxford and London: James Martin Institute for Science and Civilisation and the MacKinder Centre for the Study of Long-Wave Events, October 2011).

14 REGI is the Regional Greenhouse Gas Initiative adopted by Connecticut, Delaware, Maine, Maryland, Massachusetts, New Hampshire, New York, Rhode Island, and Vermont (New Jersey withdrew in 2011).

15 Mike Hulme, *Why We Disagree About Climate Change, Understanding Controversy, Inaction and Opportunity* (Cambridge: Cambridge University Press, 2009), 339.

16 Jonathan Franzen, "Carbon Capture: Has climate change made it harder for people to care about conservation?" *New Yorker*, April 6, 2015.

17 Marc Landy and Charles Rubin, *Civic Environmentalism: A New Approach to Policy* (Washington, D.C.: George C. Marshall Institute, 2001), 10.

18 *The Audubon Birds & Climate Change Report* (2014).

19 This approach will attract both liberals and conservatives. From the right, Bjørn Lomborg, who supports government funding of basic R&D, observed that "it is the difference between supporting an inexpensive researcher who will discover more efficient, future solar panels—and supporting a Solyndra at great expense to produce lots of inefficient, present-technology solar panels." People as diverse as George Shultz and Thomas Steyer agree. The *Wall Street Journal* ran a piece in March 2013 based on a joint interview with Shultz and Steyer titled "Common Ground on Energy, George Shultz and Thomas Steyer say bipartisanship is possible," in which both of them suggested that government support of Green energy R&D ought to attract bipartisan support.

20 International Energy Agency, "World Energy Outlook 2012 Fact Sheet," http://www.worldenergyoutlook.org/media/weowebsite/2012/fact sheets.pdf.

21 Pew Research Center, "GOP Deeply Divided Over Climate Change," November 1, 2013, www.people-press.org/2013/11/01/gop-deeply-divided-over-climate-change/.

22 Pew Research Center telephone poll conducted October 4–7, 2012, reported in *Wall Street Journal*, January 26–27, 2013, A4. These percentages have risen in some more recent 2015 polling.

23 William D. Ruckelshaus, Lee M. Thomas, William K. Reilly, and Christine Todd Whitman, "A Republican Case for Climate Action," *New York Times*, August 1, 2013.

CHAPTER 15: CENTER GREEN ON THE HEADLINE ISSUES:
HYDRO-FRACTURING AND KEYSTONE

1 Keith Kloor, "The Holy & The Hawks," *Audubon*, September–October 2005, 30–31.

2 Some Green groups dispute this premise, arguing that methane leaks from unconventional gas wells offset the lower-carbon emissions from combustion of natural gas compared to oil or coal. But a significant amount of methane leakage comes from a small number of "bad actor" wells and from particular techniques for which there are alternatives. A recent University of Texas study indicates that "Reduced Emissions Completions" (commonly known as "green completions") are both viable and likely to reduce the methane leakage resulting from natural gas production. See http://www.edf.org/climate/methane-studies/ UT-study-faq#1. The answer to methane leaks, which do appear to be a serious problem, is to regulate and prevent methane leaks, not to abandon a fuel source significantly cleaner than coal.

3 "Grant Makers Spend Millions on Groups on All Sides of Fracking Issue," *Chronicle of Philanthrophy*, October 10, 2013, 9.

4 The critical question for the Green movement in relation to coal is whether to support the development and use of technologies to permit coal to burn cleaner, usually referred to as "carbon capture and storage," or CCS. Some Greens say no, arguing that these technologies will just prolong the life of coal-fired generating plants and postpone the transition to renewables. But others, with a more realistic sense of the time it will require to wean the world off of coal, say it is critical. David Hawkins at NRDC points out that the new coal plants built between 2010 and 2030 will, without CCS, emit 130 percent of the carbon produced by burning coal in all of human history. CCS will not prolong the life of coal, but it will allow the planet to survive the time it takes coal to die.

5 U.S. Energy Information Administration, "Frequently Asked Questions," http://www.eia.gov/tools/faqs/faq.cfm?id=73&t=11.

6 Study by Michael McElroy, Harvard School of Engineering the Applied Science, and others; see *Wall Street Journal*, May 20, 2012.

7 Tom Fowler, "Exxon Declares Gas King," *Wall Street Journal*, December 8, 2011, http://online.wsj.com/news/articles/SB10001424052970203501304577084594165136990.

8 Thomas H. Darrah, Avner Vengosh, Robert B. Jackson, Nathaniel R.

Warner, and Robert J. Poreda, *Noble gases identify the mechanisms of fugitive gas contamination in drinking-water wells overlying the Marcellus and Barnett Shales*, www.slideshare.net/MarcellusDN/. See also N. R. Warner et al., "New Tracers Identify Hydraulic Fracturing Fluids and Accidental Releases from Oil and Gas Operations" in *Environmental Science and Technology* 48, no. 21 (2014): 12552–60.

9   "Grant Makers Spend Millions on Groups on All Sides of Fracking Issue," *Chronicle of Philanthropy*, October 10, 2013, 9.

10 Lynn Cook, "Fracking Gets More Neighborly," *Wall Street Journal*, March 11, 2014, B2.

11 Coral Davenport, "Keystone Pipeline Pros, Cons and Steps to a Final Decision," *New York Times*, November 18, 2014.

12 Coral Davenport, "Keystone Pipeline May Be Big, but This Is Bigger," *New York Times*, April 22, 2014, F2.

13 Gail Collins, "Republicans Pipeline," *New York Times*, November 7, 2014.

Index